CW00727595

# 1975
## (1984 minus 9)

# Hans Keller

# Music, Closed Societies and Football

### First published as
### 1975 (1984 minus 9)

TOCCATA
PRESS

Copyright © 1986 by Milein Cosman Keller
First published in 1977 by Dobson Books;
reissued in 1986 by Toccata Press

Printed in Great Britain

To
MILEIN
but for whom the resolve
mentioned in Chapter I
(pp39 & 48) might have had
a chance of failure

I owe the documentary evidence of Chapter I to Walter Wallich — the producer of the original radio talk of which this chapter is a transcript that has remained virtually unchanged. I am profoundly grateful for Mr Wallich's substantial piece of research.

My thanks also to Messrs. J. M. Dent & Sons Ltd and the trustees of the Dylan Thomas estate for permission to quote the lines on p.70.

Chapter II, III, and part of Chapter IV have previously appeared in *The New Review,* parts of Chapter V in *The Sunday Times* and the *Spectator.* This does not mean that I am submitting a collection of essays: from Chapter III onwards, I was conscious of writing this book.

H.K.

# Contents

# Preface

*Thinkers of the World, Disunite!*

I don't know whether the as yet gentle reader shares my aversion to prefaces. One skips them with an uneasy conscience. After all, or rather before all, one might be missing something. Shaw apart, however, one never is. They are not written before the book, but after, and not because something is missing in front, but because the writer can't stop. The authors of *Don Giovanni* overtures are few and far between. We others are at our most narcissistic when it comes to explaining what it is all about. Either the book does the explaining, or no preface will get us out of the mess.

But this preface is different, you expect me to say. By no means; it's the same as all the others, except that most of it is being written in the middle of the book — a fact of no perceptible consequence. Yes, and there is another difference: I do actually think that the book explains itself; in fact, the title is supposed to explain it comprehensively. Yet this preface is not, perhaps, pure self-love: what the title insinuates is something unwelcome, so I thought I'd rub it in before the reader tries to miss it. Though the book is about what happened in 1975, and the state of things we'd reached in 1975 in areas of life I know, '1975' is, of course, meant symbolically rather than merely chronologically: less than a decade to go until 1984, less than a spiritual decade.

When I first read George Orwell's book, I hated it as much as you may come to hate mine. And I hated it with what I thought was good reason. I remember having a violent argument about it with Margaret Phillips, the educational psychologist, with whom I was then collaborating (see p. 88); although not an educationist, I had a less pessimistic view than she about the possibilities of disasters open to humankind. I felt that my attitude of mild optimism — I never went as far as conceiving of the possibility of an end to wars — was well fortified by the results of psychoanalytic research. Man, I suggested, could not live on hate alone, rather blatantly disregarding the possible implications of Chapter I below.

What I have meanwhile learnt, not only about lovelessness, but about pure evil perpetrated with, in fact by, the best and easiest of consciences, has made me change my mind — gradually, yet radically in the end. There is, in short, no limit to the degree to which man can cheat himself into believing that he is good and full of love and concern and respect — especially for those he wants to control; after he has accomplished the major task of self-deceit, the successful cheating of others is a minor matter.

The more responsible his position, the greater is the likelihood that he will cheat himself to the limits of his astounding capacity — other psychological things being equal, that is (which, alas, they usually are). And to whom is he answerable, anyway? Prime Ministers or heads of organisations or institutions or business concerns or the departments of any of these are not easily sacked unless they are found stealing the crockery, which is a trivial offence compared to that of imposing on people. Thus, I don't think it is an exaggeration to say

10

that actual irresponsibility easily becomes a function of formalised, institutionalised, mythical responsibility.

Alfred Adler, the half-forgotten founder of wholly forgotten Individual Psychology, a splinter group of Freudian psychoanalysis which moved into opposition, postulated the 'will to power' as an elemental human drive; it is a pity that in the excitement over Freud's more searching discoveries, and as a result of Freud's own hostility against the apostate, the latter's preoccupation with power has not received anything like sufficient attention, though Thomas S. Szasz[1] has remarked[2] that psychoanalysis itself has 'repressed' the concept of power — at the moment a more serious, more dangerous repression, to his mind, than that of infantile sexuality.

The adage, 'power corrupts', on the other hand, has undeservedly lost much of its force through over-use: the truthful platitude's tragedy, this. Besides, in order for power to corrupt, you've got to have it, and unless you assume it by force (for which purpose you needn't be a dictator, but can be a parent or teacher), there have to be people willing to give up at least some of their essential individuality in order for you to be installed as a powerful person and exert your control without let or hindrance. The only area in which I have seen such 'leadership' succeed without any permanent loss in terms of human dignity, of sheer humanity, is that of the string quartet, where no valuable decision is ever arrived at in committee. But then, more string quartets founder than succeed, and those which succeed do so on the basis of elective affinities that make it possible to surrender

---

[1] Professor of Psychiatry at the State University Hospital of the Upstate Medical Center, Syracuse, of whom more later.

[2] Oral communication.

individuality without loss of personality, the surrender being minimal, and temporary anyway.

Otherwise, the danger of power and of the inhibition or reduction of that personal intellectual initiative which is a useful distinguishing characteristic between us and the other higher mammals is ever-present in art as much as in organised life. The symphony orchestra is a frightening example, especially the string section, where the collective playing of the same line not only produces chronic distonations behind the acoustic screen of a united, 'full', 'beautiful' tone, but makes individual solutions of phrasing problems impossible, and the participation in wrong or accidental solutions inevitable; the wind section's position is more advantageous in degree only, not in kind — unless the conductor is such a bad leader that it is possible to lead him. For the rest, the choice of my example of the permanent symphony orchestra (whose days I consider numbered, anyway) is not just due to my being a musician; I think the orchestra is a perfect illustration of a little human world having gone wrong without anybody noticing anything amiss — except, of course, those victims who haven't been totally destroyed in the process. There is, in fact, no happy orchestral player, and there are few who don't hate music; music-loving talk in the interval of a rehearsal is downright unprofessional. The talented musicians are legion, on the other hand, who have tried, or are trying, to escape from the orchestra, almost invariably facing financial sacrifice, a lowering of their living standards and security. Even amongst orchestral leaders — who, after all, have a better chance to retain some of their individuality than the rest of at least the string band — the proportion of emigrants, temporary or permanent, continues to be striking; fairly recent, distinguished cases in this country include Manoug Parikian, Hugh Maguire, and Erich Gruenberg.

Until 1959, the string quartet and the orchestra had been the only organised groups of which, football apart, I had been a member. In 1959 I joined the BBC. At that moment, I thought that while my earlier life, virtually all of it, had been marked by an exciting, if at times perturbing, instability, I was now starting a sheltered existence and had better beware of the danger of being shut off from sundry possibilities of gaining insights into life. I could not have been more pitiably wrong.

It had been my free, freelancing days that had been sheltered — not economically, to be sure, but so far as protection from the seamy side of human existence was concerned, to wit, organised collective life, by which I mean 'managed' life of any kind, anywhere, even in the BBC, which is a magnificent employer (and if *I* say that, it must be). But the seaminess of collective life has nothing to do with conditions of employment, nothing with evil bosses and victimised subordinates — or if it has, the victims are as evil as their masters, the unions as regressive as the managers. The evil, that is to say, is collectivity as we know it and accept it, with effective power on the one hand and the happy abrogation of individual judgment on the other: they were all nice people before they started being responsible, discreet, self-satisfied team-workers, successfully hiding their selfishness, and their loss of a self, behind the all-saving concept of the team. 'Mr X is just as important as I am,' says the manager. 'Without his contribution, we would be nothing.' For one thing, if he's just as important, he should get just as much money, or the manager just as little, for power does not deserve a higher salary. For another thing, in a well-definable way, the manager is right: he's just as unimportant as Mr X, for they have both forgotten the importance of being human — one in his search for power, the other in his search for the next best thing (since power, by sheer accident, happened to elude him), which is a father to hand his conscience to, with compliments. In that sense, they are both evil, each de-personalised after his own fashion, and all one can do when one finds oneself in the middle of such a fantasy world, commonly known as the 'world of action', is one of three things: turn one's back in disgust and go home, or give in, or fight it all. I am a fighter — but one who doesn't want to kill or maim anybody, which makes the fight a little more difficult, but by no means impossible.

In the course of my BBC years, I have, musically speaking, been in charge of more or less everything, with the sole exception of opera — not because, from the BBC's point of view, I'm all that marvellous in all other areas, or unmarvellous in the operatic field, but because it just so happened: plenty of things just so happen in collective life, whereas individual life is unflinchingly purposive, if you want it to be — which, admittedly, comes about but rarely. But the only reason why it comes about rarely is that few individuals are psychologically capable of doing without the calming blessings of some collective effort or other. When they are, they stand out, unmistakably, albeit in the middle of a team. Mind you, the team manager rarely thinks so.

I started off as Music Talks Producer in my BBC life (I have no 'career'). After a few months, I put in for, and was promoted to, the job of Chief Assistant, Chamber Music and Recitals, which meant that I was in solitary

14

charge of that area — William Glock, the Controller of Music, a non-power man if ever there was one, minding his own business, or what he elected to be his own business, the then Thursday Invitation Concerts (his single chamber venture), the Proms, and the Royal Festival Hall Concerts of the BBC Symphony Orchestra. After a few years, he invited me, mildly pressed me, to clear up the orchestral area — so I became Chief Assistant, Orchestral and Choral, and was in sole charge of orchestral music, again with the exception of Glock's own concerts. These were the sixties, when I was a manager all the way — an important consideration in the context of the doubts I am throwing on the factual (as opposed to the psychological) reality of management.

Came the much-discussed 'BBC rebellion' against *Broadcasting in the Seventies* which I initiated (as distinct from 'led'!). *Broadcasting in the Seventies*, now partly abandoned, was the BBC's plan for generic broadcasting (see Chapter IV, p.264), which many of us 'Supply' staff opposed on cultural grounds: we pleaded for the Third Programme principle of mixed, contrasting broadcasting — and, for that matter, still do, though there may well be fewer of us now than there were then. Speaking personally, and reiterating what I said to the Annan Committee in 1975, I am in favour, not so much of a reversion to the past, as of a natural evolution — towards what the Third Programme should have been but wasn't: a Third Programme without snobbery, without specialist esotericism, without the implied blessing bestowed on secret societies. There is esoteric knowledge, of course, but you can't have it both ways: you can't expose it exoterically.

I next became Chief Assistant, Regional Symphony

15

Orchestras, and am now Chief Assistant, New Music. In addition, for well over a decade, i.e. ever since its formation, I have been chairman of a working party of music heads of European radio stations which plans the two annual International Concert Seasons of the European Broadcasting Union.

The purpose of this autobiographical note is, simply, to show that I have been around. My views on management and control, which would never have developed if I had continued my sheltered freelance existence, are considered idiosyncratic, bizarre, even mischievous — by well-wishers and ill-wishers alike: 'Hans is a necessary part of BBC demonology', one of the BBC's most civilised top people is said to have recently remarked to a colleague. As my wife — a past master at mixing metaphors — would say, the demon is on the other leg, not the leg that kicks people (in which case they usually kick back, more or less successfully), but the leg that gently keeps them in their place, prevents them from presuming above their station, whatever that is: I don't see how you can find out without trying them in various stations; talented people are unpredictably adaptable and, what is more important, more fruitful if you are interested in fresh fruit, they adapt jobs to their personalities. But even once they have been tried out, the chances are that the wrong people have been doing the trying and assessing — for the simple reason that in collective life, there are more wrong people than right people, more people who accept yesterday's norms, especially if these norms got them to the top, than people who interest themselves in today's discoveries about what has been wrong with yesterday's norms — what has been inhuman, regressive, degrading, illusory. And don't forget that the most human, progressive, respectful, realistic people apply these very norms year in, year out — although they wouldn't dream of doing so if they were left to their own moral devices, uninfluenced by the ineluctable immorality which collective ideals impose on a person's conscience while he isn't watching — and all such ideals make jolly sure that he isn't watching.

My position, then, has been called extreme, eccentric. In relation to which centre? Charges of eccentricity, more often than not, are monumental *petitiones principii*: there has hardly been a step in the cumbersome progress of the human mind (yes, intellectually there has been progress, however slow and undramatic) that wasn't glaringly eccentric when it was taken. To accept a stable, static centre means, as a matter of geometrical fact, to go round in circles.

The circumstance that I have been around, and haven't made any noticeable hash of it, ensures that nobody is going to tell me that I am a dreamer who has been safely secluded from the world of action and doesn't know what it's all about. On the contrary, I have come to the long-considered, long-delayed conclusion that it's all about nothing — that 'management' and 'control' don't exist. They do, of course, exist as illusions shared by the 'controller' and the controlled: this is how society and societies and corporations and associations and institutions have to be run, until further notice, and it's because they are run like this that chaos is avoided, justice maintained and, above all, the ultimate purpose, the group-aim, achieved. It isn't, you know; I do, anyway.

I have been a manager, I have been managed, and I have proved consistently unmanageable — which, I presume, makes me a demon. It also makes me one of the two or three people I have been in touch with throughout organisational life who haven't been maimed by it. Of course, amongst the maimed, the unmaimed are the odd men out: the fewer, the odder. At the same time, those who have become psychologically handicapped are not difficult to diagnose — by anybody not maimed himself. As a matter of natural course, some of my closest friends are in the BBC. As a matter of utter perversion, organisationally speaking, some of them are on the lowest 'grades', while others are on my own, elevated 'grade', or yet higher: a person's grade or station, believe it or not, does not influence my personal relationships — and to me, unaffected as I am by the myth of management, all relations are personal relations, and in personal relations one does not manage or manipulate anybody, or shouldn't. Now I'll give you the opposite case, without committing any indiscretion: the identity of the individual in question will not be disclosed, directly or by possible implication; he is retired, anyway. A distinguished figure on the level of a head of department (not my own), he had spent all his life in sternly organisational contexts of one kind or another. While he was a kindly person who didn't wish anybody any harm so long as he did not feel threatened (which he never was), the degree to which he, a highly respected manager, was psychologically mutilated would pass all extra-organisational comprehension: so far as I could make out, he did not have a single friend at his place of work, not a single genuine human relationship with any of the many people with whom he had close permanent contact.

Nor was this because he had developed an independent, self-sufficient mentality that prided itself on its autonomy — on the contrary: he was extremely worried about what was thought of him, especially by his bosses, whose word he invariably took for reality. To an observer who was unaffected by the social criteria valid within the group (and only within the group), criteria which aimed at what was known as 'professional conduct', he seemed to be moving in a lifeless dream-world, in which Big Brother was amiably watching him, and he wasn't all that little a brother himself. He seemed to regard all life, certainly all professional life, as a political game, and was not readily accessible to the suggestion that he ought to speak for himself. Small wonder: he was quite right, of course, in thinking that he spoke for plenty of other people too.

Management, to be sure, is a game played to perfection, a ritual enacted with ever-renewed fervour, by managers and the managed alike. The psychological reasons are obvious. Under the regressive influence of group life, which was recognised by thinkers about human behaviour long before Freud came in and showed how it happened, the double urge develops to be the parent one would have liked to be as a child, and to return to childhood more straightforwardly and whole-mindedly, henceforth assured of parental protection.

In my experience, the question which of the two regressive paths an individual takes, or whether indeed he wants to have it both ways, does not so much depend on his particular personality, as on the psychological opportunities the group offers to him: so far as varieties of regression are concerned, the human mind is infinitely adjustable. The afore-mentioned not so little brother was a virtuoso at having it both ways — one moment a pathetic schoolboy when facing senior management, the next moment an equally pathetic picture of far-sighted managerial wisdom when facing his subordinates, but only at rare moments himself, moments in which one had to provoke him, psychologically speaking, into what he would have been if he hadn't been maimed. The horrifying experience, then, was of somebody who seemed artificial when, for once, he was being natural.

During my few months as Music Talks Producer, I did not notice any of this; I just enjoyed myself hugely and rather naively. The Music Talks Producer at the BBC is rather a separate radio station, and good luck to him: nobody has much of a chance or desire to interfere with him, and he has no opportunity at all to interfere with anybody. It can hardly be an accident that my predecessors — Alec Robertson and then Dr Roger Fiske — as well as my successor, Robert Layton, kept their vastly contrasting personalities intact despite many years of service, which I would describe as faithful and faithless in well-differentiated measure.

Things began to dawn on me as Chief Assistant, Chamber Music and Recitals, after the initial flush of excitement had subsided over having got the job I had put in for, and over now being in a position of musical 'leadership': at that time, I still thought that was something to be proud of, a heavy responsibility for better broadcasting, for more musical broadcasting, which one had to meet, whatever the cost.

Whatever the cost? What a glib thing to say, to feel. I presently discovered that I hadn't lived; the very praise showered upon me made me suspicious. Did I want to be praised by people whose aim in life was to make a success of their jobs, their 'careers', who had abrogated the highly unofficial duty to look beyond that aim, and, maybe, sideways? What if sideways turned out to be ahead, and ahead, if not sideways, then perhaps a little diagonal?

The truth — I submit there is such a thing as ethical truth — dawned slowly, but all the more tellingly. Programme x was a wonderful idea, series y a still better one, programme balance z the only logical solution to the problem of duplications and clashes of works. My staff — at that time, shame upon me, I still thought in terms of 'my' staff — had to be persuaded of our obligation to do just these things, and if, looking sideways, one spotted unhappinesses on the way, personal frustrations, neglected artistic urges, that could not be helped.

Or could it? Once again, the attitude many a distinguished colleague showed in pursuance of his aims, or the group's aims, made me suspicious. One of the most outstanding amongst them was ready to walk over corpses, some of them still wriggling, all in a good cause — the unconditional furtherance of our art. Mr A had to be persuaded to stay with us because we needed him, although a more satisfying job, more truly in line with his specific abilities, had been offered to him elsewhere. Mr B had to . . . never mind. The truth had dawned. Human beings are not a means towards an end, good producer 'material', good management 'material': despicable managerial concept. They are an end. The greatest programme in the world wasn't worth harming a human being. What was more, my superior judgment, and my ability to handle people (at that time I still thought in terms of 'handling' people!), for which I got that much more money than they, might not be unassailable; if an organisation happened to have invested me with a bit of omnipotence, that gave me no right to use it, except an

21

organisational right, and I wouldn't be seen dead with a mere organisational right, with mere invested authority. The authority of knowledge and ability, yes, but that had to *show,* whether it had been legitimised or not: it didn't need any legitimisation.

I am happy to say that I only remember a single occasion when I actually imposed my will, and I am still unhappy about having done so. At the time, in the chamber music section, Leo Black — now a widely known, distinguished musician — was one of 'my' producers, and I did not agree to his including the Nielsen Wind Quintet in a programme he had devised, because it 'wasn't good enough'. Leo Black grumpily disagreed, but far from having a proper discussion on the matter, far from showing proper respect for his opinion, I simply ruled the work out of the programme. To the best of my recollection, it was the only time I 'ruled', and I shall never rule again — even if my opinion is more objectively supportable than it was in the case of the Nielsen Quintet. In my defence, let it be said that for the rest, throughout the past 18 years, I have always kicked upstairs, more than anybody I know or know of, trying to exercise my authority that way, and never downstairs.

And I have learnt about one ultimate value without which there are no human beings to speak of, and one ultimate vice with which there are no human beings to speak of. The ultimate value is the independence of individual conscience, while the ultimate vice is its cession, capitulation, loving surrender, arrested development, collective envelopment. There is no collective wisdom; there is only unacknowledged, collective stupidity. Man has lived for quite some time now and still hasn't discovered, once and for all, that a group doesn't think.

22

Why hasn't he? Because he likes to feel that what the group does for him, the ideals with which it replaces his thoughts (which were strenuous enough while they lasted), are thought.

I have learnt that if the independence of individual conscience is an ultimate value, interference with individual consciences — my ruling that the Nielsen Wind Quintet wasn't good enough — is the gravest danger to truth-finding and man-helping alike: my ruling did not help the truth, or Mr Black, or anything or anybody else, with the possible exception of those who hated Nielsen's Wind Quintet, and who could have switched off, anyway. The fact that we can easily make people like our controlling them does not make our control more respectable, realistic, responsible — even though 'responsibility' is measured in terms of how many of them we control: it is used as a euphemism for power. We in Western civilisation have never yet seriously tried not to interfere, not to control, not to tell others what's good for either them or those we want to control with their help. We say it wouldn't work: there has to be law and order. So far as I have tried it, it has worked beautifully, with plenty of thoughtful law introduced by individual consciences, and plenty of pre-creative disorder without 'anarchy'. The very connotation of this concept begs the fundamental human question: who says that without a ruler there is disorder, lawlessness and confusion? What have we achieved with the essential help of rulers, 'controllers', managing directors, chairmen, and all the other means of paternalisation, in either the so-called capitalist or the so-called communist world? If and when we achieved anything, it was unity at the expense of human dignity, of sheer, mere grown-upness.

When I hear that somebody is 'a wonderful team-worker' (in science, in cultural administration, in any type of organisation, in the orchestra, or, of course, in a team sport itself, such as football) I know he's had it — unless, that is, he never had it in the first place: anybody who has ever formed a team with a dog, or more than one dog (as I did as a child), knows that the dog is the perfect team-worker. He has just enough intelligence to understand what you want from him, and just too little to understand that what you want from him is in your interest rather than in his: you're giving him enough sausages and pats (salary and recognition) for him to mix up his interests with yours. Below all, he loves being controlled. Though he calls himself a higher mammal, he is so corrupt, so sub-animalic, that he may die when you die, though he won't die when his wife dies, or her puppies do.

Chapter I (originally a radio talk, which I have not revised) is a flash-back from 1975 with a vengeance — to a society under a highly effective ruler. As Chapter II is designed to show, you miss Chapter I's point if it makes you feel sadly good about our (your) own goodness, and 'thoughtful' about those terrible Nazis, or terrible anybodies for that matter: what I am on about is what happens to conscience, yours, mine, anybody's, once it is projected on to a group ideal. The end of humanity happens long before any ensuing massacre. It happens when somebody starts to save the world, or his country, or his corporation, or anything that needs other people's consciences, that needs nonentities taking charge of entities. Of course, the nonentities may have been entities in the first place; the loss of personal identity goes with the job, with 'responsibility': it isn't me that's controlling

24

you, it's Germany, Marxist ideology, BBC 'policy' — something bigger than both of us. As a matter of fact, there's nothing bigger than either of us so long as we retain our moral integrity — which most people are ready to hire out, the hire fee being their salary. Quite a few people are even prepared to sell it, the price being an amalgam of salary and power, the latter measurable in terms of the former. Thenceforth, their minds are at rest: where humanity has been abolished, there are no more human problems.

Conversely, the entities which are being taken in charge inevitably run the mortal risk of gradual de-humanisation and depersonalisation. Speaking purely empirically, I should say that at the outside, about one person in thirty in our civilisation preserves the dignity of his individuality in a well-organised, 'loyalty' - conscious, collective context. The others become well-cared-for children, more loyal to their parent substitutes than they had ever been to their parents, because as children they rarely had anybody to kick instead of hitting out at their parents, whereas now they have — if only their secretaries.

An independently-thinking, young colleague of mine, stimulated by my psychological and moral objections to the BBC's annual reporting system (which I regard as regressive, degrading, and factually useless anyway), made a private investigation amongst staff he knew about their attitude to the BBC bosses' annual reporting on their subordinates. Some were for, many against — but the only group that was wholly against were the secretaries. Why were they unanimous? My answer: because they are the only group that hasn't anybody to report on, to be parental about — it's as simple as that.

Life generally is, once you banish all double-think.

Chapter III describes the climax of double-think: what had promised to be the twentieth century's leading method of safeguarding the individual psyche, of promoting its capacity for choice, and of resisting interference with it (including the therapist's), has led to the formation of a secret, moralising, soul-destroying society whose former human entities, and current inhuman non-entities, behave in a predicatable, stereotyped way in the service of what has become a group ideal which allows less intellectual and ethical freedom than do the dogmata of the most fanatical creed. Indeed, if there were such a thing as a dog's dogma, his behaviour would be indistinguishable from that of a loyal member of the International Psycho-analytical Association, a 'good analyst' as they call him; the occasional, easily subduable bark, of which nobody (not even the dog) knows whether it's joy, aggression, or a bit of both, remains the sole, pitiable show of independence, much appreciated by the (real or imagined) loving master.

Chapter IV, at the centre of my life and my profession (the two are indistinguishable), dispels the delusion that ours is an individualistic musical society; whereas Chapter V is not by Neville Cardus, who died in 1975. *Requiescat in pace,* and I did indeed greatly respect him as a person, not least because he was inaccessible to intellectual, aesthetic, or ethical interference. But he was not a musician and I am; he believed in music criticism and I don't; and he established playful, sport-ful links between his interest in music and his interest in sport which my double interest would never allow: as will be seen in Chapter IV, art is not a game, though many would make it one. All game-playing (or watching) is

26

regression — and welcome regression at that, so long as one doesn't confuse it with art or life. Sleep and dreams are regressions too, and welcome on precisely the same terms. What commands our attention in the context of this book is that even on the game-playing level, which can be as relaxing as it is regressive, and where individualism used to flower in, and lend strength and efficacy to, team sports, frightened, safe-playing collectivity and forcible de-individualisation have gained the upper hand. Our age has given up the will to win, and our dreams centre on not losing — which, we feel, can best be done collectively: safety (in numbers) first.

But unless we regain the power to think and feel for ourselves, in all intellectual and emotional situations, and unless we show total respect for that power in other people, and total contempt for all attempts at conversion, we're going to lose anyhow — transitively: we shall lose the dignity of being human, a loss which is never noticed when it happens. It is this threatening loss my book is about, or rather that part of the threat that had been realised by 1975.

The moral? The title of this preface — a crusade against all crusades.

# CHAPTER I

# Vienna, 1938

In 1938, I was due to take my matriculation exam — my A Levels, if I may translate meaningfully. For years I had been scared of this event — as indeed had all other schoolboys, good or bad: in German-speaking countries, the matriculation was one of life's major traumas, and people had matriculation dreams right up to their death, while books were written about suicides which took place out of matriculation-fear. Franz Werfel's *Der Abituriententag* ('The Matriculation Day') was one outstanding novel about such a suicide.

But in March of that year, a month or two before the date of the examination, the Nazis invaded Austria. The Austrian Chancellor, Dr Kurt von Schuschnigg (whose brother was to become Austrian radio's head of music after the war), abdicated on my 19th birthday, March 11, ('to avoid the shedding of fraternal blood' — *Bruderblut*, as he called it), and the Nazis proceeded to invade Austria. On March 12, Hitler made his entry into Vienna. While it was, of course, carefully stage-managed, the difficult question remains how far the Austrians welcomed the *Anschluss*. In any event, their enthusiasm tends to be underplayed nowadays. There had been a strong illegal Nazi party; there had been thousands if not millions of more passive sympathisers. It's not for me to guess proportions. Anyhow, the Vienna correspondent of the *Völkische Beobachter* went through

28

the usual motions:

The streets of Vienna are ablaze with a veritable fire-storm of frenzied enthusiasm which beggars description. The crowds are beside themselves with delight. As news came of the German troops' approach, people openly embraced and hugged each other in the streets. They still can't quite believe that they have won. The German city of Vienna, and with it the whole of Austria, has arisen. Swastika flags flutter from every window and balcony. Austria is a National Socialist State! Outside the official German tourist office, whose windows display a photograph of the Führer, the crowds gather. The sparkling, happy eyes of the people are the most moving thing I have ever seen.

With the Nazi invasion, the imminent trauma of my matriculation suddenly ceased to exist: from the moment go, one was, intermittently, running for one's life, and the school and study aspect of it assumed, to put it mildly, a dream-like quality: if one passed one's matriculation, one would not, as a Jew, be allowed to enter university anyway, while abroad — if one was lucky enough to get out — an Austrian or German matriculation certificate would not be recognised. Nevertheless, one did one's empty duty. After all, one had been preparing for this event for eight years; besides, going to school and doing as if one cared about the matric created the illusion, however thin, that life was going on as usual, that one might eventually survive. For many, though, life was not going on, not at all as usual anyway. According to an official enquiry carried out after the war into the events of those days,

the best available estimates are that the very first wave of arrests in the day of March 1938 caught more than 70,000 people. Thereafter, a regular trickle of arrests and disappearances continued.

The father of a girl friend of mine was arrested on March 13: he had, as a barrister, conducted and won an action against the *Völkische Beobachter*. He was taken to Dachau concentration camp, and slowly tortured to death. Friends who met him there in later months were unable to recognise him.

Now, in view of the large Jewish contingent in my own school, the physical separation of the form into Aryans and Jews, the former yelling 'Heil Hitler!' when the uniformed form-master entered (who had replaced our Jewish form-master), was not too frightening: it was easier, at that adolescent stage, to stand by silently and think 'You fools!' if there were many of you. But when we heard that our former Jewish form-master, whom we all venerated, had been savagely beaten up and his flat plundered, the thought of 'You fools!' wasn't quite good enough. He is now a university professor in America — doing better, no doubt, than he could ever have done without the holocaust. This is the paradox, but it only affected that tiny proportion of German and Austrian Jews who were not, eventually, gassed.

The matriculation came, and I passed without noticing, as it were. But one thing I did notice, and that was the official reaction to my German essay. For the Aryans, there were five titles for choice, four of them on such subjects as 'Adolf Hitler's *Mein Kampf* and the Concept of National Socialism'. The fifth subject, the only one for the Jews, was 'An Analysis of Poetic Realism in German Literature'. Well, when it came to the prize-giving stage, the German teacher, a physical cripple in SA uniform, made a speech in which he pointed to the deplorable fact that mine had been by far the best German essay: 'It's high time for Austrian culture to be rescued. We must

30

have reached a low point in degeneration if it is possible for a Jew to write the only outstanding German essay.'

The ensuing months were spent on unsuccessful attempts to get out of the country, and on being beaten up in between. My father, who was wealthy, was dying — and it was his money which made it difficult for me to obtain a passport.

Soon after the Anschluss, this order appeared in the Austrian Legal Gazette:

The Commissioner for the Four Year Plan and the Minister for Internal Affairs of the German Reich decree as follows:

*Para. 1* Every Jew is ordered to declare his entire property, both at home and abroad, valued as of the date of this decree.

*Para. 2* Property within the meaning of this decree means the total and entire possessions of those affected, irrespective of whether they are liable to tax or not.

*Para. 3* Whoever fails, negligently or with malice aforethought, to comply with the above instructions, will be liable to a fine and/or 10 years' penal servitude. In addition to the punishment, the Court may order confiscation of the property.

My father had made a full and frank declaration, and the official view was that where so much had been declared, there must be much more, undeclared, where that had come from. So long as the Nazis did not feel sure that they were getting hold of every penny available, I would not get my passport. I remember my father calling me into his bedroom and saying that anyway, he was glad that we had lost all our money: he had always been worried by my growing up as the son of wealthy parents, and by the danger of my attributing an importance to money which it did not, in reality, possess:

'Only when one realises that money's of no importance whatever does one begin to live'. He himself had been both poor and (as a successful architect) wealthy in his own life, and from the point of view of life's real values, he hadn't noticed the difference. He said he didn't care two hoots about losing all his money; he didn't, incidentally, know that he was dying.

In order to try and get a passport, one had to queue up at various places to obtain the necessary documents, and what usually happened was that one queued up all night without achieving any result, except that the SA or SS came to visit these queues occasionally, for the purpose of beating them up. As an official contemporary report to Police Headquarters had it:

Sympathy for Jews, or compassion with their fate, was manifested only rarely, and where such feelings were nevertheless expressed, however hesitantly, the majority of onlookers turned on those concerned with great energy. Any who showed excessive sympathy with the Jews were pointed out to the Police. Some of these were themselves arrested.

One such occasion sticks vividly in my memory, because at that stage I felt as if Western civilisation had abandoned us: this time, I queued up in order to obtain my British visa, or rather the document confirming it (since I had no passport to put it in) — something which very few people were able to obtain, and which I was fortunate enough to have been granted because my sister was married to an Englishman who had under-taken, if necessary, to support me for the rest of my life, so that I wouldn't be a burden to the state. Now, I had to queue up outside the British Consulate in order to get this document. We were a small and eminently beatable queue, and we talked, with some excitement, about the chances of our being beaten up while we stood there. In due course, an English Consulate official came out and asked us in a stern voice to behave in an orderly fashion, and not to make so much noise. I took the opportunity to step forward and ask him why it was necessary to stand out there in the road, when it was extremely likely that we would be beaten up sooner or later: couldn't we wait inside, since there were so few of us? 'This is quite out of the question', he said, and vanished through the door, which was duly and audibly locked. Within an hour, we were beaten up.

There were other pleasantries, such as being arrested for short periods in order to clean some Nazi barracks; if one said that one wanted to ring home, where one had a dying father, in order to tell him that one would be late, one was told 'Let him die'.

At least, I was released. Such arrests could have more serious consequences, as witness a circular by the Gestapo of 24th May, 1938:

TO: All district commissariats in Vienna.
SUBJECT: Arrest of Jews.
ENCLOSURES: Interrogation sheets and index cards.
It has been decreed that undesirable Jews, especially those with a criminal record, are to be arrested and transferred to Dachau concentration camp.
The arrests are to be organised by District Police Commissariats. Only German — that is, Austrian — and stateless Jews are affected. Jews of more than 50 years of age are to be arrested only in special circumstances.

Some 2,000 Jews were arrested following this order and transferred to Dachau.

On November 7th, 1938, a junior official at the German Embassy in Paris, Ernst vom Rath, was shot by a 17-year-old Polish Jew, Herschel Grynspan, whose parents had been expelled from Germany and sent back to Poland. Rath did not immediately die — and I thought to myself that if he died, a violent pogrom was an extreme likelihood. I therefore decided to follow the news closely, in order to stay at home or go into hiding when the news of his death came. The day after his death, however, I overslept: I had wanted to be at the Jewish Community Centre, where I would get one of the necessary documents for my passport, at 6 a.m., in order not to be at the end of one of those enormous queues; but woke up at 7. I hastily dressed, put the unread *Völkische Beobachter* into my coat pocket, ran out into the street, and caught a taxi. The unread paper contained the news that Rath had died. At the corner of the little street where the Community Centre was, I paid off the taxi — to find, to my surprise, that the street looked peaceful and abandoned: I didn't see any queues. But there was a Jew standing at the street corner, and I walked up to him and asked him whether the Centre was open, and whether one could queue up for the document in question. 'Yes', he said, with a sad face, 'just walk over there, right up to the main door.' A pity that I did not, at this stage at least, have a look at my paper. I walked along to the main door, outside which stood another Jew. I walked up to him and said: 'It looks terribly quiet around here. Is the Centre really open? I want to queue up for my document.' 'Yes,' he said with an equally sad face, 'just step in here.' I opened the door — but, instead of Jewish officials, I faced an SA man who threw me against a wall with considerable zest. When I picked myself up, I found myself in the company of a number of Jews who had just had the same experience. 'Vom Rath is dead?' I asked one of them. 'Of course,' he said. The Jewish guides outside the building had been posted by the Nazis; whoever refused to play the game would be shot.

This was the notorious November pogrom, the *Kristallnacht,* from which, eventually, only a small proportion of Jews escaped with their lives; the vast majority rotted away or were tortured to death in concentration camps, or were ultimately exterminated, gassed. Here is a confidential report by one Lieut. Fast of the SS, who was in charge of a small detachment taking part. It is dated November 12, 1938, and is addressed to one of his superiors at the SS headquarters for Lower Austria:

After my detachment had been detailed for special duty at midnight on November 9, I was ordered to report to the office of the District Commissioner at 1 a.m. Also present were leaders of other SS detachments, representatives of the SA and of the police, as well as the Special Commissioner for the Aryanisation of Jewish property.

The District Commissioner gave us a strict briefing. In response to the cowardly Jewish assassination of Third Secretary vom Rath in Paris, fierce popular indignation had already turned its wrath upon the Jews of Germany. Among other things, several synagogues had been set on fire. It was essential, the District Commissioner continued, that in Austria, too, popular indignation should rouse itself against the Jews this very night. If, as a result, any building and property belonging to the Jews should catch fire, this would be a matter for the local fire services, and detachments of the National Socialist movement were not obliged to take a hand. Within the framework of the operation, the police would have the following duties:

(1) Looting was to be prevented, and so was the destruction or damage of Aryan property.

(2) Towards the end of the operation, the Jews were to be taken into custody for their own safety — especially those

35

of working age. Popular indignation was to be given full reign until 6 o'clock in the morning; until that hour the police were to avoid all confrontation with the demonstrators. Care should be taken that all those involved in the operation should wear civilian clothing.

At the time, I knew none of this, of course. After a few hours in the Jewish Community Centre, we were taken, in lorries, to various primary schools which had been allocated for the purpose and set up as temporary prisons. Upon arrival, we had the first of several Gestapo interviews. The Gestapo officer had a printed form before him, from which he read his questions. Among the questions I remember were the following: 'Since when have you been a homosexual?' 'I am not a homosexual,' I replied. 'Did I ask you whether you were, or did I ask you since when you have been one?' When I did not reply, he wrote in 'five years'. 'How many Aryan girls have you seduced?' 'I haven't seduced any Aryan girls,' I replied. 'Did I ask you whether you had, or did I ask you how many you had seduced?' Again, when I didn't reply, he wrote in 'five'. After this comprehensive survey of my biography, he turned the sheet round and said 'Sign'. I started reading it — whereupon he said, 'Did I say read, or did I say sign?' I duly signed, and the document was carefully filed away.

Between 150 and 200 of us were then driven into a classroom which would normally have space for 20 or 30, and which was to be our abode for the next six days. For three days, we didn't get any food, but the fact that we didn't get any water for more than a day was worse. There were various types of beatings, and what was, perhaps, most interesting psychologically was that in the middle of every night appeared a special SS detachment,

36

called *Verfügungstruppe*[1], which consisted of unpaid volunteers (unpaid, that is, for this special task) who went through a violent beating exercise purely for the fun of it. At the other end of psychological interest was the composure and behaviour of the orthodox Jews, of whom I was not one. Quite often, we were chased through corridors, with SS men with rifles on either side, who beat us with those rifles while we ran through. What *I* did when such a corridor was in sight was to stop and wait until I had a long free space before me; then I bent down, covered my head with my hands, and ran through the corridor as fast as I could, so that I got most of the knocks on my behind. The orthodox Jews were above any such evasive action. They slowly walked through those corridors, in an upright position, with the result that you couldn't identify them when they came out at the other end — but, at the same time, without showing the slightest sign in their behaviour of having been touched, telling each other the same Jewish jokes at the other end as they had before the operation started. I was stunned: this was one of the deepest experiences of my life, about which I later published an article, a few weeks after my escape from Austria. There they were, people who seemed quaint, curious figures in ordinary life, now behaving in a detached manner which was far beyond the rest of us. In particular, I remember a newspaper boy whom I had known because I always bought my papers from him. He must have been about sixteen or seventeen. When he came out at the other end of such a corridor, I literally didn't recognise him; it took me minutes to discover who he was. But his behaviour was of the

---

[1] 'Disposal Squad' — which may not mean much but then *Verfügungstruppe* didn't mean much either.

orthodox kind, and when I asked him how it was possible for him to behave like that, he laughed and answered, 'Well, we have had a few thousand years' training, haven't we? What difference does one more such incident make? These people haven't reached the stage where they know what they're doing — so you can't even blame them.' Then he told me a Jewish joke which was appropriate to the occasion.

After three days, we got our first food, paid for by the Jewish Community. Most people were sick after it; I myself wasn't hungry any more by that stage and ate very cautiously and little. On, I think, the fourth day, one chap suddenly went beserk, if beserk you can call it, and started shouting 'Criminals, murderers, sadists . . .' He was shot dead, whereupon another chap, likewise, decided that he had had enough, and jumped out of the fourth-floor window. Now this wouldn't do at all, having a Jewish corpse in the street, so we were told to stand with our faces against a wall, by way of punishment, without the slightest movement; whoever moved would be shot: the SS stood with their rifles behind us. This exercise lasted about four hours — in which circumstances it was amazing to note how much you could move without moving, by gradually shifting your weight from one leg to the other.

As for events in the outside world, here's the Nazis' own statistical survey:

In Vienna, 17 synagogues and 61 prayer houses (described by the newspaper Der Stürmer, as 'not real houses of God, but dens of iniquity') were set on fire, 7,800 Jews arrested, including 1,226 who already had permission to emigrate or who were listed as wishing to emigrate at the centre for Jewish emigration. 4,083 Jewish shops were plundered and closed down, 1,950

38

dwellings ransacked. In Germany as a whole, damage amounted to 25 million marks, and 7½ thousand shops and stores were destroyed.

These figures were revealed at a meeting of representatives of the Ministries of Finance and Economic Affairs. Hermann Göring, who presided in his capacity as Commissioner for the Four Year Plan, exclaimed: 'Good heavens! Why couldn't you have killed off a couple of hundred Jews instead of destroying so much valuable property?' In fact, 91 Jews were killed during the pogrom according to the official German statistics. The number of those who committed suicide has never been established. Göring later made a speech in which he promised that within a year, Vienna would be 'judenrein' — free of Jews and clean. *That* kind of promise the Nazis tended to keep.

Now, to give a full description of the events of those days of imprisonment would be repetitive and boring; suffice it to say that more often than not, when something frightening was in store for us, we were told of it beforehand, so that we could fully savour our anxiety for hours before the event. As a result, when, on the sixth day, we were told: 'Tomorrow, at 6 a.m., you will be castrated, and at 8 o'clock you will be executed', we believed it. By that time, mind you, most of us were beyond the will to survive — almost too tired to be capable of fear. Nevertheless, at one moment during that night, the thought flicked through my mind: 'If, by any remote chance, I should succeed in getting out of here, and in dying in a bed, I swear to myself that I'll never again be in a bad mood, whatever the circumstances of my life or death.' I'll come back to this one later.

We were not castrated at six o'clock nor executed at

eight. Instead, we were transported to a proper police prison, where we met proper, ordinary criminals — veritable saints compared to our guards and officers. In the course of the morning, after a series of the usual violent incidents, there was another Gestapo interview. This time, the atmosphere *seemed* slightly more courteous. 'Sit down,' the officer said as I approached his desk. I could not believe my ears, and was right not to: as I sat down, the chair was of course, pulled from under me. Nevertheless, the questions seemed less Kafkaesque than at previous interviews, and I decided to be on my guard, just in case there was some point in giving a skilful answer.

'Why are you bleeding all over?' 'Oh, well, I fell down a whole flight of stairs as I came up here.' '*Fell?* You fell down a flight of stairs?' 'Yes, I stumbled and fell.' 'Did anybody beat you?' 'No.' 'Did you *see* anybody beat anybody?' 'No.' 'Nothing at all?' 'No.' He adopted a more solemn voice: 'Have you any complaint about the treatment you received?' 'None whatever.' While I answered, I heard an excerpt from an interview at the next desk: 'Do you know why you are in here?' 'I believe because I am one of the murderers of vom Rath.' 'That is correct.' My own interrogator now proceeded to a series of questions which could not but raise hopes in my mind: 'If we released you, how soon would you be able to leave the country?' 'Immediately, and I would leave tomorrow.' That, of course, was a lie: for more than eight months I had tried, in vain, to obtain a passport. 'Have you any proof that you can leave immediately?' 'It so happens I have,' I said. 'I have a British visa and I have the relevant document on me.' I pulled the British Consulate's confirmation out of my pocket. He read it carefully, then shouted: 'Form "B".' In due course, four identical forms were placed in front of me which, this time, I *was* required to read. They said that in no circumstances, for the rest of my life, wherever I was, would I say a word about what I'd seen and experienced while being imprisoned, and that I was aware that if, at any stage, I were to disclose what I had seen and experienced, I would meet with just punishment, wherever I was. I signed, perjuring myself joyfully: unless this was another funny game there really *was* hope. The officer then shouted 'D'!, which made my heart sink again, because I thought it might mean Dachau. I was pushed into group 'D', then, and the excitement about a possible release had totally overcome my exhaustion. Where, a day or two before, I had wholly given up, accepting the end without much difficulty, the desire to survive had come back explosively.

Group 'D' was pushed into one of the corridors we knew so well, again with SS lined up on either side, complete with rifles. But though we were chased through the corridors, nobody touched us this time — which, of course, reinforced hope. This operation continued for a considerable time: we were chased through a vast variety of corridors, up and down staircases, almost always with SS lined up on either side, and always being left unharmed. We were, however, reaching exhaustion point, and wondered how long we would be able to continue. I happened to be the first in my particular group, the front runner, as it were, and running along a corridor, I came to face a glass door without being able to stop before it. I crashed into it, and as I picked myself up and got through the door, I was standing in the street. This, I realised, was my discharge from prison.

There is an excerpt, not readily comprehensible to me, from the minutes of the Regional Economic Committee for Vienna, drafted by an SS Captain by the name of Seeliger — and interesting as a psychological document, rather than as a factual report on what he calls 'the population at large'.

As for the popular reaction to the events of 10th November and the following days, the unanimous view was that it had been one of revulsion and horror, and that in the execution of the operation, scandalous scenes had been enacted which did great damage to the prestige of the Party and the Government. Two of those present declared that if another party existed in Germany, it would be the duty of every right-thinking man and woman to support it. All those present declared unanimously that pogroms and vandalisms were not suitable means for solving the Jewish question, and that the destruction, looting and devastation which had taken place had filled not only the population at large, but even large sections of the Party, with disgust and shame.

Well, neither I nor any of my fellow Jews were in touch with any of this 'revulsion and horror', 'disgust and shame'. Anyway, the first thing I wanted to do as I was out in the street was to ring my father to tell him that I was alright. As I tried to do this, I noticed the effect of what one might call a traumatic neurosis: diagonally across the road I saw a telephone box, but in order to reach it I would have had to pass an SS man who was posted outside the prison. I tried to get myself to pass him, explaining to myself that at this stage he would not possibly harm me, since I was obviously a released person, and as care had always been taken not to show the outside world what was happening to prisoners. In spite of several mental attmpts, however, I could not

42

bring myself to pass him; instead, I walked right round the block, in order to reach the telephone box from the other side, without the necessity of having to pass an SS man.

Now, the Gestapo were not as well organised as they were reputed to be, and I should not, in fact, have been released: from another Gestapo headquarters, a warrant for my arrest had been issued before I was freed. I came to know about this fact through bribing an SS officer to look up my files: he had been an acquaintance of a half-Jewish cousin of mine, through whom I advanced the payment to him. The information was that I was to be arrested because my father had money in Hungary and England, which he had not declared — neither fact true, incidentally, but that did not, of course, make any difference, and there was no point in trying to establish the truth. One consequence which seemed to flow from this state of affairs had been that I had been told, before my arrest, that a large sum of English money (I forget the actual amount, I think it was about £1,000) was needed, in addition to the official 'escape tax' which comprised all my father's available money, in order for me to obtain one of the documents needed to get my passport. My brother-in-law had duly paid the money, but I never got the document.

As a matter of fact, the Jews themselves were made to pay compensation to the German Government for the damage and devastation caused to their own property. At the meeting of representatives of the Ministries of Finance and Economic Affairs, presided over by Göring (which I've already mentioned), the following was decreed:

(1) German Jews must make restitution for all damage

43

caused by the pogrom and reimburse insurance companies for any payments they have been obliged to make. (2) As an atonement for the death of Councillor vom Rath, a fine is to be levied on all Jews totalling one thousand million marks.

(3) All Jewish enterprises, shops and factories are to be taken over compulsorily by non-Jews — the sale price to be paid into blocked accounts.

Fortunately, my father still had enough money left to pay this 'restitution and atonement tax' too. Well, in full possession of the information in my file after my release, I was, of course, determined to be extremely cautious in order not to be arrested again. I rarely slept at home and, generally, made myself as unfindable as possible. At the same time, I had to continue to try to get the necessary documents for obtaining my passport, and indeed the passport itself. Each attempt was, of course, fraught with danger since, in theory, I should have been arrested each time I appeared at one of the relevant police or emigration departments. Fortunately, inefficiency prevailed. I remember one particular instance, when the official in question looked at my name, repeating 'Keller, Keller . . . I know your name: I ought to know your face.' I remained silent; he had, no doubt, been given or shown a copy of the warrant, but had forgotten his instructions. 'Ah', he suddenly said, 'I seem to remember. You probably were one of the Jews downstairs whom we employed to sift documents, and that's where I know your name and face from.' I joyfully agreed, although, of course, I'd never been in the place.

In the end, I did actually obtain all the necessary documents, and my passport. But by this stage I and my uncle-adviser, a barrister, were very doubtful about how to manage my departure, for the border police, as well as the officials at Vienna airport, would be in possession of the warrant for my arrest: that much we knew from the information about my file. However, another event occurred which caused the absolute need for my immediate escape — or my immediate attempt to escape, anyway: my father died, and I became his sole heir. It was obvious that as soon as the fact of his death was known, there would be redoubled attempts to arrest me and not to let me go.

My uncle and I finally decided for me to try a flight from Vienna rather than a train journey. For one thing, emigration by aeroplane was rare at that time, and one might possibly hope that I would be expected at a border rather than at the airport; for another, my uncle, if he accompanied me to the airport, would know if the escape succeeded, and would be able to notify my mother and sister in London. I bought myself an air ticket for the next plane and, next morning, proceeded to Vienna airport with my uncle. As we waited in the airport lounge, we sat back to back, because we thought that two Jews being seen together at the same time might arouse suspicion. We were talking over our shoulders, when I suddenly heard a stern voice ask my uncle: 'What are you doing here?' 'I'm waiting for a friend who is arriving on the plane from Prague'. 'What's his name?' My uncle invented a name. There was a short silence, and then the voice said 'Come with us'.

As I was passing through the passport control (or trying to, anyway), the officer, looking at my name and picture said, 'Keller, Keller . . . I know that name and I know that picture; there is something wrong with you'. I shrugged my shoulders in bafflement, hoping to God that he had forgotten his instructions, as his predecessor had at that emigration office, and that he would be equally disinclined to tell his superiors that he had forgotten. 'Ah,' he said, after a short pause, 'I think I remember: you didn't surrender your driving licence when all Jews were ordered to.' I had never driven a car, and I had had no driving licence, but I immediately confessed: 'Yes, this is quite true, but I have apologised and did finally surrender it. I simply had forgotten, and I think my apology was accepted.' He shook his head musingly, and finally said, 'Come with me'. I was taken into an empty room, where I was told to undress, and every inch of my clothing was carefully examined — as, of course, was my luggage. The whole operation took a very long time, and the departure time of my plane had passed, but through a window, I still saw the plane standing on the runway. Eventually, the investigation having yielded a negative result, the officer who had taken me into the room said, 'Alright, then. Dress and get into the plane.' As the plane took off, there was the overwhelming consciousness of survival, but, at the same time, extreme anxiety about my uncle's fate. He was going to ring my mother and sister upon my departure, so I thought that if they were at the airport in Croydon, that meant that he had been released; and if they weren't, that he hadn't been. Unfortunately, when I arrived in Croydon, there was no trace of them. I was now certain that my uncle was on his way to a concentration camp. Eventually, however, I found my family: they had gone to the wrong door. My uncle had been released after an hour's interrogation, and had telephoned them.

I was fortunate; thousands of other Jews — eventually millons, six million Jews — weren't. They did not die in the war, as part of the cruelty of war, in battle; they were exterminated — the vastest extermination of human beings in the history of the world. Against this background, let's hear what Dr Josef Goebbels, Germany's Minister of Propaganda and a man with literary, 'cultural' aspirations, had to say in an official statement in that selfsame month of November, 1938.

The cowardly assassination by the Jew Grynspan has provoked, in the entire German people, a most understandable indignàtion which, in view of the unexampled turpitude of the deed and the unbelievable impudence with which it was carried out, manifested itself in anti-Jewish demonstrations. If, despite the highly justified fury of all Germans, not a hair on the head of a single Jew was so much as touched, the world should give due recognition to the German people's sense of discipline and decency.

Two conclusions emerge — one of them what I learned to regard as sour grapes. For a long time, I thought that if one happened to survive it all, it was important to have had this experience, because, otherwise, one would not really be aware of what human beings were capable of. That's to say, if my best friend had told me about the things I had witnessed — about this indiscriminate, enthusiastic, collective sadism, I should not have believed him. The trouble is that, psychologically, this realisation of what human beings are capable of at the most primitive level simply does not work in the long run. Today, although I know, purely intellectually, what I experienced, the emotional awareness of it has been repressed — or, to put it differently, I am just as incapable of appreciating this level of reality emotionally as I would have been if I had never experienced it. This

47

type of repression is probably the most dangerous obstacle along the road towards an ethical improvement of society. It's all very well to be intellectually aware of what people are capable of, but if you don't feel it in your bones, you are likely not to do enough about preventing recurrences of such sadistic climaxes.

But the other conclusion, equally psychological, has remained reality. I've mentioned the thought which flashed through my mind at the very stage when, rationally, I had given up all hope — that if, against all realistic expectations, I was going to survive, I would never again be in a bad mood. *This* one, surprisingly, still works. Whenever there is motivation for a bad mood, it is enough for me to remind myself of this thought, and the attendant emotion comes back with it, the result being a grateful elation about being alive.

# CHAPTER II

# Prague, 1975

I have come deeply to suspect my successful pieces. Since this threatens to be one of them, I had better take fierce precautions from the outset. The most successful one is, actually, relevant to my present theme: it is Chapter I, my mere report on 'Vienna 1938', which was twice broadcast and then published in *The Listener* in a shortened version. Altogether, it elicited well over 300 letters, and although I answered most of them, I don't think I liked many of them. What I disliked was not any of the writers, but that which they all seemed to have in common — one or the other type of moral satisfaction at being able to be horrified at the past, which was safely past enough to make the illusory exercise worthwhile: it can't happen nowadays, it can't happen in this country, it couldn't have happened in this country, we must make sure that it never happens in this country etc. — all reactions which got their bearers out of the present, out of the need to do something here and now. If there is any lesson to be drawn from any crime against humanity, it is that its sources, inevitably, are actively around us all the time, and within us too, otherwise it could not possibly have happened. But the last thing we want to do when confronted with despicable human behaviour is to find it as near to us as we possibly can. We passionately turn every experience, the most distasteful included, into a source of pleasure, and there is little pleasure to be

49

derived from realising that what, say, the Nazi story teaches me is that I am behaving wrongly to my subordinates, or not wrongly enough to my superiors.

The truth about successful stories, even those of a more intellectual kind, is even worse — for without exception, they chew the cud. At this late stage in our civilisation, when knowledge is being replaced, gradually and insidiously, by knowledge about knowledge, original thought is less successful than ever before: the demand of the 'educated', 'knowledgeable', 'responsible' reader and listener is for first-rate second-hand products, for simplifications which keep step with the need for that 'general knowledge' which makes a 20th-century individual civilised at the expense of culture. One paragraph of *The Critique of Pure Reason* will provoke more thought in a reader than a whole philosophy course — but then, he prefers the philosophy course because he wants his thoughts supplied, not provoked. Contemporary literature, inasmuch as it is successful, adheres to this simple principle of demand and supply, without realising, despite all its knowledge, that in the sphere of thought, nothing worth while has ever been demanded. Everything worth while is a discovery, and you can't demand a discovery before it's happened.

Don't let the reader ask me to get down to it. I am there already, and if he doesn't like it, his skipping several paragraphs won't be of any avail either: it won't be a travelogue. In the circumstances I have described, every writer is guilty until proved innocent — until he is able to show, that is to say, that he is not contributing to the accumulation of knowledge about knowledge, not to the gratification of untopical morality (the two readily go together), but has something to say that hasn't been said before, which is all that now matters. Although nobody notices, the days of literary journalism are, alas, over; what we get instead is journalistic literature which condescendingly appears in weeklies and monthlies, with the reader unaware that it has nothing to step down from. So much for my introduction, which could just as well appear in the middle of my piece — a structural feature that distinguishes all functional introductions; when the best comes to the best, they actually do appear in the middle (that of Beethoven's Op. 130 does, for instance).

There are, pardon my language, traumata and traumata. You overcome or don't overcome a personal trauma. But you cannot overcome an impersonal trauma, one which affects life as a whole, except by growing insensitive — by death. I had three traumata in my life had an intense impersonal element, and no others can be compared to them, not even the death of someone close or closest to one. The first was the most comprehensive — the Nazi period: personally, I faced the threat of execution, and impersonally, I faced the death of a world. The second, decades later, was my visit to South Africa (about which I wrote a 'successful' article, making every liberal mind feel good, without the slightest intention of doing so). The third was my recent visit to Prague, and in one sinister respect, it was the worst. In Austria, I was first running for my life, and then, in the course of my imprisonment, thought I had had it. There was extreme personal involvement in the first place, and numbness in the second: hardly a state of mind conducive to detached reflections upon the future course of human history — to a great deal of objective fear or despair. In South Africa, I first of all made my conditions (integrated audiences), and then never kept my mouth shut; the fact that I could make

51

a repeated public stand eased the trauma considerably — and I wasn't even deported, apparently because they knew I was soon going to leave, anyway. But in Prague, there was, on the one hand, no personal involvement at all, while on the other, there was no possibility of protest: whenever you urgently felt like it, you were being told, by seasoned dissidents, that you were going to get someone into trouble, not an innocent man, maybe — but then, nobody who has not the stature of a Dubcek is innocent in a closed society. That, in itself, would not be a tragedy; but deep depression sets in once you notice that, inevitably, the consciences of mediocre mentality, mediocre morality, are spotlessly clean. For the uninvolved visitor who is not prepared to have his conscience corrupted at short notice, temporarily and slightly (and there are plenty of those), the result is hell — for that is the place from which you can't, morally, escape, and *in* which you can't act right, whichever way you try.

In my factual descriptions, I shall indeed have to take care not to get anyone into trouble — not to make certain people too readily identifiable: where cowardice is a *sine qua non* of continued existence, one has an unqualified moral responsibility towards the coward.

I had been invited, in a spirit of sham internationalism, to sit on the jury of 1975's International String Quartet Competition — if international is the word: there was no quartet from the West. As this book shows, my wife, an artist, could be expected to be intensely interested in Prague, which she had never seen before, and in anticipation of her joy, I accepted the invitation. Not that this was the only reason: I tend to join competition juries because I abhor competitions from the artistic point of view (in art, one does, not better, but something different), and the best way to fight or repair something is from within. The string quartet as such, moreover, is one of my central preoccupations, and as I had just been on the jury of the European Broadcasting Union's International String Quartet Competition in Stockholm, I was anxious to find out how the other side did it, especially since I am on the committee which is planning the EBU's next International String Quartet Competition (in Helsinki in 1978). My first reaction of slight dismay ensued when, having been informed of the generous fee I was to receive, I found out, more or less accidentally, that I would not be able to convert the money into sterling. In due course, I was to learn that things are not being kept secret accidentally — which made me immediately think about our own laws of 'confidentiality' and 'discretion': two frequent euphemisms, these, for keeping things dark, in order to protect those who do so and nobody else. We see the need for the concept of a 'white lie'; the need for the concepts of 'white confidentiality' and 'white discretion' is equally realistic, equally ethical.

The Czech plane to Prague was jolly empty and quite pleasant; I persuaded myself that I would at least have an interesting time. My flight ticket was free, as was the excellent beer on the plane, and my wife's ticket much reduced: right, I said to myself, let's beat them at their own game, let's over-value material advantage for a bit. I didn't know what I was saying; presently, I would. Retrospectively, I must confess that those humourless, humanity-less faces of the air hostesses should have warned me, but I thought, well, that's the way the Czechs wear their faces, I haven't seen them since my childhood, not on home ground. It is the way indeed, but it wasn't in my childhood. However, this denial, on the plane, of obtrusive if (for the moment) merely psychological reality was to be the last time I was forced to be wise after the event; within minutes of our arrival, I forced myself to be wise beforehand, to lovingly nurture that paranoid attitude for which I have no talent, but without which, in a closed society, you always see the truth too late if you see it at all: do in luney-land as the lunies do, psychologically speaking, or you're sunk, cognitively speaking: you lose touch with what is their reality.

What opened my eyes on arrival—I mean, what closed them to the world of reason, of reasons rather than motives — was the three-stage passport control, complete with scrutiny of our faces and the photographs on our visa, complete with stamps, note-taking, signatures; complete, too, with those three passport officers wearing the same faces as the air hostesses: they must have had them made at the same place. I looked at my wife, she looked at me; I think the exchange of glances meant, 'It's a bit early, after two or three minutes, to have had enough'. To pass the intellectual time while the last passport officer was pondering the advisability of admitting us to the holy land, I thought of our own documentary rituals, records, scrutinies, of annual reporting systems, of the appointment boards on which I had sat (I always preferred those which I faced) — of the all-consuming human need for degradation, for what our American friends call, quite rightly, infantilisation. With superhuman strength, I overcame the wellnigh irresistible impulse to say, winningly, 'Take your mouldy visas, we're going home', and was therefore admitted to the next stage. The customs control, however, was easier — easier, perhaps, than our own: we suspect people's belongings, they just suspect people.

We were met—by a welcoming party of two. One was an official from the Czech Philharmonic, the other a woman who assured us that she didn't really have anything to do with anything, that her subject was philosophy, and that she was here out of sheer friendliness. While we stood there, waiting for our luggage to be put into the car, I immediately ventured a mild philosophical challenge — with that icy friendliness which, from her 'Welcome to Prague!' onwards, I had quickly picked up from her, by way of amiable revenge. I asked her about the state of philosophical education in Czechoslovakia: was there any preferential treatment of any particular philosophical school? After giving me to understand, curtly, that the objectivity of their exposition of, say, 'idealistic philosophy' was unequalled, she emphasised, with dignity, that, needless to add, the world was being inspected from the point of view of scientific materialism — which circumstance no doubt made their survey of the rest of philosophy all the more detached and objective. Apologising for my ignorance, I asked whether any important philosophical developments had taken place in recent times in Czechoslovakia. With ill-concealed contempt, she said yes, and I did not proceed to ask why we hadn't heard about them.

In the car, with a total absence of contact underlying a continuous flow of conversation, I decided to lay it on thick, in the hope that something might happen which might lead one to accept the possibility that human beings were talking to each other.

My father's background was Czechoslovakian (Austrian at the time, of course); he was born, and spent his childhood in, a German-speaking village near Karlsbad. My grandmother continued to live in the

55

country — in Prague, where she was arrested by the Nazis when she was in her alert nineties, taken to the concentration camp of Theresienstadt, and later exterminated. My father's brother, likewise, lived in Prague, until he escaped; he was the editor of one of Europe's three leading newspapers, the *Prager Tagblatt*, a supra-political, pre-war-*Times*-like affair. It was read throughout the German-speaking world, and published, for instance, Winston Churchill's warning articles about the Nazi danger.

Now, in the car, though not much was happening in me, emotionally speaking, on the conscious level, the names of the roads suddenly occurred to me where my grandmother had lived and where my uncle had worked: I had forgotten them since childhood. A good opportunity, I thought, to test the lady's reactions to my background. But I would leave out the bit about my grandmother, so as not to elicit automatic sympathy; in any case, as I was to learn later, the central point of interest about Theresienstadt is that it was liberated by the glorious Soviet army. 'Panska 12,' I said. 'All of a sudden, I remember it from my childhood. My uncle was the editor of the *Prager Tagblatt*. Incidentally, my grandmother lived in Lützowova.' An interminable second of stony silence was followed by the information, delivered in guide-like fashion, that Panska 12, still a newspaper building, was now the home of a communist youth paper, called the National Front or something like that; everything is called something like that.

We were taken straight to the competition offices in the House of Artists (the pre-war parliament), where I was given my fee in advance, as well as the first instalment of the money I was to get for my living expenses. The operation was handled efficiently and with aplomb — the

56

first indication we had of the overriding importance attached to everything to do with what they call 'economics' and I call money: the capitalist's obsession with money is as nothing compared to the Marxist's elemental passion, in a Marxist society, to evaluate everything, organisational efficiency, ability, success, life itself, in terms of money, of the work that produces money, of art that is immediately successful and so produces money . . . As an element of national pride, West Germany's 'economic miracle' is as nothing compared to the 'miracle' (yes, they used the same word) which the Czechs said their latest government had achieved economically; and so far as one could see in 12 days, they were right. Even some dissidents who had not altogether lost their Marxist conditioning were full of admiration — so much so that one hardly dared asking them what, ultimately, all the money, all the money-earning was supposed to be in aid of, though they did agree that freedom (where they noticed its absence, which was chiefly when it was too late and they'd been sacked or silenced) was a pretty tough price to pay for money. Academic and aesthetic discussions, too, would inevitably be crowned by a joke, invariably meant seriously, about money and livelihood. The final reflection in one of our jury discussions — on a problem of authenticity — was that 'musicologists have to live'.

We were put up at the Intercontinental which, built by Pan-American, is now government-controlled. It is, in effect, identical with all the other Intercontinentals in the West — which, however, lack the special room-bugging service that is said to be provided in Prague. I have no direct evidence that our invaluable comments were, in fact, recorded, but we had sufficient warnings from sundry sources to transfer the most invaluable parts of our conversations to the crowded bar downstairs.

Another feature which distinguishes this Intercontinental from the capitalist variety is the number of policemen and military who swarm through the hotel, day and night; one never quite knows whether they live there or not — but if they don't, they certainly choose curious places to hang around in, such as the corridors along the bedrooms. However, the most gall-provoking aspect of these policemen was, again, their faces. I hadn't looked into this kind of de-humanised Gestapo face for a few decades, but I recognised it immediately; and although there is, in normal circumstances, quite a little difference between a typical German face and a typical Slav face, the two become indistinguishable under the liberating, de-nationalising influence of collective persecution mania *cum* megalomania. As in the good old days, moreover, you could depend on being offered an opportunity to make the most of those glares: when you passed a policeman, you could place a 1/5 on-bet with your wife that if you turned round, you would find that he himself had turned round too, still glaring at you, though now with traces of unspeakable sadness in his eyes — about not being able to do something about whatever he thought deserved attention.

A comparison with Israel, visited professionally about nine months before, inevitably urged itself upon me: lots of police, lots of military, lots of fear-inspired investigations and examinations — yet right at the other end of the humanity-inhumanity scale, right on top of the world in terms of her anxiety to preserve maximal individualism in the context of a war-like situation, potentially regressive; in fact, every policeman, every soldier was actually a person. I was walking along a corridor in the Israel Broadcasting Authority building in Jerusalem, on my way to a studio where I was going to do a broadcast. Outside the studio door sat a soldier of about 20, grinning, pointing a machine gun at me . . . I found this greeting slightly disconcerting: 'That's a nice way to welcome a Jewish boy!' I said, hoping he would understand English. He did, but did not avail himself of verbal language in his reply. Instead, he shrugged his shoulders in the characteristic manner of an old European Jew and winked. In Czechoslovakia, needless to add, Israel is (and I quote dependable sources) 'World Enemy No. 1'. What a confrontation. But then, in a way, she is.

'What did you think of that woman who met us?' I asked my wife during our first session in the crowded Intercontinental bar. 'Spitzel' (police informer) she said, her regression to the German colloquialism (I had asked the question in English) indicating that her mind had indeed gone back to the same past as mine. 'Funny,' I said, 'I tried to be as paranoid as possible in that car, and thought I might have overdone it when I arrived at this diagnosis. Now that *you've* made it, I don't think I did. She was absolutely in style, wasn't she?' 'Yes.' We never saw the philosopher again.

'Back to so-called reality,' I said. 'I've got a job to do.' And I started studying the 'Regulations' of the 'International Prague Spring Music Competition'. Article III, Paragraph 6 struck me with vehemence:

To avoid conspicuous differences in the appraisal of a candidate by individual members of the jury the scorings by the two members of the jury who gave the highest and the lowest number of points respectively are not taken into account. These two scorings are crossed out automatically.

Why 'avoid conspicuous differences'? There could be no terser manifesto against the value of individual opinion, against the discovery of new truth — which, ineluctably, is individual achievement: if majorities were discoverers, there wouldn't be anything left to discover; and indeed, so far as one is able to penetrate the total Marxist's world view, he thinks there isn't — not so far as animate objects are concerned, anyway.

I made a mental note of this paragraph, determined to raise the matter when an opportunity offered itself — which happened 12 days later, after the jury had reached its verdicts and criticisms were invited that might be taken into account in future competitions. All of us, I said, were seasoned international competition jurors, and we must all be aware that the history of competitions and the history of performance showed that not infrequently, prize winners proceeded to go under without a trace; and that, conversely, artists who had only been supported by one or two jurors came to assume world stature. Since the word 'democratic' had been used more often than any other adjective in the course of our jury sessions, I submitted, in the politest possible way, that the democratic spirit proved itself by its respect for minority opinion — and that in art, at any rate, the minority was usually right anyhow.

I failed. Various reasons were advanced in support of the invalidity of the highest and lowest marks, but the argument with which everybody — well, almost everybody — seemed to agree was that for what were described as 'tactical' reasons, a juror might give a very good quartet unrealistically low marks in order to let another quartet, highly marked, advance to the next round or win the final. It was pointed out to me, moreover, that the same system had, upon occasion, been adopted in the West.

I did not go on to say that in that case, one was either working as a psychotic group, or as a bunch of mutually suspicious delinquents, or (more likely) a bit of both; and that mine had not been submitted as a 'Western' case, but just as my thoughts, which were supposed to be realistic. Nor would most people have understood if I had told them that what I felt I was learning here was not that the West was good and the East bad or vice versa, but that the social and personal consequences of the established Eastern world view showed the naked eye what, when viewed under a microscope, was wrong in the West: that we were all in the same boat, but that we in the West, the more insightful amongst us, were, not unnaturally, interested in the question why it leaked, that we did in fact allow each other a wrong answer, confident that the right one might thus be found. There were one or two of the Eastern jury members who would have understood me, but they probably understood me without my pursuing the argument — which, within the official jury context, had no chance.

Of the 12 jury members, four were from the West, an Austrian, a Swede, a Swiss and myself. Amongst the practising musicians on the jury, the most distinguished were the chairman, Antonín Kohout, who is the cellist of the world-class Smetana Quartet, and Josef Vlach, the leader of the Vlach Quartet: him I only knew fleetingly, but with Kohout I had (or so I thought) established an elective affinity many years ago, on a purely musical level. But that was at the Summer School of Music at Dartington, and later in a BBC studio. Now we were in Prague, and I didn't recognise him; in fact, it was not easy to recognise him as a musician, an artist. What was recognisable was the perfect party member; for all I know, he may well be a member of the higher aristocracy — the Central Committee, whose very name is never enunciated without a shudder, without admiring or resigned awe, as the case may be. I soon learnt that there were, in fact, three categories of people — party members, 'workers', and, well, Category III, which I don't recommend: you are made to feel that you belong to it. If you are a university professor, you are likely to be working in a factory, and if you are a child, you are likely to be told to which category you belong, because your dad does.

From Kohout's lips, however, flowed the real thing—from the moment he rigged, with imposing democracy, the election of the two deputy-chairmen. Article I, Paragraph 7 said that:

at the constituent session convened by the Committee of the 'Prague Spring International Music Festival' the jury elects two Deputy Chairmen from among its members. The Chairman and the Deputy Chairman form the Praesidium of the jury.

Now, with truly divine objectivity, Kohout announced that one of the deputy chairmen would be from one of the democratic socialist republics, the other (stressed strain of politeness in his voice) from the West. Scarcely had I settled down to wondering how the hell he knew, when two names were proposed out of nowhere. One of them, surprise, was the Russian delegate, a member of the (late) Beethoven Quartet; the other, equally sensationally, was a citizen of a neighbouring country who was in frequent and joyful touch with

Prague (and spoke Czech), i.e. the Austrian who, I later discovered, had already been invited to join the next (violin) competition. Nobody objected to this Praesidium (not even I: not knowing these people, I had no grounds for objection, nor even any idea whom to propose instead), and it was elected before you could say jack up.

Not that it mattered, I thought. Little did I know. When I was vice-chairman at the Leeds International Piano Competition, it didn't mean a thing. I took over when Sir Arthur Bliss, the chairman, uncharacteristically wanted a snooze; that was all. But here it was clear that I hadn't lived. A proper Praesidium, at the slightest provocation or none, goes next door and discusses things *in camera*. No white confidentiality here, for there is no conceivable thing that can, in justice, be discussed in the absence of the jury. For rigging purposes, on the other hand, a Praesidium can be of great help. There was this question of advance from one round to the next. A certain number of marks had to be reached. I noticed that one of the quartets was only fractionally below the required minimum, and made a little speech to the effect that it would be pedantic not to let them advance. The chairman thought that mine was a rather good point, and marched out with the rest of the Praesidium to discuss it all. When they came back, and before we knew where we were, he happily announced that he proposed to accept my representations, and to let quartets x and y advance to the next round. Quartet x was the one I had mentioned; quartet y, well below, I hadn't mentioned at all — but it was, surprise, the only Russian quartet competing.

After this particular session, I thought the time had come to kick. I discussed the problem with a musician of calibre and, possibly, courage: I don't know. But he certainly knew more about these democratic methods than I did. And he advised me to shut up — for two reasons: the Russian member of the jury, an old gentleman, would have a very difficult time if he got home without the Russian quartet having shone; and the quartet itself — talented young people, after all — would be in difficulty, their instruments taken away from them or no good instruments lent to them . . .

Artistically, the competition yielded nothing, which was a little surprising, since the participants were Czechoslovak quartets and that one Russian ensemble: usually, you get pretty strong contingents from the Slav part of the world, at least as far as sheer accomplishment is concerned. The one thing one could be sure the entire jury genuinely agreed upon was not to award a first prize at all, and let the second be shared.

But competition apart, there was quite some time to have a look round, and to talk. Mind you, unless you were lucky, you had to do the talking: nobody in a good job or responsible position, music or art or anything, would open his mouth in reply to any question which might interest any reader of this book — even if you were alone with them. The answers, moreover, were stereotyped and automatic; what seemed a conversation a second ago had turned into the pseudo-contact one has when talking to a parrot, and a parrot with a jolly meagre vocabulary to boot: 'It depends'. 'That is a complex question.' 'That's a very general question' — with the implication, 'Please, don't ask me any specific ones.' White discretion. What was a face a second ago, highly developed, expressive, and unlike any other face, had turned into the face of one of those air hostesses. Individual fear as well as collective enthusiasm can produce de-individualisation, and I shyly suggest that we study faces, and changing faces, a little more deeply at our own places of work (say, the Post Office) and play (say, the House of Commons). In all dimensions, here and there, sameness is the danger signal, if not the death certificate – sameness of faces, reactions, competition marks, posters, photographs, flags . . . 'Forward with the Soviets towards a realisation of Leninist ideology': you even got it across one of the university buildings, and you couldn't move a step without facing such a reminder. Photographs of Czechs embracing the Red Army, or of the Red Army embracing Czech children, must have been rare, but copies were not: you always saw the selfsame photo — in shop windows, windows of official buildings, at exhibitions; and it was indistinguishable — the worst of all samenesses — from Nazi photos. The Czech flag was always paired with the Soviet flag; the two were all over the place, and not only on May 1, which was a orgy of sameness.

Negative sameness, sailing under the flag of 'tolerance', is even more deadly: execution by tolerance is something the Nazis, unfortunately, hadn't thought of; otherwise, my grandmother would have been allowed to die in her bed. What happens is that every rejected part of Western civilisation is turned into a museum — above all, religion, of course, together with the churches and synagogues and the believers in them. The Altneu Synagogue in the former ghetto — the oldest existing synagogue in the world (c. 1280) — is a museal place of worship on Friday night and Saturday, and a proper museum the rest of the week: you buy yourself a round ticket to inspect it as well as other sights in the Jewish quarter, such as the ancient cemetery. I wanted to see the live part of the museum, so we went to the evening service on a Friday night. 'We are

65

the last garrison,' a believer explained. 'We have no rabbi; but then, you don't need a rabbi for praying.' 'Have you got a *Khazen* (cantor)?' 'Well,' he said, switching from a mixture of German and Yiddish into English, 'an imitation *Khazen.*' I turned to another old Jew: 'How are things otherwise?' 'There is no antisemitism in Czechoslovakia,' he said with a wink that reminded me of that Israeli soldier. 'If there's something wrong with you, you are a Zionist.' His son had emigrated to the United States, and father and mother were allowed to visit him — but not together. This is a general ruling, one of the hall-marks, in fact, of a closed, paranoid society: it's difficult to get in and it's difficult to get out. What would the state lose if that man and his wife vanished? At the same time, there are, of course, limits to tolerance itself: all monasteries and convents have been closed down — with the help, no doubt, of the strong, time-honoured anti-Roman Catholic feeling which, near-identical with the anti-Habsburg feeling of the day before yesterday, had thoroughly prepared the ground. For the rest, it won't do any harm to inspect our own life under the microscope, in case we find museal death in it too: what, at the outset, I called 'knowledge about knowledge' gives us the clue. Music, for instance, has, for a long time, been suffering from a mortal disease, called 'musicology': I have not yet heard an 'authentic' performance of, say, the Matthew Passion that was alive.

Dissidents come in shades, and those who can't get out try to make the best of what, in the circumstances, they are trying to regard as a workable job. ethically speaking. Of course, only those will talk to you who have been dropped, or whose husbands have been dropped: Category III people. They console themselves with the thought that 'the leading intellectuals are all sitting at home, boiling. Something must happen, sooner or later.' Frankly, I don't see why it should, or how it could.

'It was far, far worse in the pre-Dubcek era. Now we are not a police state.' 'Really? Why not?' 'In Russia, if you are a dissident, you'll land in a mental hospital, more likely than not. There's no such danger in our country. And secret arrests and long-term imprisonments without trial have stopped.' 'If your husband were arrested to-morrow and imprisoned, without trial, for ten years — apart from expressing surprise that it's still happening, would you be able to do anything about it?' 'No.'

'I love my country, and I and my wife want to stay so long as there is any possibility of improving things and working for a better future. After all, economically, our government has done wonders.'

'My husband is a philosopher and a writer, but he can't publish anything any more. He is a Marxist, but not the right kind of Marxist. All publishers are government-controlled, which makes censorship, in effect, automatic, though legally there is no censorship. He sits at home and writes, and he sits in the factory and writes: when he lost his teaching job, he was put into this factory, but his pals soon realised that he wasn't any good at "work" anyway, so they provided him with a table and a chair, and he sits in a corner all day, writing. He can't survive without thinking, and he can't survive without writing. He is naïve about money, and doesn't realise that I am earning most of the money needed to keep our family alive: I've opened a separate bank account and don't show him what I earn. He wouldn't survive that either — knowing that he was not really providing for the family.' I am not mentioning this lady's own profession in order to make

67

identification absolutely impossible; suffice it to say that she is doing very well indeed in a freelance capacity, and that she, too, was prepared to praise the government to the extent of saying that it was no worse than the American government. 'But,' I said, 'if and when the American government stinks, you can, as an American, say, and try to prove, that it stinks: is this not an essential difference?' 'True, but we love our country. In spite of his frustrations, my husband and I would never forgive ourselves if we didn't try to make it all work.'

Such conversations, real exchanges in an atmosphere of total de-humanisation, felt like psychological festivals. It goes without saying that a member of the Central Committee would, quite genuinely, not know what I was talking about, though 'humane' would probably be the second most frequent adjective in his vocabulary, right after 'democratic'. At the final session of the competition jury, when criticisms were invited, I said it was a bad idea, in one of the rounds, to have the competing quartets play three works in succession, with hardly an interval between them: no established string quartet would be prepared to operate like a sausage factory, in either a concert or a radio recording. The chairman, his party manner at its most relaxed (stress on 'party'), did not even withdraw with the deputy chairmen in order to discuss this one. With paternalistic magnanimity, he opined that mine was an exceptionally important criticism, and that he was particularly glad that such a musical and *humane* point (his italics) had been raised, not by a delegate from a democratic socialist republic, but from one representing a country as remote as England; from the interpreter's (excellent) simultaneous translation it was not clear whether this 'remoteness' was meant ambiguously, but if it wasn't, the chairman merely forgot to mean it.

Remoteness, in any case, is the despicable word — despicable not only in the chairman's context, but also in ours: moralistic wallowing in the past is one thing, moralistic wallowing in the East not another. Charity should stop at home — nor do I mean having a go at our own new left, the Maoists and second-round Marxists (the first round having happened half a century ago). Musically, I shall have a go at them (in Chapter IV) but politically, I find them so stupidly well-meaning that I'd rather have a go at you — who thinks that he sees through them.

You don't, you know — not so long as you accept the need for loyalty to any collective ideal, sheer collective self-defence apart (if you can call that an ideal). The dignity of the individual and the individuality of conscience are indivisible: this is what a visit to an ideological society teaches one. The dangers to mankind are not bad people coming to power: they wouldn't stay there for a minute without good people having surrendered their individual consciences to a group ideal, and thus supporting them. Plenty of individual crimes are committed with a bad conscience and followed by remorse; but throughout the history of mankind, all crimes against humanity have been committed with a good conscience, followed by moral satisfaction; some of them, like the crusades, are still not seen for, or felt as, what they were, and the very term 'crusade' continues as a metaphor for a collective movement against evil. Some ends may or may not sanctify some means, but the indivisibility of individual conscience is an end, and each time we try to control another conscience, tell people what's good for them, act 'in their own best interests' which we know all about and they don't, we regress, and try to make them regress, to the parent-child relationship, with the parent functioning as superego. Our civilisation is long enough, and surveyable enough, to entitle us to come to the sober, empirical conclusion that from the standpoint of retaining and attaining the values on which we all agree, the most bizarre individual conscience is more fruitful, or at the very least more harmless, than what seems the most commonsensical or the most idealistic collective conscience.

Both individual and collective consciences try to silence selfishness; but it is the collective conscience alone that silences the self in the process, and so ultimately creates a world — it may be a little firm, an organisation, or more than half of our actual world — not for its inhabitants, but against them, wherever and whenever they don't serve it. Crusaders are degraders.

The uniform has long been recognised as a doubtful distinction, but uniform attitudes, uniform reactions, uniform faces are welcomed by all of us if we happen to like the group ideal which they serve: when we admiringly say that someone behaves like a proper x or y or z, there is something wrong with him and us, because we have no basic human right to expect him to behave like anything or anybody. The way down to behaving like a proper member of the Central Committee is steep and fast, the way right up to behaving as oneself steep and slow. The end of the world could easily be its uniformity, the cosy night of total dependence, the *Liebestod* of frictionless de-individualisation. Stepping off the plane at Heathrow, I greeted our not very brilliant daylight with the resolution never, never, to be, or to tell anybody to be, a good party member, whatever the party, real or metaphorical.

Do not go gentle into that good night,
Rage, rage against the dying of the light.

70

Prague Sketchbook 1975

Milein Cosman

# Psycho-Analytic Congress, 1975

At the time of writing, Freud is still spinning in his grave like a top — in view of the German section in the programme brochure of the *29th Congress of the International Psycho-analytical Association*, which was held in London from July 20 to July 25, 1975, 'under the auspices of the British Psychoanalytical Society' (no hyphen this time, and good luck to the Americanising, simplifying Briton concerned). So far as my first-hand knowledge goes, Freud was one of the three greatest stylists (ruthlessly clear and simple throughout his writings) in the whole of German literature — amongst its genuises, anyway. The other two were Arthur Schopenhauer and Franz Kafka — whose areas of insight, fascinatingly enough, not only overlapped with Freud's, but, like his, might have seemed predestined to produce obscure, imprecise language (and indeed did — in the hands of lesser immortals). For most, darkness is there to hide in; for the self-chosen few, it produces the self-evident, creative need for light.

In order to demonstrate the sub-intelligent amateurishness of this shoddy brochure, however, we need not meditate on such elevated heights. One of the English titles was, *The Implications of Recent Advances in the Knowledge of Child Development for the Treatment of Adults* — which, I suppose, is fair enough, even though, amongst grown-ups without obsessional traits, *Recent Advances in Child Psychology and the Treatment of*

*Adults* would have done very well indeed. But now listen to the German translation, which I am meticulously re-translating into English: *Implications of the More Recent Advances in the Theory and Practice of Child Development for the Treatment of Adults.*

Do you realise what this means? There was a whole 'Programme Committee', or 'Organising Committee', or whatever body it was that was anonymously responsible for the programme book, who must have accepted that the concept of 'the practice of child development' made sense. For the first time in my long and rich love relationship with psychoanalysis — though not, as it turned out, for the last — I granted cordial admission to an element of lively ambivalence, and felt like recommending *a course of strict association* temporarily to replace free association, until a minimal level of responsible realism was reached, a workable minimum of sheer intelligence.

Admittedly, the quaint appearance of this brochure, which seemed to have been preserved from a rural fête, insistent misprints, inconsistencies, ungrammaticalities, mistranslations and all, was not without its charm. But we have to remember that parochial charm is one thing, international parochialism another. For the rest, if the brochure had not given one an inkling of things to come, some of them anyway, I would not make such an hors-d'oeuvre of it.

Now let us have an extended word before the main course. In 1975, Walt Whitman Rostow, Professor of Economics at the University of Texas, started an outstanding radio lecture on inflation with these words:

The first thing you should know about a speaker is his

bias. This is particularly important if he is talking about an issue of public policy.

I wish that this eminently rational requirement were met by all self-respecting speakers and writers on issues of public policy — and that they knew when they were talking about an issue of public policy and when they weren't. As this chapter will gradually show, I regard psychoanalysis, its influence and development, as a latent (but none the less potent) issue of public policy, and a comprehensive statement of bias, is, therefore, an absolute ethical requirement — and a scientific one, too, if you are prepared to accept the discipline of psychoanalysis as a science, or at least a pre-science. I don't really care much whether you do, but I do care about the methods of the acquisition of truth: so long as psychoanalysis remains loyal to (1) observation, (2) whatever little experiment is possible (if the analysand wishes to experiment upon himself: self-analysis is the ideal experimental field) and (3) induction, it has a substantial claim to being at least a pre-science; whereas if and when it unconsciously poses as a pure science which, like mathematics and logic, depends on deductions from self-evident truths, it assumes the intellectual status of a religion or a psychosis. I can see the reality value of religion; I can even see the realistic insights proffered by psychosis in demonstrable circumstances (or rather, schizophrenia: everything is schizophrenia nowadays), though I don't quite see why, à la R. D. Laing, one should wax more sentimental about them than about other insights.

What, moreover, I will never see is the justification for intellectual dishonesty, conscious or unconscious: if and when you are a religion, say so, and say why you want to be, and what the likely or possible gain in the acquisition of knowledge might be. Jung, disreputable as, in my opinion, he was intellectually, at least showed an (ill-disclosed) uneasy conscience about religion and its reality value; unfortunately, he wanted to have it both ways, rather than each way in turn (like the more honest, first-generation analyst Oskar Pfister, a Protestant priest for whom Freud had such great, if ambivalent respect, harbouring as he did a lifelong ambivalent attitude towards religion anyway).

But instead of facing this issue (it is a philosophical issue, one of theory of cognition), the brochure of the Congress talked about 'individual scientific papers'— which made me, inveterate logician that I am, look for the individual unscientific papers, or the collective scientific papers, or the collective unscientific papers, of which latter there were quite a few, in all conscience. Only, they were called 'dialogue papers', because psychoanalysis has a superego thing about remaining in touch with trendy verbiage, as an uneasy reality-test; the rest of thinking mankind still can't see the difference between a dialogue and a conversation, except that a dialogue can be written, which the dialogue part of the dialogue papers was not.

It will be noticed that I have already plunged (not slipped) right into the middle of my statement of bias, of which I can now give a balanced and factual resumé. 'Resumé' remains the word, even though it will be a jolly long one: in our civilisation's central area of intellectual mystification, i.e. that of what I call misapplied psychology, the reader must know exactly where he stands vis-à-vis the writer.

After many years of patient and personal investigation —which, in the words of a psychoanalyst of the old guard,

Willi Hoffer, produced an 'unequalled knowledge of psychoanalytic literature'—I came to the definite conclusion that what, outside analysis, are known as the psychoanalytic dogmata, are in fact a single man's discoveries of world-shaking truths (shaking the mental world, that is): the dynamic unconscious, repression (*Verdrängung*) in the strictly analytic sense, infantile sexuality and its consequences, the Oedipus complex (at least in Western civilisations), and the validity of free-association technique. My investigations included a regular course in self-analysis extending over several years, which I had decided upon after I had found that it was impossible to obtain a training analysis without paying for it—what to me, then, were unfathomable sums of money: I was glad enough to keep myself alive. My model for self-analysis, or my inspiration anyway, was not Freud himself, but a chemist who, having found that he shut up on sundry hetero-analytical couches, decided to test analytic theory (which, to begin with, he loathed) all by himself. He published some of his impressive results, and Freud wrote him a charming preface, praising his contribution to psychoanalytic knowledge, and remarking that if he, Freud, had found himself in the same situation. he would probably have acted likewise—pro' d unanalysable by any other person.

My psychological interests have, in fact, always been overriding. Music is not an 'interest'; I'm a musician, and to suggest to a musician that he is interested in music makes as much sense as suggesting to you that you are interested in liquid, food, or sleep. However, my first essay in the English language did not appear in a musical journal, but in the *British Journal of Medical Psychology*. That was in my twenties and, according to the then editor, it was the first paper published in his journal that had not been written by a medical man.

Gradually, my knowledge of analytic literature became more and more 'equalled', and indeed readily surpassed; in fact, the chewing of the Freudian cud began to bore the pants off me to the extent of my ceasing altogether to follow up the literature.

Instead, I thought what I could do myself. The psychoanalysis of music and social psychology[1] apart, I became ever more interested in the logic, the ethics, and indeed the psychology of psychology, until, in the Summer, 1971 issue of the *History of Medicine,* I published a paper on 'Music and Psychopathology', which was based on a lecture previously given at the Summer School of Music in Dartington. In it, I subjected our concepts of neurosis and psychosis to a critical scrutiny, and defined situations in which these two conditions could serve so-called 'normality', intensify realism.

I submitted that

the concepts of normality, neurosis and psychosis have acquired such ritual meaning not only amongst the generally educated, but even in the medical and indeed the psychiatric profession, that a re-examination of their denotations is advisable whenever they are applied beyond the simplest and most concrete cases or situations.

I proceeded to point out that modern society, and modern psychiatry with it, had produced a curious reversal of professional and lay attitudes towards mental illness. Time was when the man in the street, still more in

---

[1]See Margaret Phillips, *Small Social Groups in England,* London 1965; owing to what she, in her 'Acknowledgments', accurately calls my 'later professional preoccupations', I had to withdraw from an extremely fruitful collaboration.

the village, regarded the mentally abnormal as evil, awesome, contemptible, while the medical man pleaded for an objective approach, uninfluenced by moralistic evaluation: that much was common knowledge. What, I suggested, we didn't want to notice was that while extra-professional attitudes towards mental abnormality had become ever more tolerant (to the extent of creating intellectualist world-views according to which there was something wrong with someone with whom nothing was wrong), well-hidden evaluation, devious moralising, had crept into sundry professional attitudes towards psychopathology—the GP's, the psychologist's, and above all, ironically so, the psychoanalyst's and psychiatrist's: both 'neurotic' and 'psychotic' had become terms of civilised professional abuse, self-castigation included.

The very fact that there is a degree of realistic justification for the devaluation of neurosis and psychosis—to be in touch with reality is better than not to be—firmly anchors the professional's concealed moralistic approach which, in any case, is almost unavoidable by dint of his position in the therapeutic situation. He is in a parental position, whether GP or specialist; and the counter-transference—he himself regarding himself as the father, on top of the patient's regarding him so—will colour his reactions to the patient (quite especially if he is not an analyst); they will be none the less violent, basically, for being unconfessed and therefore only expressible in the most harmless-sounding of forms. Condescension, the need to step down from an assumed position of superiority, is one of our most elemental passions. Whether we have children or not, we love to see the world in terms of good boys and bad boys and mixed boys; the chief thing is that they are the boys and we are the men, in a position to tell them off, always wiser than they at their best, whatever their special aptitudes.

Owing to the confusion surrounding the concepts of 'normal' and its alternatives (the latest psychiatric okay words for 'normal' and 'abnormal' are the more cautious 'integrated' and 'disturbed' respectively), the concepts of 'neurotic' and 'psychotic art' were used, I submitted, without any scientific validity whatever. I did indeed confine myself to art because I am a musician, but my conclusions are of further-reaching significance: 'neurosis' or 'psychosis' can, though of course it need not, produce superior 'mental health', otherwise unobtainable, in cognitive areas, both scientific and artistic. My extra-musical example, meanwhile, was Franz Kafka:

If we retain the reality-test as the ultimate guide to normality, Kafka's art is supremely normal just because it uncovers norms of psychological reality which nobody (except depth-psychologists) had dreamt of—one specific kind of dream apart: the nightmare. There is no doubt, then, that given Kafka's genius, his abnormality, his 'disturbedness' was a *conditio sine qua non* for his objective discoveries, which he achieved against the heaviest possible psychological odds.

I submitted that two conclusions emerged from my examination of Kafka's case. First, we had to distinguish sharply between the psychopathology of the artist and that of art. Secondly, the relation between the artist's mental health or mental illness and his art's health or sickness must needs be intricate, and vary from individual to individual.

90

There are two alternative theories about this relation—generalisations which, it seems, have not much more reality value than has a perceptive fantasy. On the one hand, there is the popular theory that mental abnormality is a help in creativity. Quite apart from the fact that the incidence of neurosis and psychosis in genius has been shown to be statistically insignificant when compared with other sections of society, there are too many known instances of mental abnormality unfavourably affecting creativity to make this theory worth considering if it is couched in such general terms. But on the other hand, there is the opposite, professional theory, popular amongst psychotherapists who value a restful night—that *ceteris paribus*, the more normal the artist, the better his art. Again, as a generality, the proposition is not much more than professional wish-fulfilment: my single, simple example of Franz Kafka speedily leads it *ad absurdum*.

Having arrived at a position, then, where grave doubts had to be thrown on the sheer operability of the concepts of neurosis and psychosis, unless they were confined to certain areas or functions of a given individual's mind and never applied to an individual's total mental organisation, and unless it was constantly realised—how could it be, in the rough and tumble of intellectual life in general and moralistic diagnostic reactions in particular? —that they could produce their own opposites, abnormal realism as it were, in one and the same person, I was both stunned and elated, after about two years, to come across the work of Thomas Szasz (*The Myth of Mental Illness, Ideology and Insanity, The Manufacture of Madness, Psychiatric Justice, Law, Liberty, and Psychiatry, The Ethics of Psycho-analysis, The Second Sin, Ceremonial Chemistry*, and sundry important papers, essays, and newspaper articles). I quickly came to realise that this rebellious psychoanalyst and professor of psychiatry (for whose precise job description see p.11) was the most independent psychological thinker since Freud—which in itself, admittedly, wasn't saying all that much, since there hadn't been many independent psychological thinkers since this giant had left the scene: people depended either on Freud or on his followers, so that it was extremely difficult to find anybody in the psychological and psychiatric world who wasn't either a Freudian or an anti-Freudian.

I sent Szasz the afore-mentioned paper, and his reply was characteristic. He expressed gratification at our independent arrival at certain identical conclusions, and added that this just showed that two times two made four, however hard the experts tried to make it come out five. I have not, meanwhile, turned into a Szaszian; in fact, -ans and -ists with a person's name attached to their description—Christians, Freudians, Mohammedans, Marxists, Maoists, Wagnerians, Schoenbergians—are humanity's leading inhibitors of thought. But I accept Szasz's basic ethical discoveries and his scientific critique of pure psychiatry (my title for what he's done), as I accept Freud's basic psychological discoveries; and this is my statement of bias. Above all, Szasz's demonstration of the concept of 'mental illness' being a mere metaphor is incontrovertible.

In my psychological life, I have been lucky enough not to be incarcerated with what Szasz calls the 'experts' for any length of time. I read one or two papers to the British Psychological Society, one jointly with Margaret Phillips, another under the chairmanship of J. C. Flugel, himself one of the broadest minds in the history of psychoanalysis. A few years ago, however, I had an experience which prepared me more properly for attendance at the psychoanalytic Congress. I had the honour of being invited into the holy of holies, the inner chamber of the sanctuary, the esoteric circle *par excellence*, presided over by none less than the widow of Ernest Jones (the Freud biographer) herself, where, normally, only those who have subjected themselves to hetero-analysis are allowed to open their mouths. I was to deliver a 'paper' (I never use any paper, script or notes) on the psychoanalysis of music, but as I got going, lovingly watching my audience, I noticed in those unspontaneous faces, heavily burdened by collective, and collectively resigned, wisdom about the unconscious (especially mine), that nobody knew or cared what I was talking about—partly because they didn't seem to care much about music anyway (even though it gets a jolly sight deeper than psychoanalysis), and partly because I made the basic mistake of saying things which they hadn't heard before. But first and foremost, I wasn't one of the boys and girls, if boys and girls you could call them. Let's face it: I hadn't been brain-washed, or if I had been, mine must have been a rotten, cheap laundry. Szasz's definition of a psychoanalytic institute would have sprung to mind if I had known it; it certainly stuck in my mind throughout the Congress, the way diverse cigars (of which more in due course) stuck in distinguished, knowing mouths there:

Psychoanalytic institute: a school where the faculty, composed of old and middle-aged men and women, called psychoanalysts, systematically degrade and infantilize the students, composed of psychiatrists themselves fast approaching middle age, who eagerly submit to this degradation ceremony in the expectation, often unfulfilled, that, after being completely deprived of all independent judgment and the capacity to form such judgment, they will be able to inflict a similar treatment on others, call it psychoanalysis, and charge high fees for it.[2]

Let me hasten to add, however, that this was not the spirit in which I approached the prospect of the Congress. If there was any spirit at all, it was one of mitigated loyalty, nostalgia almost: our own Institute of Psychoanalysis had been extremely generous to me in my youth, exceptionally allowing me free access to its unique library, with the result that when it came to that 'paper' in the inner sanctum, I was able to quote from downright medieval issues of *Imago*. There was a chap writing there, a now forgotten Hungarian by the name of Mosonyi, who was one of the few analysts ever who understood music; Freud and Szasz, for instance, are equally clueless about the art (which doesn't prevent them from talking about it). But I'm afraid the high priests, who disliked any erudition except their own, seemed inclined to think that I made it all up as I went along, hiding my heresies in alleged quotations from the prophets — those obscure bits which nobody ever reads anyway. When it came to so-called question time (statement time, that is), they as much as declared that they neither understood, nor saw any point in understanding, what I had been trying to say.

Now, my spirit of partial loyalty to the Congress — after all, this assembly was about what I consider the most important pre-scientific development in modern times — was shattered well before the moment go. It was

2 *The Second Sin*, Doubleday, New York; Routledge & Kegan Paul, London, 1974, pp. 82f.

94

when *The New Review* applied for a press-card for me and there were difficulties, hesitations. To begin with, I only hit my own roof as it were, strictly in private, granting the Congress the benefit of my residual doubt. But when I subsequently found out, from reliable sources, that there was genuine fear of the press, or of certain sections of it, anyway, and that in the end, some of those fears were thought to have been pretty well founded, my mind was made up: I had to regard the Congress as a closed society, and whatever its merits, *qua* closed society it deserved contempt.

Of course, there always are harmlessly (if wilfully) closed societies, maintaining childlike (i.e. would-be parental) secrecy towards hated parent figures (i.e. alleged childish idiots). The most outstanding example in our own century, and indeed perhaps the most realistically secretive society altogether, was Schoenberg's *Verein für musikalische Privataufführungen* (Society for Private Musical Performances), which

was not quite like anything that had been organised before. Its rules, as promulgated on February 16, 1919, were strict in the extreme; for its purpose, the propagation of new music, without regard to cliques and in a non-commercial atmosphere, was felt to require regulations of a very special kind. *Critics were not only not invited to the performances of this unique organisation; they were forbidden to attend* (my italics).[3]

From the point of view of my present argument against collective confidentiality, the trouble about Schoenberg's then view that all official Viennese critics were childish

---

3  Dika Newlin, *Bruckner — Mahler — Schoenberg*, King Crown Press, New York; O.U.P. London, 1947, p.263.

idiots (i.e. unmusical, believing themselves to be musical) is, simply, that he was right: that much we can say, being wise after the event. But in any case, two circumstances of this marginally bizarre society have to be noted if we want to assess its secrecy fairly. First, while Schoenberg tended to keep his own work out of the society's limelight, he did agree to no fewer than ten public rehearsals (without performance) of his First Chamber Symphony, then a stumbling block even to most of the most mature musical understanders: if he kept the society's musical activities a secret from the critics, he at the same time disclosed a conventionalised secret, i.e. rehearsals, to all music lovers, his aim being, straightforwardly, maximal understanding, as well as maximal prevention of the type of incomprehension that poses as disdainful understanding.

So far, the organisers of the psychoanalytic Congress can plead a comparable attitude, even though the resistance to, and misunderstanding of, psychoanalysis by our newspapers and magazines can hardly be compared to the total war on new music waged by the critics of 1919 Vienna. However, even if we decide to grant the Congress the right to a certain degree of caution on this first count, my second circumstance obliterates any such excuse: by no conceivable token was new music an issue of public policy in post-First-World-War Vienna; whereas if, at this stage in the history of what, at the time of writing, is our fast-sinking civilisation, we accept public health as an issue of public policy, we have to include mental health in it, so long as we, or most of us, or some of us, think there is such a thing. Since most of us, and all analysts except Szasz, do think so, the difficulty or delay I faced until I received my press-card has a sinister aspect: outside those time-honoured, well-practised concealments of conversations which 'children don't understand', there is no remotely justifiable reason for discussions of what are, ultimately, issues of public policy to be held *in camera,* or, at any rate, in relative secrecy. There is all the less reason, and all the more of a motive, if these discussions develop on the highest professional level where, from a public point of view, the power lies. Had I not been I, accredited by both the Editor of *The New Review* and indeed a leading psychoanalyst, but, say, a reporter for a popular newspaper, I might well not have received my visa.

I choose my nationalistic metaphor advisedly, upon grave and stressedly ambivalent reflection: I know precisely what our analysts mean when, at this stage in the history of their discipline, they don't want rubbish printed about it, but I disapprove with all my mind, even if my heart may beat for them. From 'Prague, 1975' (Chapter II, pp49ff), the reader will remember my thoughts about the closure of that society, and my thoughts about the semi-closure of this one are, I fear, identical: all such closures are in the alleged interest of those ruled, but, in reality, spring from a psychotic fear on the part of the rulers, who act in what is, or what they feel to be, their own interest. Only, in the case of a psychoanalytic society and its gatherings, the voiceless ruled aren't there: they are the patients. But the philosophical, logical, ethical, and indeed psychological position remains the same: *it is for you, and you alone, to decide what is in your interest, not for a communist central committee or a psychoanalytic congress* (or, for that matter, your boss or personnel officer). Significantly enough, whenever I raised this issue of secrecy and the fear of publicity with analysts, the defence advanced was the effect printed reports might have on patients. Had the patients been invited to say whether they minded the effect such reports might have on them, or whether, perhaps, they desired it? Or was their therapeutic infantilisation so complete that there was no point in asking them, just as there is no point in asking a child whether, by any remote chance, he's interested in the facts of life?

Did I say facts? Did I say life? The greatest disappointment of such a congress is the discrepancy between its terms of reference and what happens within them — or rather, what happens instead of them. The deepest layers of human life, its most complex and conflict-ridden facts are supposed to be under dispassionate discussion, but what you get instead is, not just the atmosphere, but the tangible and demonstrable reality of often total unreality, of a collective fantasy life based, as in the case of 'Prague 1975' (Chapter II), on the surrender of individual consciences — scientific consciences in this instance. When you are allowed to attend a fervently religious meeting or service, any orthodoxy, you are at least fascinated by the mystery of it all and have a vaguely uneasy conscience because you don't really know what they are talking about, but do know that you're missing something. But here, at this Congress, you did know what they were talking about, and you did not, alas, miss a thing; in fact, more often than not, you could play the private game of foreseeing the next sentence, as when listening to a boring piece of music. Not that audiences minded foreseeing the next bit; on the contrary, the fulfilment of intellectual expectation affords gratification and reassurance.

'Psychoanalytic theory: the work song of the Freudian boatmen'[4]; it's got to be a simple tune. How simple, how downright stupid it can at times become when somebody likes the sound of his own voice you really cannot believe unless you are there to hear it (or, of course, unless you are an at least equally simple-minded anti-Freudian).

The point — my metaphorical point, anyhow — is that a work song has to be sung by many in unison, which imposes certain restrictions on its intellectual complexity and indeed its psychic realism. We have all encountered the 'good Roman Catholic', the 'good Christian', the 'good Jew', the 'good communist', and we all know what he's going to say before he says it. You may think that I am maligning the fraternity, I mean the siblingity, when I say that the ambition of every good mediocre analyst who's lost his individual conscience (if he ever had one to speak of, his boring superego and static ego-ideal apart) is to be just that — a 'good analyst' in the religious sense. But no — I'm merely quoting, although, just as in the case of Chapter II, I am intent upon keeping my psychoanalytic sources anonymous and inextricably mixed up so as not to get anybody into trouble, amply as some of them would deserve it. And what I am quoting is no less than a reminder from the platform, at one of the all too rare moments of (mild) tension, when one or two of the boatmen allowed themselves a bar or two of rudimentary counterpoint, weak enough to be heard as mere homophony. At this stage, the distinguished speaker said, in a calming fatherly or motherly tone (and I wrote it down while he or she said it): *'We are all good analysts, but have different viewpoints.'* I looked around

---

[4] Thomas S. Szasz, *op. cit.*, p.83.

the church, I mean the synagogue. Was nobody sane enough to yell? Let it be said in fairness that one or two cigars did seem to roll uneasily in their mouths, but on the whole, the priest's reassurance was gratefully accepted, and you could smell the guilt feelings about latent, not to say lurking dissension evaporate: they stank, a tribute to the decline of independent thought. 'Different viewpoints', then, were the pinnacle of individualism; different views would, I suppose, have turned their holders into 'bad' analysts, a fate worse than death because if your conscience is outside yourself and condemns you, there's nothing you can do about it except buy a single ticket to hell; whereas with an internal conscience, even in a situation of extreme self-condemnation, I should optimistically advise the purchase of a return ticket.

Let it not be thought that when I diagnose unreality, I merely mean delusions. In psychological and psychiatric circles, it is often forgotten that there is an at least equally dangerous, and certainly more widespread, threat to realism, and that is sheer stupidity. Moreover, just as collective delusions are more readily attainable than individual delusions, because there's nobody left to see them for what they are, so collective stupidity spreads like wild fire until there's nobody left to see it for what it is. At this Congress, solemn statements and light-hearted aphorisms that were utter inanity were legion; not one was challenged. My prize goes to the venerable American analyst Leo Rangell, a past president of the International Psychoanalytical Society from Los Angeles, whose interminable reflections were lovingly described by a colleague, at coffee time, as an example of 'post-presidential narcissistic intoxication'—

a description which might have sounded more interesting if it had come out of a less narcissistic mouth. As it was, I was more interested in the emptiness of Dr Rangell's remarks than in their psychology. He was one of the many leading Freudian-cud-chewers; what made his speech exceptional was that he chewed it so badly—hence this prize-winning effort: 'So much has been lost in the zealous quest for the first year or months of life. I have a patient for whom, to understand her anal phase, is to understand her life.'

Again, I looked round me. Was there anybody, a single body with a mind left on top of it, who fathomed the bottomless stupidity of this would-be ultra-Freudian pronunciamento? No facial muscle moved, except in slight, prayer-like relief: at its nadir, the work song had turned into a sacred song, probably because the original Freudian dogmata had so far been slightly under-played, to the extent of anality not yet having been mentioned once. My admiration for Freud's discovery of the anal phase and its role in the development of personality (quite especially in our culture!) is second to nobody else's; the title of a panel discussion I mentioned in my hors-d'oeuvre is a product of anality, albeit not the most distinguished. But no life has yet been understood in terms of any pre-genital or genital phase; it would hardly be worth living if it were thus explicable. No wonder they don't want that patient to hear what her analyst has been saying; if I were she and heard him and had enough negative transference left, I would, at the next session, show him with great (anal) precision where to get off. But then, the likelihood is that far from taking this kind of explanation of life's mysteries amiss, she has already been stupefied to the point of accepting the divine message with glee; I know more than one highly intelligent ex-patient, discharged as cured after years of analysis, who immediately drops into a diagnostic or self-diagnostic stupor whenever he is confronted, or feels he is confronted, by psychological problems, or psychological 'interest'—in other people or himself. Some of these models of mental health spend most of their intellectual leisure on such a Pavlov-dog-like retreat from intelligence.

Nor is it only ex-patients who are thus afflicted—and here I come to the first of the three centres of gravity of my piece. (A musician has to get used to more than one centre of gravity: the 'Jupiter' or the 'Eroica' symphony has two each, one in the first movement and one in the last. The fear of both mixed and varied metaphors is, in fact, unreasonable: five dimensions or five co-ordinates, for instance, can make perfect metaphorical sense. So long as you stress your mixtures and variations, there is no reason why you should renounce what is one of the quickest and, potentially, most exact means of communication; the very fact of a *varied* metaphor will always remind everybody that it is, after all, only a metaphor. If, for instance, the metaphor of mental illness had been used with well-defined variations — all three hearts of the mind are affected, or all three gall-bladders are — instead of the medical and psychiatric profession forgetting that it was a metaphor, Szasz could have saved himself a book or two.)

My first centre of gravity, then, is the diagnosing and self-diagnosing stupor occupying the intellectual leisure time of the profession itself—at any rate, when these people find themselves within the confines of their closed society, unaware that a spy is listening: in Prague and at

102

the Grosvenor House Hotel at Congress time, everybody seems to have been a spy, or at least an undesirable pressman or broadcaster, who disagreed without being a good communist or a good psychoanalyst. I give it to the reader as a hard fact, closely checked and unexaggerated, that in all but one of those conversations I heard in the corridors (or overheard, or took part in), and which I found immeasurably more engrossing than all those mouldy papers and discussions, the adjectives 'paranoid' and/or 'psychotic' played a central role—applied either to a speaker heard in the course of the Congress, or (in jest, of course) to the partner in conversation, and/or (in jest, of course) to the diagnoser himself. Before I examine the single, honourable exception, let it be realised what my hard fact means. Just as in Prague, you could absolutely rely on the words 'economic' and/or 'capitalist' cropping up centrally in every conversation, so at the Congress the conversationalists' self-imposed intellectual restrictions were such as to turn an exchange of thought into a defensive word play, fortified by magically degrading terms. The only difference was that at the Congress, the magic was often supposed to be semi-jocular. Alas, a joke needs a surprise element rather than total expectability, so it was only those psychoanalytic Pavlov dogs who would muster a smile, though everybody laughed at his own diagnoses when they were meant to be funny—and sometimes, painedly, when they were not.

Once I had ascertained these unconscious rules of the game, I decided to test them, and the underlying need for a diagnostic escape from reality, on the first suitable occasion—if at all possible with an interesting and relatively thoughtful analytic mind. The opportunity presented itself out of the blue in a 'dialogue'—this time there's no need for anonymity, he will agree—with Eduardo Cortesao, the charming and ethically conscious Portuguese analyst who, as Peter Fuller has pointed out[5], 'has first-hand experience of psychoanalytic practice in a revolutionary situation', and thinks 'that the psycho-analyst could not and should not endeavour to dissociate himself from historical processes' (a slight illogicality here: if he can't he won't, whether he should or shouldn't).Together with another analyst, we were discussing Dr Cortesao's view that one should talk to everybody rather than put up the shutters, and that one should exchange views with the Russian psychiatrists rather than merely evince *a priori* hostility to their methods, which we deem to be in the service of political repression and persecution: Dr Cortesao spoke apropos of the photostats of various serious newspaper reports and articles ('Psychiatrists blame Russia', 'A Criminal Abuse of Psychiatry', 'Soviet Repression: Western Scientists are now at a Crossroads of Conscience', etc.) which were laid out at the Congress for collection by anybody interested.

'So you think', I mused, 'that there would have been a point in talking, professionally, to Nazi psychiatrists, that there is a point in discussing psychiatric and ethical problems with the Soviet psychiatrists responsible for the certification and commitment to mental hospitals of political dissidents? That there is a point in fraternising with *criminals*?' I stressed the last word for the purpose of my association test, which proved tediously successful. 'You mean *psychotics*?' he inevitably asked. 'No', I said,

---

[5] 'A chat of analysts' in *New Society*, July 31, 1975.

preparing for the supreme challenge, 'I don't mean psychotics. The criteria for psychosis are more controversial today than ever before.' What I did not add was that if the magic term 'psychosis' were used in those friendly chats with the Soviet profession, they would soon turn into a slanging match in which the two sides would call each other psychotic: it could easily be shown that according to Soviet symptomatology, every single psychoanalyst (not to speak of you and me) can be diagnosed as a case of either 'creeping schizophrenia' or 'paranoid psychopathy'[6].

'What I mean', I added with ethical zest, 'is what I said—criminals, by which I meant bad men, evil men.' The sadly expected reaction ensued. Dr Cortesao put up the shutters after all. There was disarming naivety in his utter unawareness of the paradox into which he had plunged headlong: he was keen on talking to the Soviet psychiatrists, but he was no longer prepared to go on discussing the selfsame problem with me, even though, until my challenge, he had shown intense interest in our conversation. But now, he thought to himself, 'This isn't an analyst', and within half a silent, thoughtful minute, he asked: 'What precisely do you do?' 'I'm a musician,' I said, meticulously avoiding any reference to the psychological side of my life. 'Ah!' he said, and swiftly started to talk about music.

Now, the one exception to the rules of the defensive fantasy game played in the corridors was quite something—a veritable breakthrough into reality, however short-lived. The situation was another such conversational interlude; two analysts and myself. One of

[6] See V. Bukovsky and S. Gluzman, 'A Manual on Psychiatry for Dissidents', in *Survey*, London, Winter-Spring 1975, pp. 195 and 187.

them was what is known as normal, the other was what is not known as normal—highly aggressive verbally, and a bit of a weirdie in his demeanour. But it was this man, whom an unsympathetic observer might conceivably have considered a raving lunatic, who caught my attention, and not only because I soon realised that here was a chance of listening to someone who had no interest at all in calling something or somebody paranoid or psychotic and have done with it or him. No, this man had actually refused to surrender his intellectual conscience and, as a result, talked meaningfully, whatever he touched upon—and always without a trace of rumination in a cow's sense:

Nothing but bloody first-year lectures. Everybody wants to bloody teach, nobody wants to bloody learn. Out of touch with bloody real life, that's what they are. I can't bloody breathe in here.

If the reader is irritated by the superabundance of bloodies, he must appreciate that after a day or two of hardly less abundant paranoids and psychotics, the bloodies felt, in their context, like a breath of real mountain air as opposed to watching others use life-sustaining oxygen masks.

On other topics, too, the gentleman was riveting. He had asked some Soviet psychiatrists what the proportion of voluntary patients was in their mental hospitals. 'They just didn't seem to understand what I was talking about. My bloody question meant as much to them as if I'd asked them how many voluntary communists there were, or how many voluntary Russians.'

Shortly after this episode, I ran into another analyst (yes, I spent as much time in the corridors as at the

Congress proper). I don't know how well he knew the gentleman, but he was only mildly amused, and not at all gratified. Not that he refused to be sensitive to the truth of what I had heard. But he didn't like the thought that it had issued forth from that particular mouth, since it appeared to him that the gentleman's personality (paranoid? psychotic?) vaguely discredited what he had been saying.

Which brings me to my second centre of gravity, a very grave centre indeed, closely linked to the first—the diagnosing-away of reality: the relevance of my introductory summary of my paper on 'Music and Psychopathology' is beginning to show. I was rather taken aback by this enlightened analyst's lukewarm response, and decided to drive my point home, on the basis of the conclusions reached in 'Music and Psychopathology'. But I was not going to theorise; rather, I would try to find the simplest, most connatural, most indisputable simile. What occurred to me was a football analogy:

I say to an orthopaedic specialist whose lifelong interest has been sport, and football in particular: 'The greatest headers of the ball I have known in my life were Cliff Jones and Alan Gilzean, even though Cliff Jones was very short and Alan Gilzean had a bent back.' 'I don't like that thought', says the orthopaedic specialist. 'I have spent my life straightening children's backs, and I have actually published a monograph on the "Conditions of Good Heading" in which I conclusively show that tallness and a straight back are *conditiones sine qua non* of great heading. Why do you think the old centre-half and the new centre-back had, and has, to be tall?' 'Yes, tallness and a straight back are very important, I do agree,' I say.

107

'But Cliff Jones and Alan Gilzean were the greatest headers I have known, and anybody who knew them didn't know any greater.' 'I don't like that thought,' says the specialist, with resigned, professional dignity.

My addressee nodded in silence. I don't know to this day whether he actually agreed, or whether he just didn't know enough about football—or whether, on the contrary, he knew too exclusively about the benefits to be derived from tallness and straight backs.

When I suggest that the corridors were more interesting than the halls, I do not wish to imply that there was no interest at all in the halls. For one thing, I should have no right to pass such a verdict: I wasn't there all the time, and when I was, the first day apart, there were several things going on simultaneously. I also have to admit that on at least one occasion, I preferred the corridors to any of the concurrent happenings in the halls—and I was not alone: as at all congresses (my experience is rich and varied), plenty of people were playing truant all the time, preferring informal personal discussions and consultations to the 'first-year lectures'. I do think that congresses, most of them, ought to own up to the fact that their official business is, largely, a ritual (papers are more easily, and more reflectively, read than heard), and that the value of the exercise lies in personal contact of which, usually, there is far too little, because people inevitably have a conscience about attending official business.

Indeed, at this assembly as at many another where I had been actively involved, I found that whatever was wrong with the exchanges in the corridors, they never descended to the level of ineptitude one often has to suffer when one listens to official speakers: there are always people who, when they have to address a crowd from a platform, lose all control over their obtuseness, which is stimulated into producing lapidary statements they would be incapable of in private; not everybody is strong enough to resist the appeal of the (imagined or real) common denominator. Thunderous revelations such as 'The id has changed the least—probably since psychoanalysis was born', or 'The fact of repression remains unaltered' nobody would have allowed himself in the corridors, even at his most self-confessedly psychotic: in an intimate circle of pals, nobody would feel the urge to announce that two times two still makes four.

For another thing, however, there was at least one extended moment when the platform deserved profound respect and admiration: on the first afternoon, the octogenarian Anna Freud addressed the Congress. Rather like the octogenarian Sir Adrian Boult when he conducted Brahms's Fourth Symphony at the 1975 Proms, she took unnecessary precautions in case of a lapse of memory. Boult had a score in front of him but didn't follow it; rather, it followed him, in that he always turned over several pages at a time in order to give his score a chance to keep abreast with his performance. And Anna Freud had a few sheets of notes in front of her; only, she didn't even bother to let them follow her, but merely played around with them.

She did not, of course, communicate any news—nor, on the other hand, did she simply recapitulate, or regale us with the kind of purely ornamental or decorative variation which has produced so many distinguished enemies of variation form in the world of music (a world of thought, incidentally, that yields countless pregnant metaphors to help conceptual thought along, whereas the usual, word-obsessed approach does the opposite—it sterilises music by verbal metaphor). What Miss Freud produced were what Schoenberg called developing variations, to the extent of offering calm insight into such contemporary expressions of adolescence (belated or not) as streaking—in terms of an easement of the repressions of pre-genital sexuality.

Without, apparently, being fully aware of the fact, she was moreover prepared to face, or at least touch upon, two of the burning problems which make psychoanalysis and indeed psychiatry an issue of public policy. Or shall we say, more cautiously, that she faced one and touched upon the other?

The problem she indubitably faced was the time-honoured one of the therapeutic value of psychoanalysis. It will be remembered that Freud himself, who never made exaggerated claims for psychoanalysis *qua* therapy, firmly placed the acquisition of knowledge through the psychoanalytic method as a top priority, or as his own priority anyhow. I remember my divided feelings when I first read him on the subject as a young man—my admiration for the fanatical searcher for truth on the one hand and, on the other, my unease about therapy being the concealing flag behind which the search for truth was going on, and for jolly stiff fees too. These divided feelings have meanwhile matured—deepened without, I hope, calcifying. No wonder, then, that I pricked up my ears as Miss Freud began to approach the ticklish subject—with more relaxed collective self-confidence, may I say, than behoves the psychoanalyst at the present stage in the development of his craft: there's moral safety in numbers, alas, and psychological security too.

Not unnaturally, Anna Freud (who had pointed out that she was the sibling of psychoanalysis, since she was born about the same time) proved herself her father's daughter. The accumulation of psychoanalytic knowledge, she suggested, would be of enormous value even if it could not be turned into therapeutic efficiency—to wit, in the field of prophylactic child psychology (my description). 'Increasing knowledge can help to equip us with the knowledge to prevent the very disorders which we now find so difficult to treat.'

But we were not told how this knowledge was going to be obtained except under the banner of therapy and therefore, to some degree or in some cases at least, under false pretences; nor were we specifically informed about the disorders we were going to prevent—or rather, what entitled us to regard them as disorders, and so practise our newly acquired art of post-natal, psychological eugenics (my description).

Which brings me to the second basic problem, the one which, in my opinion, Miss Freud merely touched upon. Once we were going to prevent anything, thus playing God to the extent of deciding what was a desirable type of personality and then helping in its very creation, we should have to be jolly sure, it would seem to me, that our divinity was of the right, supreme order, that our omniscience would tell us, in so many words, what we should prevent and what we shouldn't. My second problem is, in short, the real dogmatism of psychoanalysis and of modern mental hygiene in general.

I have mentioned the so-miscalled psychoanalytic dogmata—such as the unconscious, repression, etc.—which, on a purely empirical basis, I am compelled to regard as demonstrable truth. The real, if veiled dogmatism lies elsewhere—in the ethical field, in what the psychoanalyst feels entitled to consider, *a priori*, as evil and good, though he is not prepared to call things that, since he depends on a downright psychotic denial (ha! here I go) of the reality of his own moralism. So he calls them, in Miss Freud's words, 'disorders' on the one hand, and on the other—what? Orders? The naivety of the dogma would become too obvious. Besides, in the history of moralising, evil has always received more verbal and more concrete attention than the good; in fact, 'evil' itself is specific, whereas 'good' isn't: you can have a good meal or hear a good symphony, but you can't have an evil meal or hear an evil symphony. We know or knew all about the devil, the hierarchy of hell, about the capitalist, the communist, the Jew, the negro, and, most recently, the 'disturbed', but the undisturbed are never mentioned; in fact, according to Freud's own very profound instinct theory, we might see life as a disturbance of death, rather than *vice versa*.

So which are 'the very disorders', then, in omniscient view of which Miss Freud wants us to play God (a pleasurable enough role in all conscience, whether enacted by way of eugenics, euthanasia, or indeed capital punishment)? 'How is one to cure basic fault?' Miss Freud asked, making one all agog as to the true nature of original sin and its promised paradisical prevention; Genesis itself—as it stands, one of the more disreputable moments in God's career, anyway—may have to be rewritten in due course and placed altogether above board, thanks to our divine intervention based on research for which cured and uncured patients, tall and tiny, have generously provided the money. What precisely, then, is it that we are going to prevent? From

André Green of Paris we had heard of the existence of—
surprise!—a psychotic core (in all religions you've got to
have a rotten core), of a 'blank psychosis' in all of us.
Well, that can hardly be prevented—and indeed, why
should it. After all, at the time of writing, the
psychoanalytic concept of psychosis is moving amiably
near to Analytical Psychology's (Jung's) concept of
libido: there ain't much else, so why worry?

Fortunately, Miss Freud was, by implication, quite
clear and decided about what she was going to prevent,
about how, in principle, she was going to dis-disorder the
growing mind. Time was when the magic words were
'reality test' and 'object cathexis', the latter process
superseding the more primitive identification (intro-
jection). But with the fragmentation of our civilisation,
not to speak of R. D. Laing and indeed Thomas Szasz,
the reality of reality has, once again, become a bit of a
problem (as it was with Kant), and as for object relations
replacing identifications, the ten-odd commandments of
depth psychology (always rigorously implied and never
stated) have passed their most rudimentary stage, which
was: later=maturer=better; in fact, the moralistic
concept of 'age-adequacy' emerged well after St
Sigmund's death—as if, in certain endo-psychic
circumstances, age-inadequacy were not the shortest cut
to reality. Anyhow, we've grown circumspect, none more
so than Miss Freud, whose mind is far too alert to be
age-adequate. All she wants us to do now in order to give
proof that our mind is in order is to 'relate' to other
people, and what she wants to prevent is the inability to
relate—the mental disorder *par excellence.*

During the Congress, one fine evening, I was sitting
with one of the analysts, grown-up specimen, outside that

relaxing Hyde Park pub near the Serpentine, when a paddling of ducks, harmony animalified, swam past us. 'Thank God!' I heaved a sigh of Anna-Freudian relief. 'Look, how they relate! Fantastic. Watch every single one of them.' 'The tiny one at the back looks a bit grumpy', my friend suggested, anthropomorphically loyal to faltering humanity. 'Grumpy? Alright, grumpy. But look how, in spite of it all, he relates! He's grumpy on the basis of his relating, not without it. Now compare Beethoven.' 'Or Mozart', said the analyst, committing analytic high treason with relish; after all, this was his night off, and he was too grown up to go on when he was off. As a matter of fact, his example was much better than mine; only, so far as I am concerned, Mozart as a human being is so utterly inhuman that it's easier to understand a duck.

The moral of my real-life story, however obvious, cannot be overrated: its size is proportionate to the creeping moralism behind every type of therapeutic psychology. The stronger all those protestations which would have us believe that the patient (including the new-born?) determines his own values, the creepier the unacknowledged moralism: have you, gentle reader, ever met a single analysed person whose values, whose very world-view, proved unaffected by his analyst's psychological school, orthodox analysis or Analytical Psychology or whatever it might have been? Have you met many who did not, in fact, make a slightly de-individualised impression, 'individualistic', 'realistic', only to those who subscribed to the analyst's or therapist's religion and accepted it as reality? Speaking as one of the three self-analysts I know about, I could not feel and think more strongly about this rhetorical question of mine. No criticism of analysis or any other therapy is implied here. What is implied, urgently enlisted, is every available criticism of that creeping moralisation which provides us with this single difference between an orthodox religion and orthodox analysis — that analysis is, in fact, more of a religion than is any recognised religion, which at least does not make a secret of its indoctrination, whereas *the analytic priest denies the influence of his faith on conduct and mental attitude not only to the believers, actual and potential, but also (indeed in the first place) to himself.* Now, when it comes to indoctrination which, though post-natal, takes place before the mind as we know it is born, i.e. before the first traces of recognisable individuation, our own minds should boggle, if they in their turn have retained the slightest trace of respect for the development of individual autonomy in the psychological and indeed the old-fashioned Kantian sense: the very fact that psychoanalysis, utterly uneducated philosophically because of its founder's aversion to the study of ultimate reality, clings to his own primitive total determinism, makes it easy for the analyst to play God with a good conscience — vis-à-vis the child, anyhow: the other determinist doctrines of our time, Marxism, neo-Marxism and Maoism, produce an equally easy conscience about indoctrination.

Thou shalt relate — or at least be able to, like a duck. Why, Miss Freud? For a start, if you succeeded in realising this plan to evolve the finest humans (least 'disordered', I presume?), you would run the mortal risk of abolishing genius — and thus the means of perceiving and understanding the most complex aspects of the very reality which your philosophy (dare I call it that?)

proposes to serve. In fact, surveying the history of genius, you will find that the surprisingly small proportion of ducks amongst them might well turn out to be statistically significant. And although we, the aristocratic depth psychologists, have made no progress at all in the course of the past three-quarters of our century in grasping the nature and determinants of genius[7], there is one single thing which all geniuses whose work I understand and whose lives I have studied have in common: the ability, permanent or intermittent, *not* to relate, and to do something else instead—yes, *instead*. It is not really an altogether intoxicating thought to realise that according to Anna Freud's latest soothing words about the usefulness of psychoanalytic knowledge (however much of a hash we may be making of its therapeutic purpose), that sizeable part of our population which is being psychoanalysed at the time of writing is contributing vast sums towards the extinction of genius—and thus towards the snug, un-'disturbed', 'integrated', object-related[8] annihilation of man's original virtue—the capacity for discovering truths.

An eccentric thought? Of course. This entire chapter is a manifesto against the kind of centric thought which establishes ever-widening, concentric circles of thought-lessness around it: show me your congresses and I'll tell you (a) who you aren't, and (b) who you could have been,

---

[7]  Nor have others of course: they just clear—cloud—the air by denying its existence, the Marxists and Maoists above all.

[8] Speaking for myself, I don't have object-relations, by the way, if you want to know. I prefer subject-relations. People may be objects to children, but to imagine that we talk of the maturest human choices as 'object choices'! Don't think it happened in translation: Freud's original German term is *Objektwahl*.

capacity for moral independence and intelligence permitting.

A few weeks after this Congress had finished and I had returned to the living, I experienced what, in the context, was a significant professional shock, and I am making it my indiscreet business (see my observations on discretion and confidentiality on p. 53) to report on it with eccentric precision. For the European Broadcasting Union, as chairman of the international working party which plans its concert seasons, I had arranged an event which was to take place in Vienna's Grosser Musikvereinssaal, and in which what I regard as a very great artist was going to sing a number of Mozart arias as well as Strauss's 'Four Last Songs': the programme was designed to throw her art into relief, and to make it known to a world-wide audience; these concerts are being relayed by 15-odd radio organisations. Naturally, the planning of the unconventional concert was complex and took months. When, finally, all was solved and settled, the singer came to see me and told me that she was expecting an illegitimate child a week or two before the concert, which we therefore had to abandon. While there is no need to mention her name, I may add that she stressed that she had no desire to be secretive about this turn of events, which I was free to disclose.

A few days later, I discussed the situation with a close friend of mine—a tolerably orthodox Freudian analyst who had been a distinguished member of the Congress. It turned out that his shock was greater than mine. Mine was severe and practical; his was severely moral. His basic interest, inevitably, was eugenic: there would be a fatherless child, perhaps even motherless, or intermittently motherless, in view of the singer's determin-

117

ation to continue her professional life at the earliest possible moment—and that was bad (my simplifying words). Now, was it? How do we know? Are we entitled to say to a woman, don't have a child if you can't provide him with a father, or don't have a child if you want to return to full-time singing as soon as possible? Whose affair is this, ours or hers? The psychoanalyst's case is that we know enough by now for this reasonable prognosis—that things are more likely to go wrong than right. So what? For one thing, human nature and Western society being what they are, things are more likely to go wrong in any circumstances. For another, the analyst's preview is unavoidably cock-eyed: he knows the failures, you and I know the successes. If he calls the successes we know failures, that's his problem, not that of the individual in question. But most importantly, he is planning human society statistically rather than humanly, on the basis of the safety-first principle, eschewing risk (as if he were setting up traffic rules), and in the light of divine moral prejudices, such as that heterosexuality is better than homosexuality, when a glance at history's great homosexuals leads our automatic heterosexual elitism *ad absurdum*. (We complain about homosexual elitism!) Nor, of course, is fatherlessness or homosexuality the only hazard we have to face in the psychological planning of future generations. Reverting to the case of Beethoven once more, and considering the top security risk, physiological as well as psychological, that was his own father, we can safely say that if only Mrs Beethoven had had the benefit of the most recent psychoanalytic advice, the unfortunate accident of Ludwig's birth might well have been avoided, and with it untold mental and physical suffering—his own, that is. 'Blessed are those who were never born' says and old (i.e. pre-Israel) Jewish adage, except that it's quite often a blessing for others if they are.

One of the analysts had his birthday during the Congress. We were having coffee during the luncheon break, his wife, psychologically educated, with us. I told him about the orthodox Jews I had met who ignored their birthday (not an occasion for celebration for them), who did not know when it was, didn't even know their precise age. I then quoted the adage. 'Well, now,' he said, 'since they were, after all, born, they'd better face up to it.' Applausive smile at his 'realism' from his wife.

Face up to what? To our ceremonial identification of the birthday? To our absurd birthday ritual? Is that 'reality', just because we have conventionalised and institutionalised one particular outcome of our fantasies about birth? As I have shown in Chapter I, in 1938, those orthodox Jews faced up to life (and down to death) a jolly sight better than most the rest of us who knew their birthdays.

I am steadily moving towards a definition of my third centre of gravity, but I am not by any means close to it yet, because without an examination of the canonisation of Sigmund Freud himself, the psychoanalyst's and his congress's regressive removal from reality cannot be seen for what it is, i.e. the opposite of what psychoanalytic thought should lead us towards. In a petition signed by ten members of the International Psychoanalytical Association, and proposing 'Amendments to the Constitution and Byelaws', Clause 1 stated that 'Membership of the IPA shall be dependent upon an undertaking not to use the name of psycho-analysis in the pursuit of activities hostile to the emotional integrity,

119

liberty of thought, or life of the individual'; whereas Clause 3 demanded that 'Membership of the IPA shall be terminated if any individual, or group of individuals, expresses aims incompatible with [the preceding Clauses]'.

Never mind the aims you *express*. You should be the first to realise that what matters is the aims you *pursue*: if you take these into account, you might as well dissolve the IPA on the basis of your own amendment, or at least suspend it until further notice. From the moment the bust of St Sigmund was carried into the Congress, the emotional integrity and liberty of thought of the individual received no more than lip service—the very service most favoured, and most regularly practised, by all religions, however vast their differences. 'Psycho-analytic meetings: the Yom Kippur services of the secularised and "scientific" faithful: instead of regaling God in Hebrew with accounts of their own sinfulness, the worshippers regale each other, in the jargon of psychoanalysis, with accounts of the mental aberrations of their patients.'[9] Since Szasz made this observation, things have become a little more sophisticated, and proportionately yet more religious, especially in the corridors: 'their own sinfulness' has come back with a bang, not to speak of each other's, as the obsessional references to paranoid and psychotic behaviour show. This is banished, invariably, by verbal magic, i.e. tired, litany-like jokes, amusing only to their maker, the lonely grinner, unless somebody is kind enough to pray with him.

The degree to which St Sigmund's bust watched over the proceedings, as a loved, feared, and indeed more or less secretly hated patron saint, can hardly be overrated.

---

[9] Thomas S. Szasz *op. cit.*, p.83.

That one of the greatest thinkers humanity has produced should thus be degraded shows that recognition of the importance of indivisible autonomy should be a basic clause in the constitution of any association of thinkers (not a thinking association: there is no such thing); the only divine law worth binding any of us together is that very respect for the differences between us which distinguishes us from ducks.

To date, Szasz is the only one who, while fully appreciative of Freud's stature and achievement, has begun to tackle the mythology that surrounds the founder of psychoanalysis—an urgent task if we ever want to turn psychoanalysis into a grown-up discipline without a world-view hidden inside it, and a pessimistic world view to boot. I am quoting at length: [10]

. . . Freud used cocaine in two distinct, but psychologically closely related ways—a distinction that has been remarkably neglected in the literature on psychoactive drugs. First, he used the drug on himself, to bolster his energy in the service of his boundless ambition to leave his mark on the world. Second, he used the drug on patients and made extravagant claims for his therapeutic success with it. In short, cocaine made him a stronger man and a more effective doctor. When he found other ways of being strong and effective—as a person and as a therapist—he gave up this particular method of coping with stress. The answer to whether a person finds it easy or difficult to give up a drug habit thus lies not in the drug, but in the use to which the person who takes it puts it, and in the substitutes for it that he can or wants to employ.

It is interesting to note here that Freud's work with, and use of, cocaine evidently embarrassed his reverential

---

[10] *Ceremonial Chemistry: The Ritual Persecution of Drugs, Addicts, and Pushers,* Doubleday, New York, 1974, Routledge & Kegan Paul, London, 1975, p.82f.

121

biographer, Jones. Indeed, perhaps it is precisely because Freud himself was a cocaine 'addict' in the present-day sense of the term, and because he was also 'addicted' to cigars, that psychoanalysts have put forward such peculiar and plainly misleading views on addiction—the most revealing being that Freud was simply not an addict at all. His use of cocaine is discounted by Jones with the phrase 'the cocaine episode', and with this remarkable reassertion of the master's 'mental health': '. . . as we now know, it needs a special disposition to develop a drug addiction, and fortunately Freud did not possess that.' In exactly the same way, neither Jones nor other 'orthodox' psychoanalysts consider or classify Freud's smoking as an addiction. On the contrary, Freud's cigar, like his couch, became a significant symbol of the psychoanalyst's professional identity.

These two habits of Freud's, and their interpretation by respected psychiatric historians and psychoanalytic theoreticians, should, in my opinion, command our closest attention. For, to repeat, when the founder of psychoanalysis gives up cocaine after using it for three years, his followers cite this as evidence of his mental health! And when Freud smokes cigars immoderately and cannot function without them, that prompts them to incorporate cigars into the ceremonial chemistry of the psychoanalytic ritual! Perhaps Freud could give up cocaine but not cigars because he could feel that he was 'himself' without cocaine in his body, but that he was not 'himself' without a cigar in his mouth.

Freud, meanwhile, continues to create the psychoanalyst in his own image, and will continue to do so until the robot realises that in a mature intellectual world, there can be no such thing as a 'Freudian', and that as from puberty, if not indeed the latency period, identification means, ineluctably, depersonalisation— not a terribly difficult proposition to understand for a psychoanalyst, one should have hoped. The array of cigars at the Congress, though not dramatic, was impressive—especially in the corridors, where the listener turned into both lecturer and, of course, interpreter. A strictly statistical survey would have been difficult and, perhaps, unfair: Americans smoke more cigars than we do, anyway, and the American contingent was heavy. Besides, the threat of bronchial carcinoma has turned some cigarette smokers into cigar smokers (though more of them into pipe smokers). But the fact remains that this was the most cigar-infested assembly I had ever seen, and that it was in the middle of the Congress that a simple autobiographical consideration suddenly came to me: although I know a lot of people, the only cigar-smokers I know are psychoanalysts.

I am not being facile or flippant. The symbol is there, easily diagnosable; what it symbolises is what matters. Anna Freud's and the Congress's relatively easy-going attitude to the problem of therapeutic ineffectiveness, to the fact, never clearly defined, that plenty of people may be paying plenty of money for nothing — at times even for worse than nothing — would have been impossible without the dead (and, in this respect, rather ruthless) saint having given his pretty explicit blessing, his own conscience being that of the discoverer rather than that of the helper anyway: all of us who try to discover on the one hand, and try to help on the other, know this inevitable conflict within the superego, though only some of us are prepared to acknowledge it — as with the help of Anna Freud's eugenic, prophylactic meditations. Now, she, at least, is her father's daughter. The real father as a saint is one thing, the substitute father as a saint is quite another, because as soon as you canonise him, you are demanding obedience to him from a group, not just from yourself: the one is but your own problem, the other everybody's. That psychoanalysts, of all professedly thinking people, should indulge in such wholesale regression involving, yes, moral corruption throws a discomforting light on our reserves of individual courage (itself a pleonasm, this, which few would notice if I did not so describe it!) — and let us not ignore the fact that by 'reserves' one means, or should mean, something simple and specific, to wit, an amount kept on hand to meet unlikely demands. I personally would go so far as to say that the crisis of our age is the crisis of courage: far from lacking collective ideals, we've got too many of them, because the very fragmentation of our culture proves many of us too cowardly, too scared, to do without them (see Chapter IV, pp 229 ff). What is lacking is the ability to fight alone, the ability not to 'relate', not to love yourself by losing yourself in the evil service of the common good.

At the same time, a moral maze, always unfaceable for many, will inevitably produce outstanding ethical honesty on the part of the few who've got it in them. I know a psychoanalyst who, quite generally, feels unhappy about being paid for what he is doing. No doubt there would be plenty of colleagues who'd volunteer to psychologise this one out of him without charge, as an honorary collegial service; meanwhile, he has my unreserved respect, because his patients have, as individuals. For the selfsame reason, I love a private remark quoted by Anna Freud at the Congress when she tried, quite successfully, to catch fish in Kleinian waters: many decades ago, one of the early, classical analysts, Sandor Ferenczi, when discussing with her both the infant's radically positive attitude towards monogyny and its reproduction in the transference situation, remarked sorrowfully: 'In reality, one should only have one patient.' I like the bit about 'reality': it shows total commitment to the so-miscalled patient[11] as person. For the rest, the two problems converge: the solitary patient would have to pay a lot to keep the analyst alive, for which purpose he would have to have a better 'reality-sense' (adjustment to environment: getting money out of it) than his analyst would have, poor dreamer.

Another classical analyst, the afore-mentioned Willi Hoffer, once rang me, again decades ago, and said, 'I've got a patient for you.' 'You've got a *what?*' 'There's this teenager, I can't do anything about him. He's facing a schizophrenic breakdown, and it'll come. But you might postpone it. He's highly talented musically, and you, with your combined psychoanalytic and musical knowledge, would be able to do more than anybody else. It's a rich family, the fee doesn't matter. Ask whatever you like.'

I was very young and felt extremely flattered. Besides, the mention of a fee, let alone a high fee, turned me all spiritual; at that time, I got £1 per 1,000 words from *The Music Review*, and such 1,000 words meant many hours of original musical analysis before you put pen to paper. I asked £3 per session and felt a bit of an imposter; nor have I any reason to change my feelings retrospectively, except that I didn't know at the time that a considerable (though nowise essential) part of our society's most respected professional activities were as bogus as was the medieval witch-pricker's. I have learnt. Until this day, I don't know whether or not I deferred that boy's

---

[11] The original objector to the term is, of course, Szasz.

breakdown; it certainly ensued. Meanwhile, *I* had a marvellous time, psychologically speaking: I had never been in close touch with a real schizophrenic before. What the sessions did for him is another question, which I am unable to answer. All I know is that his parents paid *me* for *my* psychological education, and that this was a professionally approved course of action.

I need not labour the comparison. On both sides of the Iron Curtain, the money motive, both survivalist and psychological, produces the most serious ethical problems—which are no longer much talked about, for two reasons. First, the money motive has been politicised out of recognition and has become proportionately boring, whereas it is not, fundamentally, a political problem at all, but one for each individual conscience. Secondly, we think we know all about it anyway, whereas in fact we deny it where it harms most, i.e. where the customer pays for being controlled, deliberately or not—by the teacher, the doctor, the dentist, and the psychiatrist. The priest, special services apart, receives his money from elsewhere, which makes him the agent of his church, synagogue, mosque, or the state. The psychoanalyst enjoys the worst of both worlds: though he is paid by the patient, the often total surrender of his conscience to his patron saint makes him, at the same time, the loyal agent of his synagogue.

Both the danger of the money motive and indeed the power of what Szasz calls the therapeutic state, and what I simply call collectivism, have been beautifully, tactlessly, and repeatedly discussed by him, and I do not propose to reiterate. But there is one mortal danger inherent in the therapeutic situation to which he does not seem to me to devote sufficient attention, for reasons

126

which, I think, flow from his theoretical (anti-psychologising) position, and it is this danger that constitutes the present chapter's third centre of gravity. It will be remembered (will it?) that the first two were: the analyst's diagnosing and self-diagnosing stupor, and the diagnosing-away of reality. The third, likewise, is concerned with what, by now, we may call *the symptom that is psychiatric diagnosis*—a symptom which, like no other, aims at, and succeeds in, solving the diagnoser's own problems in what he is able to regard as a 'realistic' fashion. To put it bluntly, but without exaggeration, the psychoanalyst is the agent of his own difficulties. Aren't we all, you might say. Many, not all. And those who are do not, all of them, use human beings as their professional material, their 'objects'. Where they do—teachers, managers, critics, politicians—they are all potential enemies, not of society, which protects them, but of the individual, his integrity, dignity, and indeed his maximal maturity.

I think the reason why Szasz fights shy of throwing this fact into relief is that, objecting as he does to the psychological degradation of intellectual opponents, he does not wish to thus degrade his own opponents in his turn—that he does not, in fact, want to fall victim to what I have described as the symptom of diagnosis. But we have to think this one out—and thought out, what may seem a complex intellectual situation becomes elatingly simple. The psychoanalyst's habitual *argumentum ad hominem* is indeed irrational and contemptible; if he knew something about philosophy, he would be aware that since antiquity, this type of argument has been known and despised as the most primitive logical fallacy, based as it is on the pure intention to discredit the arguer

127

or debater or, simply, view-holder with whom one happens to disagree; the *argumentum ad rem* has always been recognised as the only legitimate approach to logical controversy or disagreement. So far, so clear: if a psychoanalyst happens to object to the proposition that in all conceivable circumstances, twice two is four, it will be of little logical avail to him to call the proposer an obsessional neurotic, preoccupied with numbers, figures, and rigid, universal legislation. *A priori,* then, the *argumentum ad rem* is the only justifiable mode of logical attack, and has been accepted as such ever since man started thinking about thinking—itself no doubt a deplorable obsessional activity.

What psychoanalysis (rather than the psychoanalyst) has contributed to the possible solution of controversy is the depth-psychological approach to a demonstrable fallacy *a posteriori*; after the fallacy has been established, it is logically permissible and, of course, desirable to ask oneself how it came about, to *explain* the *argumentum ad rem* by the *argumentum ad hominem,* to enquire into the motives rather than the reasons which make one's opponent think that in certain circumstances, twice two is five.

It is thus that we are able to turn the tables on the analyst's psychologising, that we are entitled to psychologise it in its turn, to apply the *argumentum ad hominem a posteriori* to his applying it *a priori*. All we have to make sure of is that we are really arguing from a position of logical strength, that we have, in the first place, submitted objective evidence of his fallacious attitude. I suggest that this is precisely what I have done throughout this chapter — the most dramatic single piece of evidence being, perhaps, the polite character assassination of the only analyst, or one of the very few, who clearly saw the unreality of the Congress, and whose capacity for insight I had to compare to the heading ability of Cliff Jones or Alan Gilzean.

Once we accept the palpable likelihood, then, that the analyst, unless he is ethically careful (not just psychologically, analysedly, glibly so, knowing everything about his weaknesses vis-à-vis the patient, counter-transference and all), is the agent of his own difficulties, psychological as well as financial, that the patient may easily keep him alive in both dimensions, it becomes clear to us why some of the simplest therapeutic solutions and/or possibilities of training never occur to him, have never yet been as much as discussed. Above all, I am, of course, thinking of the possibility of self-analysis (just as, in my teaching capacity, I always insist on self-teaching, with the result that the student can often get rid of me *before* any transference situation develops). It is inconceivable that Freud himself, and that chemist I mentioned earlier in the present chapter, and finally I myself, are humanity's only three specimens capable of sustained and elucidating self-analysis without hetero-analytic assistance. Yet this enormously important, virtually uncharted territory is never as much as approached by the profession without reference to hetero-analysis; on the contrary, the development, analysis and resolution of the transference situation have been elevated to an absolute religious truth, compared to which the Immaculate Conception of the Virgin Mary is, within its own religious context, a minor and dispensable technical detail.

I have encountered only two analysts who showed the slightest interest in my own self-analytic experience, and

I greatly respect them for their ability to free themselves from dogma. But even one of those two seemed to imply that my success was due to my exceptional personality, by which, I suspect, he didn't mean anything particularly 'good' from his point of view; in fact, without saying so, what he probably meant was a particular narcissistic[12] constellation, without which he just couldn't imagine it having happened—an unwillingness to 'relate' to an analyst.

No doubt I lost through not participating in an analytic transference situation; no doubt I gained immeasurably more than I lost by not having my brain washed—and I readily accept that my particular brain is of a nature that makes it prefer its home laundry. My point is that there must be plenty of brains which are, in that respect, like mine.

I know people who have emerged from analysis with impressively increased autonomy; I know one person who, after five years of analysis, stresses that it yielded absolutely no result, though his analyst happily thinks it did; and I know people whom analysis has crippled, in that they have replaced any symptoms, real or alleged, by the symptom of psychiatric diagnosis (self-diagnosis included), into which they seem to put all their energy, so that they appear incapable of sustaining a mere conversation without it, as well as its attendant psychoanalytic moralising. At the early stages of the Congress, I had lunch with an analyst who, rather anxiously, wanted to know what I thought of it all. I

---

[12] 'Narcissist: psychoanalytic term for the person who loves himself more than his analyst; considered to be the manifestation of a dire mental disease whose successful treatment depends on the patient learning to love the analyst more and himself less.' Szasz, *The Second Sin*, p.82.

remarked that there seemed little awareness of how, in the wrong hands, analysis could maim, and gave him one or two examples. He riposted that the defects of the profession were like the defects of any other profession. 'What about music critics? Some of them maim too.'

The one parallel I accept here is that critics, likewise, are the agents of their difficulties, which they work out on people. But the differences are that critics are, alas, expected to hurt, and that they are not employed or engaged by their victims, many of whom would in fact gladly pay them to shut up. It may not, indeed, be without significance that this analyst picked music critics as the first analogy that occurred to him. Partly, his choice was no doubt due to his awareness of my critical activities on the one hand and my hostile attitude towards established professional music criticism on the other; but beyond this realistic reason, I smelt a ministrative motive—the analyst as evaluating critic, objecting to moralisations, it is true, but replacing them by his own with all the greater fervour. We might ebulliently drive the comparison one step further and think in terms of founding a Schoenbergian Society for Private Psychological Discussions which psychiatrists and psychoanalysts would be 'forbidden' to attend.

Perhaps such manifest grotesquerie (by no means pointless or reality-less) would, at last, alert analysts to the absurdity of their own secret society — whose credentials are, of course, derived from its medical background, whereas what realistic psychoanalysis ought to do is help in the fight against parental medical secrecy and its concomitant terminological obscurantism. We have a long way to go — a steep path up to a full recognition of the dignity of the individual, up *from* the

131

regressive position where one can't live and let live without playing the parent, recognition of counter-transference or not. Meanwhile, I should like to awaken the analyst's conscience, the more respectable part of his superego, not the unconsciously moralising one. This year, we shall have the next Congress, and here is my challenge to it: I want to be given sixty minutes, please, to talk about 'The Creeping Moral Philosophy of Psycho-analysis: The Need for an Open Psychoanalytic Society'. Members of the psychoanalytic audience would be allowed to intervene as often as they liked; I should — fairly, I hope — incorporate their criticisms in my lecture, as I went along. For it wouldn't be a 'paper': papers are phoney. You either write or you speak, and each mode of communication has its function and character.

I have little hope that the Association will allow me to gate-crash. Why won't it? A public answer, simple, honest, unpolitical, would be welcome. Your hygienic and eugenic policies, confessed or not, are themselves an issue of public policy: that much, at least, I suggest I have here demonstrated.

To the first publication of this challenge, the International Psycho-analytical Association responded as expected: its congresses 'are not open to non-analysts'.

# CHAPTER IV

# Music, 1975

## I. Another Statement of Bias[1]

Both Chapters II and III were about closed societies. Music is not a society, even though musical society exerts its influence on it. Nor is our musical society closed — but it used to be, before the disintegration of tonality, the ageing of key, the loss of the Western world's common musical language. And here we encounter a fundamental paradox: in life, closed societies produce de-individualisation. But closed artistic societies produce, on the contrary, a flowering of individual achievement. How do we explain this seeming contradiction?

Our age's confusion between life and art has led the non-artist to believe that he does not, as such, exist — that he is an artist too. He is being encouraged by psychoanalyst and ex-psychoanalytic anti-analyst alike: a psychoanalyst recently remarked to me that what the patient submitted in analysis was really a work of art, and no less a mind than my brother-in-law-in-arms (brother would be too collective), Thomas Szasz, recently remarked in private, apropos of the case of the paranoic[2] judge Schreber on which Freud had written his famous

---

[1] Cf. Chapter III, pp 84f.

[2] The adjective 'paranoic' has gone out of psychiatric fashion, but I propose to retain it: 'paranoid' as sole adjective ignores the difference between 'paranoic' and 'paranoid', which parallels that between 'schizophrenic' and 'schizoid'.

treatise, that the harmless (but compulsorily committed) man's delusion of being a pregnant woman seemed to show, at that historical stage, a 'compassion with the role of women—*poetry*' (Szasz's spoken italics). *No* to my acquaintance, no, Professor Szasz: there is no unintentional art—no art that does not aim at the clearest possible communication of something new and generally (rather than merely personally) true, addressed to the communication's widest possible audience (not very wide, of course, in the case of, say, a late Beethoven quartet), and expressed in terms that are uniquely suitable to the message: something which could not be expressed, or expressed as well, in any other terms. A piece of music that says something which could better be said in words is, at best, mediocre, and certainly superfluous; a paranoic delusion is not even mediocre poetry, and it is equally superfluous—except, of course, from its 'creator's' point of view: *he* needs it as much as the composer may need his mediocre piece. Compassion for the role of women may well be the stuff of poetry, but there's a long and responsible way from the stuff to the poetry: it's the way from a diary to an autobiography and thence to biography, from self-expression to expression, from discovering oneself to discovering the world in oneself, isolating that part of oneself which is relevant to the world.

Schreber's delusions communicated his problems to those who were prepared to listen and able to understand; our psychoanalyst's patient communicates his problems to an audience of one—not because his communication is a yet more complex work of art than a late Beethoven quartet, but because this single-man audience has been trained to understand that particular type of uncontrolled and, therefore, unintentional communication, because he has established himself *in loco parentis*, as a father confessor, and because he is being paid for the job. The artist communicates his problems to you and me inasmuch as they are yours and mine, and it is we who pay him for the job—at times posthumously, if the widest possible audience does not assemble in his lifetime, the message being too new for comfort, and maybe too true.

Now, the utmost clarity of expression of something new inevitably means two things. In the first place, it means the clearest possible language (including its grammatical logic, whether verbal or musical or indeed pictorial), which in its turn means faithful adherence to common terms of reference, and indeed to wider entities than terms, i.e. structures, or common principles of combining terms—common, that is to say, to the creator and his audience, present and/or foreseeably future. But in the second place, since the discoveries the artist conveys are psychological (and let us, for the purpose of our discussion, include in this category any metaphysics, real or imaginary), his language must needs contain a personal element—if, that is to say, he uncovers new psychic realities, never articulated before, and thus, at the time of expression, exclusively his own: later, when the universality of his truths is experienced and perhaps even intellectually realised, his 'personal language', though still recognisable, will be absorbed by the generally available, instinctively comprehensible reservoir of common terms and structures of reference. It is thus that the personality of a genius, his individuality, can express itself most fully and lucidly and widely if he has a firm system of common terms of reference to draw

135

upon: against its background, he will be able to define the personal side of the language he uses—and thus to communicate the new as if it weren't new, as if it were implicit in the old. Prospectively, he creates surprises; retrospectively, inevitabilities—those cogent thoughts of great art which, although they feel utterly individual, characteristic of the creator's personality, strike us as ineluctable at the same time: thus, and only thus, it had to happen.

I have chosen the metaphor of a generally accessible linguistic 'background' with intent: for me, it is no longer a metaphor, but has become a technical term and, as such, an essential element in my theory of music, which includes a theory of musical understanding. I've pinched the term—and its opposite, 'foreground', of which more anon—from the Austrian theorist Heinrich Schenker (1867-1935), nor is this all I have pinched from him: from the point of view of the harmonic structure of tonal music, he remains the most insightful, most genuinely musical investigator in the entire history of analysis. But within the context of my theory, 'background' means something very different from what it meant to him and still means to his followers, though there is an overlapping area between his denotation and mine. However, I mean by it the sum total of well-defined expectations which the composer creates in the course of a structure, but most of which are never met: they are as thoroughly suppressed as they are implied. Instead—and this is where the composer's personal contribution to the 'language of music' (Deryck Cooke's concept[3]) comes in—we hear

---

[3] His *The Language of Music* is, in turn, one of our age's most important answers to the simple-sounding question, 'How does music work?' His death in 1976 was not sufficiently mourned.

meaningful contradictions, again well defined as such, of what we have been led to expect, and the sum total of these contradictions I call the foreground of the composition.

Now, while the foreground is always heard, the background does not always remain unheard. I've said that most of the expectations are never met: some are. At the end of a tonal movement, for instance, the composer will create the expectation of a perfect cadence by sounding a dominant seventh chord (G-B-D-F in C major —to those who suffer from terminophobia, the one mental disease that exists in spite of Szasz's *The Myth of Mental Illness*). At such moments, and invariably at the end of a piece or movement that does indeed finish, the background moves to the fore and is heard; there is no foreground. They are, invariably, moments of relaxation of tension, and therefore occur, prototypically, at the end of movements or works. But what gives a composition definable meaning, aesthetic 'news value', is the accumulation of tensions between foreground and background. The proof of the pudding is in the digestion: none of the tensions I have thus analysed, either verbally and therefore incompletely, or by means of my wordless method of musical analysis called Functional Analysis, has yet been analysed in alternative terms, nor has any such specific analysis been contradicted. I would therefore submit that my theory of music has proved itself in practice. No wonder, I myself would say, for it was derived from analytical teaching and coaching practice in the first place: it did not develop from general reflections, but only from specific, eminently concrete analytic work.

In the course of the development of composition,

foregrounds move into the background of potential expectations available to all composers, players and listeners within the musical world in question—say, that of Western civilisation: what was a personal linguistic contribution becomes common property. In order to provide a paradigm, let me recall the selfsame dominant seventh. It is sounded (as in bar 63 of the *adagio* from Mozart's 'big' A major Piano Concerto, K.488—to take an example with which, upon inspection, every music-loving reader will find himself familiar), but the expected resolution on to the tonic chord, i.e. the perfect cadence, does not ensue; instead, we hear the so-called chord on the submediant, which is the sixth degree of the scale. This is what is called an 'interrupted cadence', and the feeling of meaningful inhibition, of a purposive accumulation of tension instead of its expected, anticipated relaxation, is quite overpowering—even today, hundreds of years after this element of diatonic[4] language had been invented, and over half a century after tonality was said to be worn out.

Whoever invented the interrupted cadence showed, within a progression of two chords, what meaningful music is about—and showed it at a crucial structural point, to wit, the end, or rather, the expected end: the perfect cadence which, unavoidably, we still expect was his background, the interrupted cadence his individual invention, his—and his players' and his listeners'—foreground. The reason for the extreme meaningfulness, the incisive logic of this foreground's contradiction of the background of a perfect cadence is, simply, that maximal

---

[4] 'Diatonic' refers to the scales of five whole tones and two semitones we know as 'major' and 'minor' scales: move up or down the white keys from C, or down from A.

contrast between foreground and background is combined with maximal unity: of the three notes of the tonic[5] chord which are expected when the dominant seventh chord is heard, the upper two actually ensue, i.e. reappear in the chord of the submediant, whereas the all-important root[6] in the bass is, of course, replaced.

Once the interrupted cadence had become common property (not to speak of receiving a name), it had receded into the background of possible expectations to be meaningfully contradicted by innovatory thoughts, individual inventions which communicated news before they, in their turn (say, Wagner's), became common language.

We have arrived at a position where we can explain my introductory paradox—that in art as opposed to life, closed societies (that is, artistic societies) promote the development of individual achievement. What makes them closed—fending off immigration, i.e. foreign artistic languages, and anxious not to lose any of their own 'citizens', the constituent elements of their own languages—provides them with the collective background which ensures the possibility of meaningful individual foregrounds. I have confined my argument to music because I am a musician—but colleagues in other arts assure me that my theory of music could, *mutatis mutandis*, probably be shown to apply to their arts too.

In the eighteenth and early nineteenth centuries when, with the help of our highly developed diatonic language, our Western musical society was hermetically closed—it would have been unimaginable for anybody but an

---

5 The tonic is the keynote.
6 Root: the generating note in a triad, i.e. the bottom note in its fundamental position — C in the C major chord.

unmusical person to be interested in Indian or Chinese music to anything like the extent he was interested in his own — individualism itself was at its most highly developed. It is a gigantic fallacy, repeated with Pavlov-dog-like reliability down the decades by historians and academy professors alike, to suggest that it was in the romantic era that individualism ran riot: unfortunately, it isn't always the most musical people who are given to speculating about history and its philosophy, and unmusical people go by what composers say rather than by what they do. When all the twaddle is over, it is easier to distinguish between mature Bach and mature Handel, or mature Haydn and mature Mozart, than it sometimes is, at least for stretches on end, to distinguish between, say, Schumann and Mendelssohn. Now, is it conceivable that we had to wait until the present moment for this revelation to be made? That our education has brainwashed us to that extent? What is significant is that the most pronounced individualist of them all, to wit, Beethoven, was the one composer in the history of Western music who made himself universally comprehensible when he wished to, without sacrificing the complexity of his thought, indeed its extreme individuality: hear his Ninth Symphony, not one phrase of which can be confused with anybody else's music. The significance lies in the, potentially, universal accessibility of individual, even individualistic thought, so long as it is true. The loner can do more for humanity than the good-doer, because there is no substitute for the truth, which is humanity's *raison d'être*: without the need for truth, humans would be superfluous, and the animate world could manage perfectly without them — more safely, in fact, and altogether better.

140

Psychologically and philosophically, this differential diagnosis can be made: while even the talented member of a politically closed society — whether Marxist or psycho-analytic — surrenders his conscience to a common aim and turns ends (human lives and an inexhaustible variety of human values) into means in the process, the creative member of a closed musical society accepts common means of expression for the exclusive purpose of retaining his individuality, or his appreciation of individual thought: *his is a collectivism of means, not of ends*, for he knows that without a firmly established common background, the clarity of his own foregrounds is in jeopardy — or, if he is not a creator but a player or 'mere' listener, he knows, instinctively, that he needs that firm background in order to have a chance clearly to understand whatever puzzling foregrounds he may come up against, whatever communication of new discoveries about the human mind his own might be receptive to.

And this is my statement of bias so far as the premises of my eventual submissions on 'Music, 1975' are concerned: I accept music as a demonstrable form of the communication of truth and, therefore, as something to be *understood* in the first place. In order to avoid all possible misunderstandings, let me stress that I am not prepared to commit the conventional, intellectualist double *petitio principii,* according to which 'understanding' means intellectual understanding, and intellectual understanding means verbal or, at any rate, conceptual (mathematical) understanding. The laws of musical thought are definably different from the laws of conceptual thought, and my own wordless method of analytic communication, Functional Analysis, has shown that complete musical understanding takes place without any reference whatever to concepts or terms, and can take place without any conscious reflection of any kind.

My purely musical — played, sounding — analyses are either heard and understood purely instinctively, in which case the nature of, for instance, the afore-mentioned interrupted cadence is simply appreciated through a demonstration of what it suppresses (i.e. the tonic chord), or they are also understood intellectually, but still extra-verbally, in which case the listener also appreciates *why* the cadence has the effect it has: because two notes remain the same as those expected, and the most important third doesn't.

Needless to add, such understanding, instinctive or instinctive *cum* intellectual, not only affords enjoyment, but could never happen without enjoyment: if the interrupted cadence were not emotionally enjoyed, its sense would not concern us — and, conversely, if we didn't immediately perceive, however inarticulately, what was happening in this cadence (a perception made possible by the universal acquisition, in the West, of the diatonic musical language), there would be nothing to enjoy for a musical person.

Enjoyment thus emerges as a function of musical understanding, which is not to say that there isn't plenty of unmusical enjoyment of music that happens without any musical understanding; as we shall come to under-stand, a lot of it had happened by 1975. After all, there's enjoyment of bird song too, quite prevalent among the unmusical — not to speak of the enjoyment of less animate sound effects. But so far as the art of music is concerned, my bias is in favour of understanding, in favour of there being something that wishes to be understood, something which should be understood

142

because it's true. I consider all forces that resist, obstruct or indeed abolish such understanding regressive and degrading — degrading, that is to say, the art of music as I know it, which is the centre of my life. Anybody who regards this musical world-view as naive, old-fashioned, or narrow, need not read on. All others are invited to follow me on my way to 1975, via —

## II. The Crisis of Communication: The Schoenberg Trauma

It was Schoenberg who 'abolished' tonality, or was said to have done so. If he did, we might be led to conclude that he pronounced the death sentence on my backgrounds, on any possible, feelable, ascertainable tensions between foregrounds and backgrounds — and thus on the art of music as communication. Well over half a century after the event, there are in fact plenty of people, including plenty of musical people, who feel just that. Rumour has it that I don't.

In the entire history of music, Schoenberg must be the only composer who, after the number of decades that have elapsed (in what is quite wrongly regarded as a fast-moving age) since the atonal trauma, is considered too advanced, too modern, by one part of the musical world, yet almost despicably old-fashioned by another: 'Schoenberg is dead' wrote Boulez more than twenty years ago, trying his (not altogether adequate) best, in the intervening years, to keep the corpse alive and at least metrically (if not rhythmically) kicking: he is our age's most distinguished necrophile, and there are plenty to choose from.

A third part of the musical world has simply come to

regard Schoenberg as a great composer. That alone doesn't make him great. Plenty of small composers were considered great in their own times; one or two dwarfs were even considered great after their own time. (Venturing an aside, I would submit that if we now think we know they were small, it behoves us to try to understand why others thought them big—why others heard something that wasn't there: if you do that outside music, in 'real' life, you are likely to land in a mental hospital, voluntarily, perhaps, in this country, involuntarily in the United States or Soviet Russia.)

What is a fact, in any case, is that by 1975, nobody remained who actually considered Schoenberg small. The ambivalence in Boulez's breast had indeed been indicative of the Schoenberg complex under which our entire musical world had been suffering for many years, of the ill-confessed conflicts between and *within* individual musicians and music lovers: yes, those ideas of 'too advanced' and 'old-fashioned' still cut right across individual minds, cut them into two. The fragmentation of our culture wouldn't be what it is if it only happened between people and groups, not within them; in fact, there would be little fragmentation to speak of. All cultural conflict worth discussing is endo-psychic conflict in the first place, and projected in the second.

And the fact that this conflict still exists and shows no sign of abating does seem to present conclusive evidence of Schoenberg's greatness. For one thing, nothing could be more unrealistic than to arrive at the assessment of greatness in terms of comparisons with preceding greatnesses: in every conceivable respect, Beethoven's greatness is the opposite of Mozart's, who was a perfectionist; Beethoven was an imperfectionist who put truthfulness, or even truth-half-fulness, above mastery. It is, in fact, of the essence of greatness that it produces an unprecedented situation within its musical society, present and future—and it is only in this respect that we can be certain of precedent: Beethoven demanded and indeed established his future, posthumous musical society where Bach, the 'conservative', would have renounced it if, sociologically, he had been able to think of it, and where Mozart, who *was* able to think of what the future would think of him, sunned himself in the possible glory of being remembered as an outstanding *Kapellmeister*.

For another, more positive thing, if you are too advanced more than half a century after you have advanced, you are bound to have said something new, and if, at the same time, you are felt to be old-fashioned, you are bound to have used means of expression which aim at the clearest possible comprehensibility—which welcome traditional language inasmuch as it is still usable, welcome it as a common basis, as stable terms of reference for communicator and addressee, as a reservoir of backgrounds against which individual foregrounds can be thrown into relief with crystal-clear precision. The new is great when it is clear, so long as the news is important enough. The increasing realisation of the nature and importance of Schoenberg's news is shown by the steady rise in the number of performances in the seventh and eighth decades of our century, and by the steadily increasing audiences to concerts containing his music. As a radio man, I have quite a little experience of this statistical situation.

However, there is clarity and clarity. Clear complexity seems less clear than clear simplicity, and the mature Schoenberg is the most complex and the most contrast-

145

ing composer (the two go together) since the late Beethoven—nor should we forget that without any overt crisis of understanding, Beethoven's E flat Quartet, Op. 127, was the only one among the late five (or $5\frac{1}{6}$, if you count both the Grand Fugue and the finale to Op. 130 with which he replaced it and which forms his last complete composition) that met with understanding in his lifetime—or indeed his death-time until the later years of the nineteenth century.

Yet clarity within a general language is clearer than clarity outside it, and the late Beethoven was still thinking within—and, of course, audibly against—this general language. Schoenberg, on the other hand, in those crucial years well over half a century ago, purposefully moved outside it, drawing and pulling others with him in an attack of justifiable paranoia, of realistic megalomania[7]: he thought he was history, and continued thinking so until he came to be. During his military service in the First World War, an NCO asked him whether he actually was 'that composer Schoenberg'. 'Well, nobody wanted to be him, but somebody had to be, so I volunteered for the job.'

And so he pulled and pulled, until hardly any general, collective language was left: well nigh single-handed, he opened up our musical society, establishing, by way of compensation or over-compensation, a little closed, secret society of his own—of which the social or anti-social expression was the 'Society for Private Musical Performances' I described in Chapter III, p. 95.

---

[7] Thomas Szasz has a novel theory of paranoia which, at the time of writing, he has not yet published, but which fits Schoenberg's case perfectly. I have to summarise his exposition as he gave it to me in private conversation: paranoid delusions fill in the gap between an individual's ambitions and the recognition he receives.

When I say that hardly any general language was left, I do mean every word of it: it is an irresponsible over-simplification to maintain, as many of the leading misleading minds of our culture have done, that we are now without a general language. Shostakovich and Britten, geniuses both of them, and recognisable as such in their worst attempts (where worse composers have often done better), retained enough of what was a general language to make themselves generally accessible to those still in instinctive touch with it—with the backgrounds which these composers firmly imply. But not everybody is in spontaneous touch with them, and Boulez understands the two as little as Shostakovich or Britten understood him, i.e. not at all: what was left of a general language in 1975, the year of Shostakovich's death, was— paradoxically—no longer generally accessible. Even Schoenberg himself, over twenty years before, found Shostakovich's and Sibelius's language less accessible than the language of composers on whose music he allowed himself a technical verdict; he contented himself with the nose of a 'mere' music lover:

In favour of Sibelius and Shostakovich, I said something which did not require the knowledge of an expert. Every amateur, every music lover could have said: 'I feel they have the breath of symphonists.'[8]

In fact, perhaps the most accurate test of how this general language became less and less accessible is Schoenberg's loss of understanding—no misprint here— of his own language, after those traumatic years in which he abandoned tonality. Historical chance provided con- crete evidence. He had written most of *Gurrelieder* by

[8] 'Criteria for the Evaluation of Music', in *Style and Idea: Selected Writings of Arnold Schoenberg*, Ed. Leonard Stein, Faber & Faber, London, 1975, p. 136.

1903. In the middle of the song of the Peasant (No. 2 of Part III), however, he had to interrupt the orchestration in order to concentrate on making a living—chiefly by orchestrating dozens of operettas instead. He resumed work on *Gurrelieder* as late as 1910. By that time, the atonal trauma had happened: he was past the F sharp minor Quartet (1907-8—not so F sharp minor in the finale!), the Stefan George Songs (1908-9) in which he took the official plunge into atonality (publicly announced, though not in these terms, of course, in his programme note for the first performance), the Three Piano Pieces, Op. 11 (1908), the Five Orchestral Pieces (1909) which have meanwhile achieved a measure of popularity, the monodrama *Erwartung* (1909), part of the opera *Die glückliche Hand* (1910-13: *The Knack* in my unofficial, eminently relevant translation of the title), and the unfinished Three Pieces for Chamber Orchestra (1910)—two and a bit, to be exact.

The result of this cataclysmic interruption of *Gurrelieder* was, especially as from the song of Klaus, the Fool (No. 5 of Part III), a pretty violent stylistic contrast—which was not, of course, confined to the orchestration: the accepted view that virtually all the *music,* as distinct from the scoring, had been finished by 1903 is not altogether tenable. In point of fact, I know from private sources about Schoenberg bitterly complaining that he 'couldn't find the style any more'; that in 1910, a few bars cost him more trouble than whole numbers had cost him in 1903. And indeed, when you compare such pieces as the song of the Wood-dove (No. 10) with some of the music towards the end of this secular oratorio (as Erwin Stein once described the work), you become aware of a downright change of language—or if you don't, you merely prove thereby that you don't understand either language anyway, that both of them have become as strange—and hence, as alike—to you, the member of our new open musical society, as Bach and any other pre-classical stylite seemed to Bach's own sons, who considered their father a boring old fogey. But the difference is that in that case, more likely than not, you probably don't really understand Schoenberg's later, atonal styles either, not to speak of 1975's medley of languages, whereas Bach's sons were right inside their newly emerging, closed linguistic society — which, in fact, they helped to create.

Not that *Gurrelieder* falls apart because of its change of language: Schoenberg's personality, fanatically pursuing integration, was too strong not to be able to make a creative virtue of self-created historical necessity: what, in the ears of a lesser mind, would have become unmanageably heterogeneous, turned into extreme, functional contrast (which is really what significant music is all about), once it had filtered through his stern creative conscience; and his creative conscience, as opposed to that of one or two other geniuses (such as, pre-eminently, Brahms'), was indeed *creative* conscientiousness.

What had happened in terms of my theory of music was that through the atonal trauma—which, in due course, was to become Western musical society's Schoenberg trauma—he had lost touch with his instinctive backgrounds, which he now tried to recapture. The attempt being only partly successful, he turned the friction thus produced, the very search for backgrounds, into a means of contrasting expression, selecting new, contrasting backgrounds which evinced unity with the old ones, and throwing his foregrounds into relief against the backgrounds newly gained. They were no longer instinctive, or not as instinctive as the old ones, but they were still chosen, with an intense feeling of creative responsibility, as part of the general musical language—what was left of it, alive, in him at that stage in his development, when he must have repressed quite a bit of it as a result of the creative trauma: it must have had a similar effect as what used to be called 'war neurosis', 'traumatic neurosis'—shell shock. The shell was atonal sense which was nonsense to everybody else, but which wouldn't have been sense if he hadn't known that it was capable of making sense to others, that it, in its turn, had been achieved through the use of collectively—but no longer universally—available backgrounds.

*Mutatis mutandis*, it had all happened before, of course, this artistic combination of languages—or at least of dialects, to put it very mildly—if on a far less critical scale: the finale of Mozart's great G major String Quartet, the first of the six he dedicated to Haydn, as well as the finale of his 'Jupiter' Symphony, shows a fusion of styles so far apart—pure homophony [9] and pure polyphony [10]— that they can, with concrete musical justice, be considered at least as different as Swiss German and High German, perhaps even as different as Dutch and Deutsch. But then, Mozart understood the polyphonic Bach better than did Bach's own sons—better even, maybe, than the newly atonal Schoenberg understood his own, just-past tonal language, which he had dynamically repressed. Later on, when the self-induced shock had been assimilated, he came to understand his earlier tonalism better—and, in

[9] Tune and accompaniment.

[10] Tune(s) against tune(s): it can be two despite the '*poly-*': 'bi-phony', as it were.

fact, returned to it in more than one twelve-tone guise: hear the dodecaphonic[11] *Ode to Napoleon* (1942) which, you will agree, works up to, and finishes, in E flat, despite its carefully worked twelve-tone row[12]—not to speak of the Second Chamber Symphony, begun in 1906 and completed in 1939, which is a perfect summary of Schoenberg's development as I have tried to outline it. Firmly anchored in E flat minor, that is to say, it had to be interrupted by the trauma; but when Schoenberg came to complete it, after he had overcome his traumatic neurosis, he was able to avail himself of his atonal, dodecaphonic procedures which he had meanwhile evolved, and yet adhere to the E flat minor framework. The new backgrounds had become natural to him, while the old ones—those of the tonal framework—had become natural *again*, with the result, it seems to me, that he found it easier to return to the Second Chamber Symphony after thirty-three years than to *Gurrelieder* after seven.

When the concussion occurred—one from which our musical society as a whole (some whole!) has not yet recovered—when Schoenberg's needs, his creative compulsions, were about to throw him, as he put it, 'into a sea of boiling water', he must have been a very worried man indeed—more worried than ever about remaining an artist, a clear communicator, rather than turning into a psychoanalytic patient, a free associator, or a psychotic 'poet' *à la* judge Schreber. For his articulate conscience, clarity was, in fact, the first commandment. Yet, owing to

[11] Twelve-tone.

[12] The basis of twelve-tone composition — a series of twelve different notes (the notes of the chromatic scale in a certain order), which, with its transpositions and mirror forms, rotates throughout a piece to give it unity.

the complexity of his thoughts, owing to his chronic urge towards compression (an eminently artistic urge if ever there was one), owing also to the swiftness of his advances which, out-Beethovening Beethoven, took things (backgrounds!) for granted nobody else did or could, he was in trouble long before the atonal crisis—as early as the string sextet *Transfigured Night* (1899), in fact. Like, later, the First Chamber Symphony, the Second String Quartet, and the *Ode to Napoleon*, he came to orchestrate the work, in an attempt not only to make concert performances more easily possible, but also to make the music, its new sound, more readily palatable.

*Transfigured Night* had come to be called Straussian by 1975, which was absurd: Strauss's blending, filling-in approach to texture was the very opposite of Schoenberg's; in fact, Strauss thought, predominantly, in terms of harmony, where Schoenberg thought in terms of counterpoint.[13] As a result, other things being as equal as history could make them, Strauss's music invariably proved more easily accessible than Schoenberg's. It still is, and I am not forgetting the relative popularity of *Transfigured Night*: as will be seen in a moment, the wide-ranging enjoyment of the work is not necessarily a function of its understanding—and 1975 was a milestone in the history of joyful incomprehension anyway.

When *Transfigured Night* burst upon the scene, professional and public reactions were, in fact, hostile. A Viennese concert society refused its first performance because of one chord—'that is, one *single* uncatalogued dissonance', as Schoenberg puts it in his afore-quoted essay, the chord being B flat—A flat—E flat—G flat—C—E flat. Nor is it good enough for us just to sneer.

---

[13] Tune(s) against tune(s) again.

This was the last-ditch defence of the West's closed musical society, and there was more musicality in that act of incomprehension of Schoenberg's harmonic foreground than there is in the kind of contemporary enjoyment of *Transfigured Night* which remains unaware of the harmonic adventure, the extreme tensions between foreground and background, in this first symphonic poem for chamber ensemble. If, thus, the enjoying ear misses frictions of essential structural significance, it fails to understand the very passages which the work's first audiences found incomprehensible, but it fails for the opposite reason: where they were too much taken aback to understand, the conventional contemporary ear, alienated from real musical understanding altogether, is not taken aback far enough!

I don't like talking in generalities, and the mention of a single chord won't suffice. If the reader wishes to test his own ear to see whether he is the victim of bogus appreciation, of our time's degeneration of musical understanding, he can easily do so. Gramophone records abound, and here is a selection of passages in *Transfigured Night* which, if we are at all in touch with the tensions between the work's foreground and background, we cannot but be pulled up by; pain as well as pleasure is a function of understanding:

Bars 64 ff.; bars 79-80; bars 124 ff.; bars 144 ff.; bars 153 ff., with their complex counterpoint of a theme played against its inversion [14] ; and bars 310 ff. And this, let us remember, is the music to the accompaniment of which children nowadays do their homework and grown-ups their income tax.

---

[14] Inversion of a tune: what went up comes down (same distance) and vice versa.

We have, in fact, grown to treat this early masterpiece either as a mere stepping-stone to future things, or as negligibly light music expressing the heavy spirit of its times, which, to us, has become lightweight, like everything historical, and/or geographically remote. We might, just as well, not play the work at all: if art cannot be experienced, simply, as itself, it is not being understood. This does not mean art for art's sake, to which dictum Schoenberg subscribed without knowing what he was doing[15]; it means art for life's sake, for the sake of understanding life—including, if you are a Schoenberg, metaphysical life.

The fact that it is Schoenberg's own 'fault' that musical history has raced ahead at a pace which makes comprehension of his early music difficult even for some of those who are still capable of well-definable musical understanding, does not altogether acquit them. Accepting that Schoenberg was a great composer in an age which tries its best to inhibit greatness by denying responsible individualism and promoting irresponsible individualism (psychosis), we have the artistic obligation to understand the early Schoenberg better than, perhaps, the maturer Schoenberg did himself; after all, we do not yet understand the maturer Schoenberg as well as he did! As one who has coached *Transfigured Night*, and has coached it *con amore*, I find the superficiality with which players, conductors (of the string-orchestral version),

---

[15] 'One thinks only for the sake of one's idea.

'And thus art can only be created for its own sake. An idea is born; it must be moulded, formulated, developed, elaborated, carried through and pursued to its very end.

'Because there is only "l'art pour l'art", art for the sake of art alone.' The concluding words of his famous essay, 'New Music Outmoded Music, Style and Idea', *op cit.*, p. 124.

listeners, and indeed musicologists treat this work quite astounding. Hard circumstantial evidence of such frivolity is ready to hand: in this scholarly era, when knowledge *of* something (experience) is readily replaced by knowledge *about* it, we do go on for ages about authenticity in Bach or, if we are modernistic rather than historical snobs, about allegedly 'wrong' notes in Schoenberg's twelve-tone works (i.e. notes which deviate from the tone-row, its transpositions and mirror forms), yet at the time of writing, in 1976, nobody has ever remarked quite important little problems in the notation of Schoenberg's most-played work. In bars 338 ff., for instance, in both the chamber and the orchestral version, *fff* in the first cello part leads, via no fewer than three crescendos, to an *ff* upbeat; and after the ensuing bar has accommodated yet another crescendo, we mysteriously land on a mere *forte* level! Decade in, decade out, the selfsame score has been printed without anybody noticing anything amiss, or caring if he did. What is musical life about? Is scholarly lifemanship to replace it, while living study—that which studies what it is inspired by—is abandoned?

It will be when (and if) *Transfigured Night* is fully and intelligently experienced, without any historical preoccupations while the musical experience takes place, that its significance as a stepping-stone will assume actual meaning. In this age of tired alienation, when people, and especially senile teenagers, actually enjoy incomprehension because of the opportunities it offers for not having to identify with the object of their attention, not having to bother, let alone commit themselves, they do enjoy stepping-stones as stepping-stones; in fact, they enjoy everything as a stepping-stone—historically, detachedly, so long as one step leads to the next, whence it need not be grasped as a self-sufficient event. Should there be events which can't be turned into steps, which don't produce 'interesting' associations with something else, a proud, self-satisfied, defensive declaration of incomprehension ensues. 'I don't understand x' used to be a conscious admission of intellectual and emotional failure; it is rapidly turning into a show of superiority, albeit psychotic: 'I don't understand x; hence I am better than x, because I'm showing that x isn't worth understanding, that it's confused, pretentious, meaningless, stupid.' But psychoses, alas, live on a grain of truth, and it will presently be seen that modish protestations of incomprehension have not only themselves to blame—nor even Schoenberg.

Meantime, *Transfigured Night* struck 1975's rare understander as a symphonic master-structure which is, simultaneously, extended and compressed. As a large-scale, complete symphonic build-up for a string chamber ensemble of over thirty minutes' duration, it evinces an unprecedented—though not unsurpassed—broadening of symphonic proportions without the help of sharply contrasting colours offered by different kinds of instruments, i.e. the type of texture of which an orchestral work avails itself—or, for that matter, Schoenberg's own, equally continuous First Chamber Symphony of 1906. Yet again, *Transfigured Night* contains much more, emotionally and hence structurally, than could a mere first-movement form—and it contains it well. It does not quite yet roll four symphonic movements into one: that task was left for the next Opus (5), another symphonic poem, this time an orchestral one, i.e. *Pelleas and Melisande* (1902-3), as well as for the afore-mentioned

Chamber Symphony—and, in between, for a work as economically monochrome as the sextet, i.e. the First String Quartet, in D minor, of 1905, which prompted Alban Berg to his classical essay on 'Why Schoenberg's Music is Difficult to Understand', and whose symphonic proportions are still broader than the sextet's.

Quite aside from the Schoenberg trauma, yet helping its effect along over the decades, there is the composer's lifelong preoccupation with compression, with making a movement contain much more than a movement: here indeed is one of the reasons why, despite its lucidity, his music is difficult, and although *Transfigured Night* certainly does not go all out in this dimension, its compressions do produce a characteristically Schoen- bergian type of complexity. The indubitable climax of his urge towards compression is reached in the tightly- packed, almost 45-minute-long, single-movement struc- ture of the First String Quartet; what the compressions here result in can most simply be described as a lot of things (too many?) happening at the same time—even more than one could naturally expect from a composer in love with counterpoint. The fact, entirely unnoticed by decades of investigators, that he never again attempted compression to such a fanatical extent seems to indicate that he himself must have felt that he had rather overdone it[16]; the Second, Third and Fourth String

---

16 So, it seems, did Mahler — as we learn from a lecture of Schoenberg's first published in 1975: '. . . when I showed the First String Quartet to Gustav Mahler, the great Austrian composer and conductor, at that time head of the Imperial Opera in Vienna, he said: "I have conducted the most difficult scores of Wagner; I have written complicated music myself in scores of up to thirty staves or more; yet here is a score of not more than four staves, and I am unable to read them."' 'How One Becomes Lonely', *op cit.*, p. 42.

157

Quartets, not to speak of the String Trio, unfold decidedly more transparent textures and are, in that respect, easier to understand, despite the twelve-tonality of the latter three.

Again, the circumstance that Schoenberg's first two single-movement structures, *Transfigured Night* and *Pelleas*, have a story attached to them, even though their music leads an utterly independent existence, might well be taken to show that he was beginning to be worried about the universal accessibility of his backgrounds, and thus about the comprehensibility of his foregrounds— and indeed about making his conscious complexity tell as clearly as possible: who knows, the story might help the baffled listener! When he came to write the atonal Five Orchestral Pieces, Op. 16 (1909), he unwillingly gave in to the publisher's request for titles—but, quite uncharacteristically, he did give in, only to withdraw the titles later. Throughout his creative life, in fact, his attitude towards the musical use of words, texts, stories, was ambivalent; at an easier stage in the development of composition, it might not have been—nor indeed would he have been all that worried about comprehensibility: the compression, to be sure, would have been there, but so would a safe general language. When we come to consider 1975's verbal crutches and 'mixed media' (nowadays every excuse for not writing autonomous music gets a pseudo-positive fancy term attached to it),[17] we shall be able to diagnose what has become the negative counterpart of Schoenberg's ambivalence—a reflection of it in dirty, ruffled waters as it were.

Meanwhile, two years after the single-movement structure of the First String Quartet, and but a year after that of the First Chamber Symphony, came the plunge into the sea

[17] See Section IV, below.

of boiling water, and with it the true crisis of comprehensibility, musical history's gravest trauma— for musical history is a meaningless discipline if it does not encompass the history of musical understanding. To be precise, there was more than one plunge, but the most crucial work, the F sharp minor Quartet, his official Second, shows not only the crisis itself, but Schoenberg's reaction to, and handling of it to the naked ear—to any musical ear, that is, however untutored. Schoenberg here produced the twentieth century's monument to creative responsibility, to art as communication, and if it had been understood and accepted for what it was, 1975's musical society, however critical its condition, would have been honoured by not having a mammoth chapter written about it.

Approaching what he must have known to be the highest risk of incomprehensibility in the evolution of musical composition, aware of the absolute need for the clearest possible comprehensibility in any creative circumstances, however inauspicious, Schoenberg abandoned, for the time being (which promised to be a jolly long time), the frantic single-movement compressions to which he had subjected all his symphonic structures to date, all four of them (*Transfigured Night, Pelleas and Melisande*, the D minor String Quartet, and the First Chamber Symphony) —the sole 'normal', four-movement form having been the early String Quartet in D major (1897) which he never published, and which was, fortunately, excavated after his death, and printed in 1966.

Now, in the F sharp minor Quartet, before that dive ( or that ascent?) into atonality in the last movement, and again after the finale's atonal liberation ('I feel the air from another planet' is the first line of the Stefan George poem of which this movement is a setting), Schoenberg returns to

159

the widest and deepest available formal backgrounds, to downright classical proportions, divisions, and specific methods of contrast and unification—in a ruthlessly self-sacrificing attempt to make everything as easy as possible for the player and listener alike, everything except for that boiling sea itself, in which all of them must needs find themselves together. The attempt proved dramatically unsuccessful at the stormy first performance of the work—but by 1975, it had turned out to be an enduring and triumphant success, whose nature it is now our artistic duty to examine: to be wise after the event is immeasurably preferable to not being wise at all.

The Quartet's four separate movements are conventional in their basic design, whose background harks back beyond the late Beethoven quartets; Schoenberg does, in fact, offer 'proper' classical quartet movements or symphonic movements. But they are not, by any means, the end of the story; they are merely its beginning in general terms. Comprehensibility, in other words, is never furthered by general terms alone, by large-scale backgrounds; it is the specific foreground thoughts whose understanding has to be promoted in the background, step by step: there is no real total understanding without local understanding.

And here the first movement, customarily the most complex, renders the most conscientious help, even though it does not renounce its own measure of Schoenbergian compressions. But where, in the preceding four works, compression paradoxically yielded length, it now results in brevity. The texture is more transparent than ever before; fewer things happen at one and the same time (fewer, though still quite a few!), thus allowing each of them to emerge with crystalline clarity—and, above all, each of them, each thought, every stage of this classical sonata structure remembers, in its background, what had happened to the string quartet and the symphony ever since the middle-period Beethoven: Schoenberg ensures that the understanding listener feels thoroughly at home before he is taken out of the home key and all its relatives and plunged into the sea. I submit that in the intervening years, close on seventy in fact, not a single composer, big or small (and I include Webern here, who was both big and small, or big and narrow anyway), has taken comparable care of the listener's understanding when trying something radically new, has been equally meticulous about establishing the precisest possible tensions between his foregrounds and his backgrounds—if indeed he was at all worried about this necessary two-dimensionality of all comprehensible music: by 1975, comprehensibility had become, for many, an outmoded concept.

Let me go into one particular, all-important detail of this sonata structure; my little analysis can easily be understood without any technical knowledge to speak of. Musical history's first string quartet which dropped the repeat of the exposition in the first movement (marked by that black double-bar towards the middle of the movement familiar to anybody who has ever been in visual touch with classical music) was Beethoven's in F major, Op. 59, No. 1—the first Rasumovsky Quartet—and middle-period Beethoven *par excellence*. Now Beethoven was as complex and as clear-minded as Schoenberg (remarkable how he contrived to resemble his son!) — as conscious, in fact, of the demands of comprehensibility. The omission of the repeat would be a shock, he realised; he had to do something equally drastic to make it absorbable. And what he did was, we now realise, the only logical thing to do (we

161

analysts are, in fact, invariably as clever as Beethoven, so long as he thinks of it first): he repeated a bit of the first subject in the tonic at the beginning of the development section, or rather before its beginning, *as if he was going* to repeat the entire exposition. In other words, for the purpose of clarity, he built a mental bridge, for player and listener alike, between the expected repeat of the exposition and the actually ensuing development. Or, in my terminology, he composed his repeatless foreground against the background of a repeat, thus making the omission of the repeat the more meaningful.

The innovations which Beethoven introduced into sonata form always hypnotised later composing minds by their logic. The repeat of the exposition in a sonata build-up had been about the most natural, most functional repeat in the history of instrumental forms — because it was a remindful repeat of that which the rest of the movement was going to be about. Its loss, therefore, continued to be felt as a loss: the repeatless exposition did not easily move into the background, into the reservoir of merely implied expectations.

Beethoven's means of overcoming the loss, therefore, fascinated successive generations of geniuses, who went so far as to adopt it in various large-scale first-movement structures — Mendelssohn in his first, masterly E flat Quartet; Schumann in his A major Quartet (dedicated to Mendelssohn), in which, however, he repeated the exposition nevertheless, on top of it all — a tautology or double-insurance indicative, it seems, of his fear of mental disintegration, whence my recommendation is to ignore the repeat; Brahms in his Fourth Symphony, and Mahler on more than one occasion . . .

Brahms went so far as to give us a complete history of

our story; in the first movements of his first three symphonies he repeated the exposition, and it was only in the first movement of his Fourth that he omitted the repeat and decided upon the mental bridge between expected repeat and actual development, i.e. the first subject in the tonic introducing the development section.

However, that Schoenberg should, in his very last tonal sonata movement, go all the way back to Beethoven to explain the omission of the exposition's repeat, as he does with his reversion — varied in sound, to be sure — to the first subject's first theme in F sharp minor, proves him more structure-conscious, more comprehensibility-conscious (for what is structure there for, if not to serve comprehension?), than anybody since Beethoven. But then, the two were perhaps the most uncompromising discoverers of new creative areas in the history of musical invention, and in proportion as you are a revolutionary, you have to force yourself into background-retaining conservatism in order to get your revolutions across. Those many who, in 1975, considered Schoenberg old-fashioned didn't know how right they were, because they didn't really know what exactly they were talking about anyway: Schoenberg's structures dimly reminded them of something else — and it is, of course, by reference to the known, to the background, that a structure makes itself tell. What Schoenberg does at that central stage in the first movement of the F sharp minor Quartet is that he accepts Beethoven's background on the one hand, but pushes Beethoven's foreground into the middle-ground on the other: the expectation of Beethoven's (Mendelssohn's, Schumann's, Brahms's, Mahler's . . .) innovation is taken into account too, and a tension established between that expectation and what

163

actually happens—a different *sound*, in terms of quality, though not a different basic *sense*. But the novel sound makes a confusion between the introduction to the development and a repeat impossible: we know that we are now working up to the development, being reminded, at the same time, of the repeat in the background, of the possibility that it could have happened.

And at, or just after, the most revolutionary stage in the F sharp minor Quartet—our musical society's most revolutionary moment, in fact, the moment when it finally and irretrievably opened up—Schoenberg decides, quite consistently again, to be older-fashioned still. As a matter of fact, those frantic antics in which the more playful types among 1975's composers indulged in order to produce the most contrasting, the most unheard-of juxtapositions of sound-events — or just sounds, without events — didn't get anywhere near what, demonstrably, remains Western music's most intense contrast within a narrow space; at the same time, we can't call it a violent contrast, because the violence comes first, the contrast afterwards: a soothing contrast would be the correct description — an anti-shock.

What I mean is that after the finale of this Second Quartet has plunged us into the boiling sea, after Schoenberg has, shockedly as well as shockingly, achieved his total 'emancipation of the dissonance' whose comprehensibility is, in atonal circumstances, 'considered equivalent to the consonance's comprehensibility'[18], after he has, in short, left key far behind, he not only returns us home at the end of the movement, right into the home key of F sharp minor, but actually goes back at least as far as Bach (strictly speaking as far

---

[18]  Composition with Twelve Tones', *op. cit.,* p. 217.

164

as 1500) and *treats the minor third as a dissonance,* finishing, as it were, on a Picardy Third[19], in F sharp *major,* as if the minor third were too harsh a dissonance to bear! There is no comparable instance of extreme revolution and extreme conservation being closely integrated with each other—of extreme comprehensibility warding off the threat of unprecedented incomprehensibility. For the purpose, paradoxically, an extreme background—the major third at the end of a minor-mode structure—is used as a foreground, because it is *no longer* an element in the reservoir of expectations. The expectation, once the music moves back to F sharp minor, is, in fact, an F sharp minor cadence—and, for once, the foreground's surprising contradiction of the background does not produce tension but, on the contrary, an unexpected degree of dis-tension. I have pointed out that at the end of a diatonic piece, the background moves to the fore in the perfect cadence in order to achieve complete relaxation; here, at the end of an undiatonic movement (but still a basically diatonic work), it is a wellnigh forgotten background (F sharp major) that moves in front of the music's properly implied background (F sharp minor), to produce a surprise that is the opposite of a shock. This is one of the two slight (and welcome) complications of my theory of music known to me, the other being Schoenberg's too, as we shall shortly see. Meanwhile, it has to be remembered that the finale of the F sharp minor Quartet is, after all, the only piece of music which, having produced an extreme shock, proceeds to apply shock therapy—for the

---

[19] *Tierce de Picardie*: the origin of the term is unknown. It denotes the (pre-classical) introduction of the major third into the final chord of a piece or movement in the minor mode.

purpose of showing that the shock wasn't meant as a shock, but was merely a function of drastically new expression, which the therapy (and self-therapy) makes better comprehensible, acceptable emotionally as well as intellectually.

Schoenberg's ensuing period of so-called 'free atonality' was entirely without textless extended forms: he had abandoned one means of large-scale unification (key), of making long works comprehensible, and not yet found another—*the* other, so far as he was concerned. And even when he had discovered his method of composing with twelve notes, he did not, for a long time, take up again his beloved symphonic compressions into single movements. He was, in fact, too aware that the atonal crisis was still with him and his audiences (as it still is with us, otherwise you'd be hearing people whistle atonal tunes) —that he had to make things as easy as possible in all those dimensions which had not, inevitably, become as difficult as was conceivable: the top difficulties were, of course, harmony and dodecaphony. The symphonic works of the so-called classical twelve-tone period are immeasurably more conservative in formal layout, therefore, than are the afore-mentioned, early Big Four— *Transfigured Night, Pelleas,* the D minor Quartet, and the First Chamber Symphony. Rather, the classical twelve-tone works took as their cue the F sharp minor Quartet's passion for tradition, though tonality itself was now out of the question. But the classical, sectional methods of making a structure readily comprehensible weren't, nor indeed was the classical four-movement form: Schoenberg's classical twelve-tone period was classical in more than one sense—a trait which also shows in his twelve-tone operas, *Von heute auf morgen*

(1928-29) and, of course, *Moses and Aron* (second act completed in 1932), both of which are far more traditionally organised, had to be for the sake of large-scale comprehensibility, than the much shorter, quasi-aphoristic operas of the 'free atonal' period, *Erwartung* (1909) and *The Knack* (1910-13). And the twelve-tone classic itself, the Orchestral Variations, Op. 31 (1927-28), which is Schoenberg's only orchestral twelve-tone work without either soloist or the human voice, adopts the most conservative formal background available for an extended structure—variation form, albeit vastly expanded.

But if we take both local and total backgrounds into account, internal formal entities as well as overall forms, it is in his chamber music of the classical twelve-tone period that he is most past-conscious: the Wind Quintet of 1923-24 is an outstanding example. It was, after all, in the chamber-musical area that he (and not only he!) allowed himself to be at his most complex—so easily identifiable backgrounds were a *conditio sine qua non*. And when he returned to his (and not only his!) beloved medium of the string quartet in 1927, he once again went back even further than Beethoven, twelve-tone technique and all. Twelve-tonally, this Third String Quartet is perhaps Schoenberg's most complex work altogether, using as it does two tone-rows, or rather one-and-a-half, half of the second availing itself of half of the first. But formally, the first movement is almost primitive in the historical sense, remembering as it does the reversed order of subjects in the recapitulation which was a symmetrical device practised by members of the so-called Mannheim school of composers. (The analysis in the widely-used first impression of the Philharmonia score is

167

wrong, i.e. misprinted.) It is more than doubtful that Schoenberg, the anti-musicologist *par excellence*, knew any of the boring Mannheim works in question; he probably had the device from Mozart, who made inspired use of it in one or two works of his early maturity, such as the 'Mannheim' Violin Sonata in D major, K.306. What, from the point of view of structure, commands especial attention is that once again, as at the end of the F sharp minor Quartet, Schoenberg uses a remote background—one no longer available as a dependable instinctive expectation—as foreground, and for the same purpose, to wit, surprising relaxation in demanding circumstances: the Mannheimers' symmetrical sonata form is, *ceteris paribus*, easier on the ear than the later, established form, in which the first subject does not relaxingly recur at the end.

As for the complex twelve-tone technique of the work, even here Schoenberg tries to counter-balance the refined complications of his unifying method by conservative clarification, going against his own twelve-tone rules in the process! That is to say, far from not re-using any note before the complete row is over, he starts the first movement off with an appeasing, old-fashioned ostinato[20] in the inner parts, which repeats the first five notes of the principal row over and over again, three of them appearing as doublets (which in itself is not against Schoenberg's self-imposed rules, providing as these do for immediate repetition). The object of this gradual evolution of the structure is obvious: repetition serves memorability, and memorability serves understanding.

And again, when it came, nine years later in America,

---

[20] An 'obstinately' repeated figure — recurring, that is, again and again in immediate succession.

to the Fourth and last String Quartet, the conventional four-movement scheme was still maintained. What is more, just as Schoenberg had clarifyingly mitigated, mollified his first 'free atonality', almost thirty years before, by an eventual return to the home key and a Picardy third to top it all, he now mitigates the essentially contrapuntal nature of twelve-tone technique by an unprecedentedly homophonic approach to it: the very opening, for instance, is accompanied by chords—a tune with accompaniment, almost in the old style.

It must have been shortly after the Fourth String Quartet that the shock of atonality was at last wholly assimilated, and that twelve-tone technique had become as instinctive to Schoenberg as tonal language had been. And it was at this stage that he allowed himself to return to tonal techniques, both in conjunction with twelve-tone technique, combining two methods of unification, mutually exclusive on the surface, and outside it. Logically, it was at this stage, too, that he allowed himself to resume his passion for the compressions of single-movement symphonism: the road to increased structural complexity now seemed clear. If, that is, *he* was ready for 'mixing it', both stylistically and structurally, without risking any loss of clarity, so must his listeners be—who could, ideally, be expected to have moved along with him, since he had thought of them all along, or of his ideal listeners anyway, the successors of those whom Beethoven thought of when he wrote his late quartets. In other words, if his actual listeners were not able to follow his creative development, future listeners would be— and, by 1975, were.

The Piano Concerto of 1942 still shows the outlines of the four symphonic movements which, however, it firmly welds together; it plays without even a suppressed break. It is in the String Trio (1946) which is, if I may so put it, perhaps his greatest string quartet altogether, and in his last instrumental composition, the fiddle Phantasy (1949; his 'Ph'), that the single-movement compressions reach ultimate intensity and, hence, ultimate complexity, within consistently twelve-tonal frameworks.

So far, so clear—but only so far. My immediate conclusion is an undramatic, sad denouement. Schoenberg solved his own creative life by clarification—yet, by bursting what had remained of the walls of a closed musical society, he caused lasting confusion; not ever-lasting, one hopes, but lasting long enough to produce musical history's—arguably world history's—most chronic crisis of communication.

Just as Beethoven, impatiently surging ahead, had dropped the repeat of the exposition long before the history of composition would have made this step inevitable[21] (with the result that one stage of creative development was largely missed out, i.e. the varied repeat of the exposition[22]), so Schoenberg plunged into

---

[21] There were, however, remote precedents, which I have discussed in detail in the Mozart chapter of the Pelican *Symphony*, vol. I (ed. Robert Simpson, 1971 impression) — in the first movements of Mozart's 'Paris' Symphony in D major, K.297, his Salzburg B flat Symphony, K.319, and his C major Symphony, K.338. In the 'Paris' Symphony, the apparent innovation is achieved by a reversion to older models rather than through the evolution of sonata form which came to produce Beethoven's revolutionary repeatlessness; in the two other symphonies, the development's material is not stated in the exposition, which is therefore that much less in need of a memorising repeat: to understand a development, we have to be able to recall what it is that is being developed.

[22] Consistently pursued in only one area, i.e. classical concerto form.

his sea long before our musical society's general language had genuinely exhausted itself; as we now know, it had not even entirely exhausted itself by 1975. What he told that NCO in the First World War was not, chronologically speaking, true: somebody had to be Schoenberg, admittedly, but certainly not yet. The history of tonality between 1908 and 1975 has shown beyond any reasonable doubt that Schoenberg came too soon.

This is not a complaint: early arrivals, not to speak of gate-crashings, are among the occupational hazards of genius, and the occupations of geniuses become, inescapably, our preoccupations. It is just that Schoenberg couldn't have chosen a worse moment for coming too soon: the break-up of our closed musical society, our general language, would have caused chaos in any case (or rather, as we shall note in section III below, chaoses), but since it came too soon, it caused something worse than, and in addition to, chaos, i.e. pseudo-communication.

From the moment the atonal eruption had taken place, the devil—the spirit that doesn't care what it means, or whether it means anything—had his chance. That spirit hovers over our age in any case, ready to penetrate even towering minds. 'I think that man now realises he is an accident', said Francis Bacon in 1975[23], 'that he is a completely futile being, that he has to play out the game without reason . . . You see, all art has now become completely a game by which man distracts himself; and you may say it has always been like that, but now it's entirely a game. And I think that that is the way things have changed, and what is fascinating now is that

23 David Sylvester, *Interviews with Francis Bacon*, Thames & Hudson, London, 1975, p. 29f.

it's going to become much more difficult for the artist, because he must really deepen the game to be any good at all.' The same Francis Bacon, this, who seemed to think, in an extended private conversation some years ago, that my theory of music might well apply to his art. He was drunk, admittedly, but not all that drunk, and in any case, alcohol might have been supposed to make him lose his inhibitions about declaring life, and hence art, an accident, not gain them. What did he think, then? That the theory was just another game, a game explaining the game that is art, and which sheds light on the senseless game that is life? But if art shows anything, it is that life is not futile.

Now, my description of Schoenberg's creative life has emphasised one thing all along: throughout the vicissitudes of his development, his consuming passion was to serve clarity. But having arrived prematurely, his new clarity did not get across, with the result that even those—a handful to begin with—who liked his music didn't really get it. And once this state of not really getting it had become an established frame of mind, the weaker souls among composers, who inevitably are in the majority, didn't worry too much about getting what they themselves meant in the first place, far less about whether it would precisely get across. If Schoenberg succeeded without communicating, they unconsciously and wrongly felt, why shouldn't they? And, worse luck, they did—increasingly so. From being an act of precise communication, preciser than any verbal effort could hope to be (as precise, in fact, as mathematics, and hence as comprehensively analysable, if only in musical terms, just as mathematics is only analysable in mathematical terms), musical expression descended to the level of mere stimulation, until mere stimulation was itself regarded as a virtue, by those who, at least intermittently, had renounced communication altogether—John Cage & Sons. It was in this situation that everybody began to feel guilty about Schoenberg, that most bodies' hearts were ambivalently divided: if and when that man meant something, he was now declared old-fashioned.

Schoenberg thus emerges as musical history's most tragic great figure—its most uncompromising clarifier and by far its most outstanding confuser at the same time. The psychotics who are proud of not understanding the things people have done under the protective umbrella which Schoenberg provided without ever offering it—all those alienated listeners have a little point, because there are plenty of composers around who haven't done anything, not even anything bad, whose art is beyond good and evil, i.e. simply useless, 'accidental' and 'futile' in Francis Bacon's words. At the beginning of its fourth quarter, our century's crisis of musical communication shows no sign of resolving, but every sign of being increasingly denied by those who, whether they know it or not, thrive on it. This crisis of sheer musical sense, audible sense, has not merely, not even chiefly, been produced by one musical language having split into several, one society into several.

The one language has also, over a considerable part of the contemporary scene, evaporated into none.

## III. Our Chaoses

The firmly closed musical society of two hundred years ago had its disadvantages, of course—and, if that is any consolation, our open society, our linguistic bedlam, has achieved a state of compositional affairs in which such disadvantages simply cannot occur. They, too, were dangers of non-communication, but of a very different type—the opposite type, in fact, which, with the help of my theory, is easily definable. In 1775, that is to say, the ready concreteness of available backgrounds which the general diatonic language made possible was such that unless you were somebody, you could spend your life as a successful, readily accessible composer without really doing anything, without saying anything, without conceiving of a single new thought. Your equally mindless listener, always in the natural majority, would not notice anything amiss; on the contrary, he noticed something amiss in the Mozart Violin Concertos written, all of them, two hundred years before 1975, because they did not fully meet his expectations; whereas the eighteenth century's mindless music, which can still be surveyed not only in the British Museum or in L.R.A.M. examination rooms (since it does follow the rules!), but also, nowadays, on radio and gramophone records, consists of nothing but the meeting of expectations, so that after you have heard or seen the first eight bars, you can write the piece yourself. It is, in fact, tautological music, inasmuch as it says again what is clearly in your own mind anyhow—and we know all about the pleasure which minor minds derive from having their own thoughts, if thoughts you can call them, confirmed by an outside source: the craft of criticism itself would at once cease to be a going concern if such pleasure were to dry up.

Such music is all background and no foreground, background replacing foreground—one-dimensional music, in fact, a continuous and indeed consistent exposure of expectations and their fulfilment, i.e. of self-propelling anticipations, making no more sense than was available before the music started. But that much sense, at least, it makes, and so long as it meets the rules of the general language's grammar (which themselves are nothing but a codification of expectations), it cannot be called bad. It is, in principle, schoolroom music, pre-artistic; it is craft—for craft (the mastery of language) is the background of structure (which is individual). Structure is, in fact, the total foreground of a piece, and those eighteenth-century tinkles are without it: they are merely filled-in form.

1975's player and listener had no such pleonasms to fear, except perhaps in the field of pop music, the Eurovision Song Contest, or students' stuff and the like. But for the rest of what, in a disintegrating civilisation, is lovingly known as the 'spectrum' of our creative endeavours, what we have been witnessing is exactly the opposite type of danger—all foreground and no background, the opposite type of one-dimensionality, in fact. 1775's mindless composer reminded us of nothing but his own difficulties and, of course, our own—the difficulties of keeping music alive as meaning.

What is considerably worse, whereas in 1775, mindlessness was confined to the mindless, by 1975, mindlessness had deeply penetrated the minds of the mindful—inevitably so, since they were no longer in a position to be remindful of stable backgrounds: the Schoenberg trauma had seen to that. The result—no names where young, struggling composers are concerned—was, at best, a regression of art to a game: Francis Bacon, the last artist to be himself accused of gamesmanship, has a point vis-à-vis 1975, when he talks about having to play out the game without reason, but not vis-à-vis humanity

175

as an historical whole. I speak with the widest possible experience, not just as a composition teacher, or listening musician, or a so-called critic and musicologist, but, possibly, with the most comprehensive knowledge of new scores one can attain. This is in no way a personal achievement; it is mere accident. I happen to be in charge of New Music at the BBC, and I have revised our score-reading system and our rules of acceptance and rejection in a way which makes it incumbent upon me to read any new score submitted myself—native or foreign. In addition, I read for the Society for the Promotion of New Music, as well as for competitions. So whatever you may find wrong with my diagnoses, they are not based on ignorance or inadequate knowledge—or if they are based on inadequate knowledge, this fact alone supports one of my diagnoses, to wit, the absence of a sufficiently workable language to make the creation of consistently two-dimensional—and hence consistently meaningful—music possible for any but the most outstanding few.

The game means that the composer, or the group of composers to which he owes psychological allegiance, or that group's leader, has worked out the rules he is going to follow—anxiety-ridden rules which have self-therapeutic rather than artistic significance, in that the sense of insecurity produced by the absence of dependable backgrounds produces the need for savage limitations, whatever the cost in terms of musical realism: if these limitations don't correspond to anything in you, the recipient, and so define a usable background, they might just as well not be there, so far as their role in the story of the meaning of music is concerned. They mean as much as your carefully walking from A to B in 200 steps, rather than walking from A to B, perhaps more quickly, or more comfortably, without counting your steps: by way of the game, art degenerates into a pathological symptom, meaningful only to the sufferer and to any co-sufferers—of whom, in such a threatening situation, there may well be many.

According to classical psychoanalytic theory, neurosis and psychosis used to be mutually exclusive; in fact, neurosis was an insurance against psychosis. But then, that was before psychosis, in the eyes of the observer, came in a big way: psychoanalysts used to call each other (and everybody else) neurotics then[24]. Our game-players are the ideal model for having it both pathological ways—if anybody wants the perfect combination of purely clinical diagnoses: playing the game, they behave like seasoned obsessional neurotics, singly or collectively, but since the game and its rules are mistaken for the real world of art, they exhibit, at the same time, the clear picture of a raving psychosis—complete, I may add, with both persecution mania and megalomania, again both individual and collective. The rules of the game are mistaken for the rules of a new grammar: the delusion of a background fills the gap left by the Schoenberg trauma and its explosion of old backgrounds.

1975 was quite a year for one's reflective musical consciousness—especially if one was worried about foregrounds and backgrounds—the year of the publication of the vastly enlarged edition of Schoenberg's *Style and Idea,* from which I have quoted, and of the afore-noted death of Shostakovich, who was far enough removed from Schoenberg—the post-traumatic Schoenberg, at any rate—not to be intellectually comprehensible to him, yet near enough to earn Schoenberg's

---

24 Cf. Chapter III, pp. 102-3.

instinctive admiration (see Section II). It is less widely appreciated that Shostakovich's attitude to Schoenberg —never publicly articulated, of course—was complementary, his ambivalence, however, immeasurably more intense: Shostakovich came to feel far more involved in Schoenberg's music than Schoenberg ever was in Shostakovich's.

At a considerable distance in time, I had two musical conversations with Shostakovich—if conversations you could call them: he did not speak either English or (as most Russian artists do) German, and the discussion had to develop through an interpreter—in neither case a musician, and in each case one of those Gestapo faces I have described on a previous page[25]. Possibilities of wilful or accidental mistranslation or omission could not, therefore, be excluded; certainly, the interpreter's sentences were invariably much shorter than Shostakovich's own, although a translation is normally longer than the original, because it has to cope with words and phrases for which there is no exact equivalent in the receiving language. But the gist of what Shostakovich had to say or wished to say did seem to emerge. On the first occasion, we chiefly talked about Schoenberg's music. Though emphatically respectful, his attitude was indistinguishable from the party line, and there was no sign of his 'putting it on'. In any case, he did not look like a good liar: he was a very nervous man and looked equally unhappy and truthful.

On the second occasion, I tried—most unsuccessfully —to challenge him. I had published a detailed analysis of his then new Twelfth String Quartet[26], at the end of

[25] Chapter II, p.58.
[26] *Tempo*, London, Autumn, 1970.

178

which I had invited him to say straight out whether or not it was true. There had been no reply: closed societies and their willing or unwilling representatives—and let's not forget that Shostakovich was willing—tend to be too 'realistically'-minded to give real replies. They will either not reply at all, or give a political reply, which means that they say what they deem to be in their own interest, which again they either regard as the truth, or as temporarily preferable to the truth, because it serves what they consider the ultimate truth; see the end of Chapter III, p.132.

Anyhow, what Shostakovich seems to have felt unable to reply to were two things, which I had demonstrated in my analysis with, I hope, meticulous objectivity and precision—not at all politically! Formally, I suggested, the Twelfth String Quartet could be shown to be modelled on Schoenberg's First Chamber Symphony, to the extent of contradicting the model very specifically, *à la* background, where it didn't specifically follow it; methodologically, I established that the work applied, most understandingly, Schoenberg's own twelve-tone technique, despite its tonal organisation, its acceptance of key as its basic unifying force. Shostakovich must, in fact, have studied Schoenberg's twelve-tone technique in conscientious detail, as did that other Russian genius who had shown the same public hostility to it—Stravinsky.

In our second conversation, then, and in view of what Shostakovich had told me on the first occasion about Schoenberg's methods of composition, I registered respectful surprise, together with my admiration for the Quartet—which I do indeed regard as one of our century's most effective weapons in the struggle against the decline of musical history's most developed genre of instrumental music, which is capable of more expression within narrow spaces than any other. Point by point, I tried to ask Shostakovich whether he agreed with my analytical account of the work, and if he didn't, what was wrong with it. His reactions left me with a hangover. In reply to my observations about the Quartet's structure as compared with that of Schoenberg's First Chamber Symphony, the interpreter pronounced: 'It is true that there are very strong parallels between my Twelfth String Quartet and Schoenberg's Chamber Symphony.' Parallels, mind you: the implication of an inevitable causal relation was ignored. Then, in reply to my points about the Quartet's twelve-tone technique, the interpreter said: 'Any means of expression are permissible to an artist.'

That was that. It seemed impossible to get genuinely, musically in touch. But what appeared certain was that Shostakovich had indeed spoken honestly, not politically in an opportunist sense—that, in other words, artistic politics were part of his own mental life, quite independent, by now, of external pressures: any contradictions between what he was saying and what he had said before were not due to a conflict between his views and the musical world-view of the state, but to conflicts in his own mind, self-confessed or not; he was being political with himself. Nor could the conflicts have developed between his conscience and his self, between superego and ego in psychoanalytic parlance, but they must have been conflicts within his superego: I here choose psychoanalytic nomenclature not in order to befog, but because the superego, as distinct from the traditional concept of the conscience, includes a vast, dynamic, unconscious aspect.

180

My interpretation squares with what we know both about Shostakovich's musical history, in which seeming rebellion was invariably followed by self-criticism or even contrition, and indeed about his music itself, which is hardly ever without conflict of intention—a very different thing from contrast of expression, which is conflict artistically realised and rationalised, the kind of conflict which concerns us all, whereas Shostakovich's politico-aesthetic conflicts were really his own problem.

I should go so far as to say that the First Symphony apart, and not forgetting the Tenth, nor underrating the powerful Eleventh, Shostakovich perhaps never wrote a 'good work', a spotless masterpiece in his life—which, for a genius, was quite a negative achievement. Needless to add, one prefers 'bad' (inconsistent or uneven or conflict-ridden) Shostakovich to a mere talent's masterpieces (of which there are precious few about, anyway, at this largely backgroundless stage in the development or envelopment of musical composition): Shostakovich said more even where he said it badly, because what he said was newer.

My view of his creative psychology—which, I submit, is the only one that takes all the evidence into account—can thus be briefly summarised: Shostakovich mistook his political conscience for his musical conscience, because his loyalty to Marxist ideology forced him to do so. His musical conscience, on the other hand—enormously strong and background-conscious in a mind of such profound musicality—he mistook, when the remorseful spirit took him and mistook him, for wrong, 'sick', Western aesthetic ideas, wrongful intentions—at any rate, whenever they contradicted his political conscience, or were opposed by it. This basic conflict within his superego ought to be a warning to our own society's second-round musical Marxists (the first round having happened in the now fashionable twenties, before most of us were alive or could think). Of their own special chaos, I shall write in Section VI below.

Meanwhile, I have not wilfully inserted this Schoenberg-Shostakovich episode into our considerations of 1975's chaoses, for the purpose of light relief or heavy thoughts—to help our ambivalent mourning of a genius. These incidental gains—'secondary gains' to the psychoanalyst — may or may not play their part, but the place of my episode in the scheme of our investigation is strictly functional; in fact, musically speaking, I am not sure that one is entitled to call it an episode, for I propose to show that it is quadruply thematic.

In the first place, I have tried craftily to anticipate some sophisticated readers' reactions to my description of post-Schoenbergian musical games: twelve-tone technique itself, they might have thought, is such a game, born out of our anxiety over the loss of backgrounds. The reason why I take these imagined reactions so seriously is that they would, partly, be right. Which part? Many parts, Schoenberg's own dodecaphony excepted, and Stravinsky's too—the twelve-tonery of two of the twentieth century's few geniuses, it so happens. But even among the most gifted twelve-tone composers, those who have attained the status of twentieth-century classics, the honest ear—that which identifies a technique's musicality and potential meaningfulness with its audibility, with its self-explanatory effect on a highly musical person who may or may not be musically educated—will detect quite a few who were not beyond using dodecaphony as a means, not of communication, but of pacifying self-gratification. In fact, bogus twelve-tone technique was not unknown to the most hallowed twentieth-century figures, the first-generation composers of the so-called 'Second Viennese School'[27] themselves. I am aware that it is not humanly possible to criticise St Anton, provide as he did excuses, right up to 1975, for not composing full-bloodedly, developmentally and indeed extendedly, but the fact remains that as often as not, Webern's twelve-tone technique is no more than autobiographical, his music remaining meaningful not because or in spite of it, but apart from it. Surprisingly enough, much the same can be said about the other member of the Holy Trinity, Alban Berg, a full-blooded composer in all conscience, who did retain or regain his backgrounds after the Schoenberg trauma, but who, for purely psychological reasons, i.e. out of reverence for the father, could not allow himself to write undodecaphonically when the time came, at any rate on paper, with the result that he will one day be recognised as a veritable model of phoney twelve-tone technique and related games which are being practised, until this very day, in the most elevated circles. The way in which he derives a bunch of subordinate rows from the basic set of *Lulu*, for instance, has to be seen to be believed; it certainly can't be heard. Yet to my knowledge, the myth of *Lulu's* single row has only twice been exploded in all these decades—by myself over twenty years ago, and by Desmond Shawe-Taylor in 1975 (independently: he hadn't read me).

---

[27] H. F. Redlich's uncontested title. Which was the 'First'? In the entire literature, it is never mentioned — and with reason: the only Viennese classic who went to school with another Viennese classic was Beethoven -— with Haydn. We have intimated that he duly made a hash of it.

183

Come to think of it, I personally can name only three composers who made consistent and consistently musical use of the technique, and all three were, to my mind, geniuses: apart from Schoenberg himself and the later Stravinsky, there was the Greek Nikos Skalkottas (1904-1949) who, now rediscovered, remains to be reassessed. Unfortunately, his scores are not easily decipherable—hence the delay in their publication.

The anti-dodecaphonists, then, would have quite a case. Would have, rather than have: downright reactionaries apart (a reactionary, to me, is very different from a conservative, who does not deny what has happened), there had been no more than a whispering campaign against the technique, conducted, at times, with considerable authority, but always stopping short of the last, official public step. My friend and colleague, Peter Stadlen, for instance, a former Webern pupil, has been promising or threatening an anti-paternal, anti-dodecaphonic book for ages, but somehow, it doesn't seem to be coming.

Is there a realistic inhibition at work here? I would respect it. But in any case, rather than conduct this argument on the level of what I can hear and you can't, silencing criticism by sheer one-upmanship, or else by way of the kind of public demonstration I gave in the early sixties when I whistled the twelve-tone row of Schoenberg's Orchestral Variations on television (between ourselves, I can teach you to do that too, especially if you happen to possess, like every dog, perfect pitch), I would resolve the contest on a purely empirical level, heeding nothing but the factual implications of what has actually happened.

If, that is to say, Shostakovich, who side-stepped the

Schoenberg trauma or tried to, and who, in any case, can be shown not only to have retained his backgrounds firmly and safely, but to have paid exclusive attention to audibility—if even this major, anti-Schoenbergian genius got himself quite deeply involved in twelve-tone technique, he can only have done so because of its concretely musical attractiveness as a unifying method, as a new way of establishing a background—the tone-row—within the very confines of a piece, investing it with foreground significance in the first place, at or near the start of the music. The Twelfth String Quartet is by no means the only late work in which Shostakovich 'did it'—and never in the history of music has there been less of a game-player; it was, in fact, 'academic', 'formalist' game-playing he used to object to most of all, at one here with his political fathers.

Nevertheless, probably as a psychological concomit-ant, it was the structure of Schoenberg's First Chamber Symphony that fascinated him as a consistent new foreground thrown into relief against the background of the traditional symphonic scheme (which was Shosta-kovich's major preoccupation throughout his creative life, whether in the symphony or the string quartet); it was this Schoenbergian structure some of which he, in his turn, pushed into the background, thus trans-forming it, formalising it, in order to be able to establish tensions between it and his own structure. Where concrete, musical interest offered itself, then, it was grasped despite all anti-theoretical theories, despite the would-be overriding political religion: with Shostakovich, as with all musical geniuses down the ages, music either came first or a very close second, whatever else his conscience told him about the reason for his existence.

185

1975's tragedy was that for many a major musical talent, music seemed to come last or not at all — because without instinctive backgrounds, it had to be justified in words, however delusionally, before it was allowed to emerge. But the prime justification, too — actually saying something— tended to come last.

The second thematic function of my juxtaposition of Schoenberg and Shostakovich is, in fact, an examination of the two-dimensionality of all communicative music viewed from either end of our musical world, the traumatic end and, shall we say, the extra-traumatic end — as Shostakovich no doubt would have us say? For from his point of view, there was no need for the trauma — and not only from his point of view: his close friend, right in the middle of our own musical society, another of our century's few geniuses (who, incidentally, seemed to accept my theory of music), showed himself in emphatic agreement with him — Benjamin Britten. But he, too, evinced a striking ambivalence towards the 'Second Viennese School' in general, and towards its founder in particular. Not only did he, as a youngster, want to study with Berg, not only does the development section of his Second String Quartet's opening movement show surprisingly detailed recollections of Berg's *Lyric Suite* (which, one gathers, had only been heard once, and never been seen, before the Quartet was written!), but dodecaphony itself did not leave Britten alone either, even though he, too, side-stepped the crisis, or tried to. I am not just thinking of such rather esoteric symptoms as a twelve-tone chord in *Billy Budd* (1951, revised 1960), which, needless to add, assumes dominant function [28],

---

[28] Dominant function: what the G major chord does in C major.

but of Britten's actual flirtations with serial technique or its implications — conducted with emphatic ambivalence in the *Cantata Academica* written in commemoration of the quincentenary (1960) of Basel University (*academica*!), but far more profoundly and, at the same time, individually, in what many of us regard as his greatest opera, *The Turn of the Screw* (1954).

From Shostakovich's and Britten's end, music's two-dimensionality was never in doubt, the reservoir of backgrounds never in danger. Yet they both occupied themselves, more willy than nilly, with the very composing method, or at least with clear significations of the very method, which had been designed to overcome a trauma they themselves had never fallen victim to, or indeed personally experienced. Neither of them, as a musical personality, would have dreamt of interesting himself in any method as such, without being fascinated, somewhere, by the actual music which had produced the method — yes, that way round: all composing methods worth their name develop *a posteriori,* inductively.

But if the music fascinated them as music, it must have been two-dimensional in their own sense, must have transparently concealed backgrounds which, from an harmonic point of view, were plausible to them despite the fact that they were unwilling to accept keylessness as such, atonality. And here we come to the supreme paradox at the heart of Schoenberg's victory over his self-created trauma. The many structural conservatisms we have diagnosed which helped him swim in the boiling sea and resist its heat would have been as nothing if, harmonically, he had remained at sea: not for him, the author of perhaps the most original book on *Harmony*

187

there ever was[29], the creator, in his tonal music, of the most refined harmonic complexities, to ignore music's harmonic aspect all of a sudden, to let any old note hit any old note, as 1975's notes have done more often than not, claiming, if necessary, that pitch didn't matter anyway.

What he did in the vertical dimension was something he himself never grasped theoretically, something so utterly instinctive that, given his genius, it was bound to come out right, two-dimensional, backgrounded— something which, if we accept that he succeeded, confirms the greatness of his creative mind, for which I have already adduced evidence. In his 'free atonal' period, he was without harmonic directives altogether; in his twelve-tone music, he persuaded himself that the serial organisation of his vertical combinations of notes, his soundings-together (whether chords or parts hitting or fondling each other) ensured a minimum of order. But he realised himself that, in itself, it was a very poor minimum, that the real rules of his harmony escaped him, that they might be discovered by future analysts. Indeed, within the serial framework, you have as much freedom harmonically as you have melodically within the tonal framework: additional laws for the construction of tunes had been needed in diatonic music—if only to get the background straight.

Benjamin Frankel, who went dodecaphonic in his late middle-age (I taught him the technique), O. W. Neighbour of the British Museum, Kenneth Hicken[30]

---

[29] A defective and partial translation is about to be replaced by a full and, one gathers, highly competent one (Faber).

[30] 'Schoenberg's Atonality: Fused Bitonality?' in *Tempo*, London, June 1974. Hicken's is undoubtedly the most systematic approach, but also, perhaps, the least easily comprehensible!

and I myself have, I think, shown the way towards a solution of the harmonic problem in Schoenberg's atonality (a 'mere' theoretical problem, of course!), no matter whether 'free' or twelve-tonal. I am expressing what is, in principle, our solution in terms of my theory, and apologise to the dead Frankel and the very live Neighbour and Hicken if, from their point of view, I get anything wrong in order to get it right from mine.

Schoenberg's atonal harmony is not atonal—or, if you like, it both is and isn't: the foreground is atonal, the background isn't. Step by step, progression by progression, seeming vertical accident by seeming vertical accident, his harmonies can be shown to be meaningful contradictions of expressively suppressed tonal implications which, in the background, are sufficiently well defined to produce the spontaneous expectation of resolutions or, anyway, of specific continuations that never happen: the principle of precise harmonic communication is none other than that underlying the time-honoured interrupted cadence described in Section I. It is this harmonic logic which, again purely instinctively, both Shostakovich and Britten have acknowledged through their appreciation; it is this harmonic sense which we miss in the vast majority of 1975's harmonies, inasmuch as they haven't returned to open tonality anyhow. No musical ear—and there were plenty of unmusical ears among 1975's despisers of harmonic communication—can accept the irrelevance of a meeting of pitches.

The third thematic purpose of the Schoenberg-Shostakovich story is, simply, a reminder that, at either end of the world, and even in the face of an unprecedented world crisis, genius overcomes everything: at one end,

189

the crisis is created and then resolved; at the other, its apparent inevitability is virtuosically ignored—and again we may include Britten at the other end. No wonder these extremes (rather than deliberate extremists) had a sneaking admiration for each other; no wonder they disliked each other too: you don't like anybody evading your crisis, and you don't like anybody who has produced a crisis you have successfully avoided. But when Schoenberg felt that Shostakovich had the breath of a symphonist, he extended the deepest compliment he was capable of: it was for the purpose of being able to express his own symphonic breath that he evolved his method of composing with twelve notes 'only related to each other'. My stress on the potency of genius may seem banal to the virginal reader who, naive soul, is still aware of the fact that there is a difference in kind, not merely in degree, between, say, Mozart and Boccherini, a difference remarkably independent of economic circumstances and the emergence of the bourgeoisie—but, as will presently be seen, unless he (the virginal reader) is careful, genius is about to be abolished: I was told as much in a public discussion the other year in which contemporary German music was examined in terms of contemporary *West*-German Marxism.

The fourth and last reason why my Schoenberg-Shostakovich episode is as much of an episode as is any of the episodes in the last movement of Bach's E major fiddle Concerto, where the episodes are, if anything, more important than is the principal section (a meaningful contradiction of a rondo background here!)—this clinching reason is the comparison the juxtaposition offers between a genius in a closed society and a genius in an open society, at what, before the trauma happened,

190

was roughly the same historical stage. And here we have to face the uncomfortable truth that the closed society's genius had it marginally easier: the reality of the trauma, the plunge into atonality, came to be 'prohibited' anyway, psychologically denied, and so the conservative genius could pursue his course unmolested, inasmuch as he could afford to feel that he had every artistic right to remain a member of that closed *musical* society which ensured the continuity of backgrounds, and which the Schoenberg trauma came to break up with fierce force.

But was it worth it? I say that Shostakovich had it *marginally* easier, and I mean it: while he did not have to face the trauma frontally, he was, instead, saddled with that conflict within his superego which I have attempted to describe, and which must have prevented a more harmonious development of his genius that might well have resulted in a number of spotless masterpieces— such as Schoenberg showed himself capable of creating, trauma and all: it is not, after all, part of the destiny of genius to have it easy, even though the example of Mendelssohn shows that given the absence of any need for self-punishment, an easy creative (and material) life doesn't do a genius any harm, whatever the gluttons for other people's punishment may think.

Without Shostakovich's conflicts on the one hand and the Schoenberg trauma on the other, moreover, Shostakovich's counterpart in our wide-open musical society achieved his own measure of spotless masterpieces by adhering to the technical and stylistic ideals, the general language of a closed musical society that no longer was: 'So what!' he said, or it said in him. 'I will be understood by those who have these backgrounds still—and un-complicatedly—inside them', and he was. What all three geniuses avoided with imperfect ease was any of the chaoses which continued to dominate the decades, in various guises of pseudo-orders, pseudo-systems, 'total serialisms',[31] the lot, right up to 1975, by which time it could definitely be said that only geniuses on the one hand and kitsch merchants on the other were able to compose with stable backgrounds behind them—the kitsch merchants without any foregrounds to speak of in front of them. For the rest, and for reasons which will become obvious later on, the plural of 'chaos' seems to be required for the first time in cultural history.

But the newly emerging contemporary classics, those now passing into middle age — like Maxwell Davies, Thea Musgrave, Hugh Wood and, of course, Alexander Goehr (who accepts my theory of music) in this country, are sufficiently conscious of the need for communication not to lose themselves in self-satisfying games, even though, at times, their backgrounds wobble. Lack of clarity, however, is not chaos; the continuing danger, on the contrary, is that clarity itself is experienced as an anti-model by those who are equally afraid of saying something (and hence being thought obvious) and of saying nothing (and hence feeling frustrated)—and who therefore commute the sentence of having to say some-

---

[31] Total serialism was, in the fifties, a creative world-view which, like Hitler's Third Reich, was expected to last a thousand years, and to which most leaders of the Continental avant-garde owed allegiance at some stage or other. Schoenberg's serialisation of pitches — the tone-row — was complemented by the serialisation of everything else — rhythm, dynamics, tone-colour, form, and even time itself, the 'element' underlying all these 'factors'; see Luigi Nono, *The Development of Serial Technique* (1958), republished in 1975 in a collection of all his writings (and other people's about him): Jürg Stenzl (ed.), *Luigi Nono: Texte, Studien zu seiner Musik,* Zurich.

thing or, Cage-like, having to say nothing, into playing at something. Of all chaoses, the game-playing one is perhaps the most invidious, because it sails under the self-deceiving flag of control.

Opposite ends of the world are one thing, the moon is quite another, because it is lifeless except for the life you invest it with, either by staring at it and weaving poetical fantasies round it, or by actually walking around on it or watching others walk around on it. The extension of experience into lifelessness, into chaos *par excellence*, without any desire to create order out of chaos, is one of our age's achievements, in accord with its need for dehumanisation which springs from the Francis Baconian resignation from any attempt to find a purpose in life, or indeed to put one into it. I gravely suspect that our interest in the moon, our fascination by it, would quickly evaporate if we encountered purposive beings up there; we should probably take the next inter-planetary express back.

That notorious spectrum of our creative endeavours, then, is wider than it ever was before. In music, it extends beyond opposite ends of the communicative world, with a motley of chaoses in between, right into total non-communication, accidental or deliberate. I have spoken, at the end of Section II, of mere stimulation being regarded as a virtue by those who have renounced communication altogether, backgroundless as they find themselves. The father of the anti-movement, of the apotheosis of staticism, of peaceful, amiably sneering chaos is, of course, John Cage himself, anti-St John, though he has, of course, done other things besides, playing games included. It would be simple-minded in the extreme to ignore his achievement, which was one of gently violent liberation: at the tail-end of a culture, or rather of its subsequent civilisation—Oswald Spengler's *Decline of the West*, so often ridiculed, is proving truer every decade—the burden of the past, dead backgrounds and all, is such that only the strongest shoulders can carry it, and the wisest heads are not always to be found on the strongest shoulders.

I would argue, in fact, that after the Schoenberg trauma, his surprise pupil John Cage (what a teacher-student relationship that must have been!) has proved the widest influence on our musical age, or at least made the strongest impact—affecting, like Schoenberg, sundry minds who were passionately opposed to the originator of the influence. Where Schoenberg produced a crisis of backgrounds, however, Cage 'solved' that crisis, if you like, by abolishing backgrounds altogether at the production end, letting any backgrounds at the reception end have their free play with what he was offering—which was the moon and not, mind you, a poem about it. If, after a Cage concert, the bewildered listener were to say that he might just as well walk out into the road, listen attentively to the traffic noise, and project whatever sense he pleases on to it, Cage would reply that he, Cage, was the composer of the traffic noise, for without him, nobody would ever attentively listen to it. The *objet trouvé* is *not* the model, for it is selected because it looks like something, thus conveying the selector's projection of meaning; whereas pure un-communicative Cage—prototypically, his silent work *4′ 33″ (tacet) for any instrument(s)* (1952)—sounds like nothing on earth, like something on the moon which proffers the listener-creator complete freedom; 'anti-communication' would, in fact, be a sharper definition

194

than non-communication, more expressive of the intentions behind it—which, wholly permissive, are totally destructive in effect. Cage cannot love without hating because he is incapable of respect; in fact, in one's unkindlier moments, one recognises him as a commercial traveller selling disrespect, which is more gleeful than contempt: it offers the lifeline, such as it is, of the grin.

Where the Schoenberg trauma had concealed communication, even that fanatical communicator's own, and the concealment of communication had offered Cageian pictures before Cage came in, or out of it all, the anti-master himself, by rejecting communicative selec·tion, opened the front door to chance, Schoenberg's own ultimate hate-object, while the back-door remained open to the re-entry of sense, though scarcely Cage's own: he isn't musical enough for that, nor does he want to be. But right up to 1975, many others, inspired by the Cageian spirit, had made more sense than they wanted to: they were too musical to be able to rid themselves of their backgrounds—while others again, who want to make sense, just can't, and accept the Cageian impression they make as a good if guilty second best; at least, it is an impression which has been legitimised. For let nobody think that any of our diverse chaoses has anything to do with individualism, though the creative rights of the individual are in every messed-up mind's mouth: these individualists can't take a step without at least the hope of collective approval, however small the collection of people who are expected to approve. No Beethovens around now, big or small[32], deaf to the outside world and

---

[32] Psychologically speaking, though, Nikos Skalkottas was a small late Beethoven, insensitive to contemporary audiences — or their absence, or indeed the question of their existence.

clairvoyant in the face of the inner one, confident that it will turn out to be the real world after all the incomprehension is over, that individualism means being there first: all discoveries are lonely, and all have universal significance.

But 1975 buried more than it discovered—and, what is worse, it buried things that weren't there. One of the long-term effects of the Schoenberg trauma is the art that hides the absence of art. An elemental human urge here manifests itself, primitive in the sense that it tends to cease once infantility is over; but in a regressive society, infantility is not easily over, is easily reverted to. The prototype can be spotted on any beach—the little girl with the bikini, who proudly hides something that isn't there. Once she grows up, it will be there, and she will communicatively hide it or not, as the case may be. Meanwhile, she behaves *as if.* Composition-as-if is one of the most noxious chaoses—at a time when even the most perceptive among us often have great difficulty in deciding what, if anything, is under the bra. And then Cage, always waiting, grinning in the wings, comes to our diabolic help, and makes us hear things that aren't there. What's wrong with that, you (he) may ask. Both the little girl and her spectators are happy—but only if they have an infantile or senile interest in little girls! Well, if the reader (dispirited by Francis Bacon) thinks there is nothing wrong with being happy about nothing, even though one's missed one's chance to be happy about something, he merely offers himself as evidence of what I am deploring and need not, so far as you and I are concerned, pursue my line of thought any further.

What, at the same time, is remarkable and reinvigorating about Cage's influence and infiltrations, right across that notorious spectrum he himself violently extended, is the musical, communicative use which creative minds made — whether they knew it or not — of the most unmusical and anti-communicative ideas of his. This side of the Iron Curtain, if you go out of your way to try and find what has been consciously the most anti-Cageian creative character and, at the same time, the most complete musician, you will probably land yourself, once again with Benjamin Britten. Yet the quasi-aleatoric[33] devices he used in some of his later works, the church operas as well as his last opera, *Death in Venice* (1973), with its rhythmically unbridled notation of the protagonist's — Gustav Aschenbach's — recitatives[34], are inconceivable without the effect, however indirect, which the Cageian world-view has had on our musical world: these things had not happened before Cage appeared upon the scene, and happened after he did, and a correlation (as between night and day) rather than a straight causal relation cannot logically be imagined.

People like Stockhausen, parts of their creative souls, have owed Cage open allegiance, of course, thereby curbing their own need for communication because of the complications it entailed (to whom do I say what and, above all, how?), but the point here is that even those who were, in twentieth-century circumstances, the most

---

[33] Aleatoric or aleatory music, or 'indeterminacy' (Boulez), is music which is largely or wholly determined by the player(s) (if anybody) rather than the composer. 'Who gets the royalties?' was William Walton's analytic response (oral communication).

[34] There is even more 'indeterminacy' here than meets the eye — in that Peter Pears, the dedicatee of the work and the first Aschenbach, was a co-determinator of the pitches too, which Britten is said to have picked up from private declamation.

confident communicators, big and small, took from Cage what was theirs, not his: a liberation, this, which did not endanger their means of communication, the tensions between their foregrounds and their backgrounds. The first outstanding example of its almost academic type was one of the most surprising—Mátyás Seiber's (1905-1960) dodecaphonic Violin Sonata (1960), strictly organised and structured, where, however, a short cadenza allowed the players to improvise on selections of notes; but the selections had been so craftily made that whatever the player did with the notes, they were bound to make harmonic sense: chance turned into strict determinism.[35]!

It will by now be gathered that the different chaoses, easily definable as each is, interpenetrate each other, usually in the mind of the same composer: just as John Cage himself is not beyond playing games, an unsuccessful communicator can, of course, turn into a successful non-communicator in no time, without the outsider (to whose role the recipient is reduced) noticing the difference, unless he has undergone a new kind of self-schooling, which enables him to detect what is happening behind the scenes, not only in the shape of ill-defined backgrounds, but also in the shapelessness of their ill-disguised absence. I would go so far as to suggest that without such self-training, the teaching of composition

---

[35] The composer's relevant instruction, before bar 84, reads thus: 'The players should continue to improvise on models a-g (violin) and 1-8 (piano) in any combination for about 15-20 secs. Variations on these models can be used by changing register (using more extreme registers, particularly for highest and lowest notes on the piano); the order of notes can also be changed as long as each instrument keeps to the 6 notes allotted to it.'

has become virtually impossible—although, needless to add, the impossible is being practised all the time, and in the highest circles too.

Order and chaos, too, are interpenetrative, nor does a composer necessarily do what he says he is doing, or what he thinks he is doing—and few, nowadays, don't say, don't cling to the word as they threaten to sink in the tepid, backgroundless sea into which they have been plunged. A much advertised contemporary classic of no mean stature, but without anything that can remotely be described as classical, an 'articulate' man in the contemporary sense in that his words tend to be in advance of his thoughts, has mastered the craft of irrelevant verbalisation and systematisation and musical legislation to an extent which, though his music may follow the rules of any current game of his (which are not always easy to comprehend), enables him to gloss over a double chaos—the chaos which any game hides, and the intrinsically chaotic relation between the rules of the game and the unrecognised rules of the music: Pierre Boulez, in my submission, makes sense in spite of himself, or intermittent sense anyway. He has his backgrounds, but he doesn't care about them, and would probably regard the theory applied in these pages as a load of rubbish or worse: a collection of past-ridden preoccupations.

What, to my ears, is wrong with his backgrounds is something which, owing to his extreme talent, strikes one far more forcibly than it does in the case of many another contemporary figure, whose music is in a mess anyway, and therefore does not easily betray single, almost single-minded defects—fundamental shortcomings which are the outcome of the Schoenberg trauma as I

199

have described it. In short, like so many of his contemporaries and successors, Boulez is without identifiable harmonic backgrounds. Single combinations of notes, to be sure, he writes with great skill and persuasion: one would not deny him *chordal* backgrounds. What his music lacks is any sense of harmonic *movement*, with the result that from a vertical point of view, we are often presented with a catalogue of sonorities rather than a continuous evolution of vertical tensions and distensions.

I wouldn't make such a noise about this disability, were it not for the fact that in two ways, it is patently symptomatic of the harmonic chaos with which the composer of the late twentieth century is confronted, and its effects on him. In the first place, that is, it forces him to turn his back on the dynamic, kinetic function of harmony, to do things instead of moving harmonically in order to hold the attention—and Boulez is a veritable virtuoso, unequalled among contemporaneous practitioners, in doing things instead: there are catalogues and catalogues in this world, and some of them, very few, make you turn their pages despite the absence of cogent continuity. Even over extended stretches—and some of them might strike us as being too extended for structural comfort—Boulez is able to prevent us from leaving the hall. While he does not make us wonder about the consequences he is going to take, he does make us curious as to what is going to happen next, and never mind why: when you hear a fascinating sound, you want to hear another one. Many react like Boulez; few interest us in their reactions.

But in the second place, Boulez exposes the mortal danger, the paralysing effect of renouncing harmony that can in any way be regarded as functional, and so generates its own rhythm—which indeed used to be called 'harmonic rhythm' in tonal music. We can hardly assume that with his wonderful ear which penetrates, in rehearsal, the finesses of vertical combinations of sounds as easily as all other aspects of music in performance, Boulez was born without a sense of harmony. It is far more likely, I suggest, that he let this sense atrophy, because he didn't need it, didn't want it—because he needed, in fact, to deny harmonic reality.

The audible result of this atrophy is downright sensational, and must be obvious to any natural musician and music lover, even though he be totally out of touch with contemporary musical developments. Yet nobody writes or talks about what I am now going to pin-point, because Boulez is a famous conductor, trans-continent-ally acclaimed, an in-figure whom stupid orchestral musicians love because he, as opposed to other stick-wagglers, can hear them, and because otherwise, they have ceased to care anyway, had to: if they cared, they couldn't phrase one way one day, and the opposite way the next. I think the reader who, in the circumstances, has retained a minimum of unspoilt individual judgment can divine what I am leading down to: Boulez cannot phrase—it is as simple as that.

So far as all available evidence goes, of which there is plenty, he does not know what a phrase is. In that respect, his conducting of Bach, Beethoven or Wagner is absolutely identical: with all the precision and trans-lucence he achieves, with all his so-called rhythm which is really metre, he does not bring about a single well-shaped phrase—the reason being that he ignores the harmonic implications of any structure he is dealing with, to the extent of utterly disregarding harmonic rhythm and hence all characteristic rhythm in tonal music. In the temporal dimension, he has backgrounds indeed; in fact, he has nothing else, for metre is background, whereas rhythm is the foreground thrown into relief against it.

Whoever has taught gifted young children must have a curious feeling when listening to a Boulez performance of pre-classical, classical, or romantic music: bar-line accents and half-bar accents are all he hears, instead of a musical *Gestalt*, and while he will be impressed by the exactitude of it all as well as depressed by the crystal-clear audibility of subordinate parts or accompanimental figures that shouldn't really be heard all that obtrusively, his mind will, otherwise, conjure up aural pictures of those pre-pubertal instrumentalists who, though they did not evince Boulez's virtuosity, had exactly his answers to questions of phrasing—i.e. none, except for regular strong beats.

There could, in fact, be no more decisive proof of the functionality of Schoenberg's atonal or twelve-tonal harmony which I have postulated than what I, for one (or, as will be seen in a moment, almost one), considered his disastrous 1975 performance of *Moses and Aron* which, alas, is available on gramophone records: there it could be heard that it doesn't really make any difference whether you interpret Bach, Beethoven, Wagner, or Schoenberg: with all composers who write two-dimensional—and hence functional—harmony, foreground against background, a phrase is a phrase, and rhythm, therefore, is not metre. What the habitual non-phraser does, on the other hand, is to replace phrasing by pace (everything too fast), and rhythm by 'beat', by

202

motoric pseudo-excitement. The result is that while you can hear things which you shouldn't, you can't hear things which you should, especially in a rich texture, partly or wholly contrapuntal: they're past before you can say blast you.

I felt thoroughly depressed after this event, surrounded by collective enthusiasm about nothing, about 'that marvellous performance' of 'that marvellous work' which couldn't be heard—when, the morning after, Susan Bradshaw, the distinguished interpreter of contemporary music who had taken part in the performance, rang me at my office, making me think that this was a business call, of which there are many between us. But it was psychological business, artistic business, lonely business: she had felt extremely depressed after the performance, and found herself surrounded by collective enthusiasm . . . It was a telephone conversation that threw the automatic identification of the established majority verdict with 'objectivity', and of individual judgment with 'subjectivity', into a perspective which the fascist and the democratic spirit alike find incomprehensible, imperceptible. There is no excuse for what is known as established authority, nor for the absence of real authority; there is no substitute for the authority of knowledge and insight.

Harmonic chaos, if not indeed the threatening death of harmony, is, to my mind, the most frightening aspect of our creative situation altogether. If it is agreed that a maximal differentiation of expressive means makes possible maximal expression, in the sense not of any chronic expressionism, but simply of saying as much as can be said that's new and true, the continuing abandonment of developmental harmony would mean a regressive

203

withdrawal from communicative positions attained after centuries of selfless struggle for the most comprehensive truthfulness, and maintained by Schoenberg, the chief if guiltless villain of the story, in the face of heavy if self-created odds. The primitive diatonic or mildly chromatic fumblings which some of our younger composers indulge in by way of an understandable, but plainly incompetent reaction against the threat are no cure; in fact, it is not a cure that is needed, but sheer creative conscience, independent of that gamesmanship which so readily replaces it, and dependent, unreservedly, on that ear which, as Schoenberg once said, 'is the musician's sole brain'. The way we, some of us, can still hear harmony, forehear harmony, and hence understand the creative contradictions of what we forehear, is part and parcel of the most evolved kind of conscious experience and sheer reasoning the human mind has shown itself capable of, an indispensable element of that definition and transmission of truth which, the same some of us think, cognitive life is about. There can be no decline of harmony without incisive stupefaction.

In such circumstances, 1975 offered an experience, right at the end of the year, on December 8 in fact, which made one ask oneself whether the solstice then approaching was, perhaps, conceivable if not yet perceivable in the hemisphere of harmony too—whether one worried too much: natural musicality suddenly seemed inextinguishable, where the day before one had foreseen the possibility of the end of music as we know it, or at least the likelihood of its hibernation over many decades, perhaps a century—which would not surprise Oswald Spengler for one.

It happened in the most unlikely corner of our musical

204

world, and the newest too. Let me first of all explain my frequently reconsidered attitude towards electronic music —which is really part of my attitude towards colour, especially since pitch is but a dimension of colour, as Schoenberg points out at the end of his book on *Harmony*.

There is no denying the possibilities of new expression which the production of electronic sounds offers, while the exclusion of the human player, which is a disadvantage, may well eventually be offset by new means of humanisation, unthought-of in the world of instrumental and vocal music. It is indeed mildly entertaining to find that most of the sworn enemies of electronic music are gramophone addicts. For the repeated playing of a gramophone record is really the musically dehumanising act *par excellence*: a unique performance (which it ought to be, though more often than not it's a non-performance produced by retakes being stuck together), the result of unrepeatable inspiration because all inspiration is unrepeatable, is degraded to the level of increasing — and finally utter — forehearability, mechanised out of human existence, schematicised and finally killed, without the recipient of the ever more hypnotic and ever less communicative sound-event becoming aware of the fact that he is carrying a corpse around with him, maybe because he is not all that alive himself. Electronic music, at least, is constructed in a way which renders the human interpreter irrelevant, whereas human performances on gramophone record are an insult to any score which has been constructed with a view to ever different, ever differently searching interpretations.

That said, it remains a crude fact that to date, there are but few children with the sound of electronic music in

205

their ears, and the imaginative potentialities which the new medium offers: for once, the overworked noun is justified. But instinctive invention without instinctively concrete sound-ideals is impossible, and such instinctiveness is acquired in childhood, if the instinctive is to sound as compelling as if it were instinctual. The communicative (rather than merely stimulating) power of colour, moreover, depends as much on tensions between foreground and background as the communicativeness of all other elements of expression: a colour is at its most expressive when it meaningfully replaces an expected colour.

Hardly any electronic colours (or microtones, for that matter) are as yet instinctively expected — with one of two likely results: either the electronic sound, *qua* sound, meaningfully contradicts extra-electronic (instrumental or vocal) expectations which it succeeds in conjuring up, most easily by actually using these extraneous sources (Stockhausen), but also by reminding us of them (Ligéti's *Articulation* of 1958), or indeed by combining live and electronic music, or else the finished product is, colouristically at any rate, one-dimensional, all foreground again, with the additional disadvantage that the sound as such doesn't 'click' with the listener; it probably hasn't clicked with the composer in the first place, because he didn't really have it in his inner ear before he started composing but, more likely than not, arrived at it experimentally. György Ligéti, by far the most precise and specific among advanced ears, abandoned electronic composition because he was unable exactly to reproduce what he imagined — and, paradoxically, started to imitate electronic sound in his instrumental compositions, using *it* as a background: that's advancedness for you. One gathers that he is now about to return to electronics, in view of the refined methods of sound-production which have become available in the United States.

A few outstanding examples apart, then, which succeed against the most unfavourable historical and psychological odds[26], my attitude towards electronic music is sceptical, strictly temporarily so. From the harmonic point of view, certainly, we have not yet had much functional joy from electronic sounds, all the less so since the manufacture of unheard combinations of pitches (frequencies) is child's play — and isn't: once it becomes child's play all will be potentially well.

The greater and more gratifying my surprise, therefore, when I heard Luciano Berio's *Chants Parallels* on the afore-mentioned date—when the first hearing in this country of the work's first public hearing took place on Radio 3: the seeming pleonasm is factual and exposes one of the difficulties of electronic music—the eventlessness of the public event. It took Berio close on two months to prepare the tape. It was first played in public in Paris (on April 7, 1975), being 'staged' by Radio France and promoted by the European Broadcasting Union, which had, in fact, commissioned the work. This public hearing was directly relayed by various European radio organisations; the only audible element in this directness, the only live factor, was, of course, the applause after the playing of the tape. For purely practical reasons, the BBC deferred the relay, applause and all.

---

[26] By now, Stockhausen's *Gesang der Jünglinge* (1955-56) is an almost old-fashioned classic, and his *Hymnen* (1966 to '69 — an electronic *cum* vocal *cum* instrumental work) would be if it weren't so long, battering us into submission. His *Telemusic* (1966), too, must be included among the exceptions.

At the beginning and end of what turns out to be an extended ternary arch, not shorter (23′) than some mature Haydn string quartets with their four separate movements, the composer shows himself intensely aware of the need for backgrounds, not only by using the (electronically treated) human voice, but also by establishing an almost primitive harmonic basis with distinct pentatonic[37] implications — a 'popular mode', as Berio has described it. But the work does not confine itself to five notes; on the contrary, it contains three more pitches than the chromatic scale has to offer — fifteen frequencies, in fact. They are used against a well-implied harmonic background, with the keynote, A, being heard throughout the piece, like a combination of an ostinato and a pedal[38]. I went to the trouble of asking the composer whether my hearing a background, a framework of A-chiefly-minor (but also pentatonically major) was a projection, whether my ear read things into the music rather than drawing them out of it. He said — by no means, my hearing confirmed his creative intentions. Now, while I do not wish to suggest that Berio has here created a major masterpiece, while repeated hearings will, in fact, disclose a deliberate primitiveness of structure, the invaluable facts remain, first, that the music makes harmonic sense throughout despite its use of unusual pitches and, secondly, that its structure as a whole is so clearly conceived, palpably two-dimensional

---

[37] 'Pentatonic', in this context, refers to the most prevalent five-note scale, which many folksongs in different parts of the world use. It is, of course, a 'gapped' scale, leaving out the fourth and seventh degrees of the diatonic major scale — C-D-E-G-A in C major.

[38] A sustained note sounding with changing harmonies.

stage by stage, that it holds the attention throughout, even though it is an exercise in staticism, 'beautifully relaxing' (as one studio manager described it to me) rather than exciting, with the level of tension between foreground and background being low, the rate of relaxation (of the background's emerging to the fore) high.

A liberating event in the contemporary situation — liberating not like Cage: liberating us from Cage. But then, Berio is a musical composer. A curious statement to make, this, but tragically relevant in the midst of our chaoses. The trouble is not that there are many unmusical composers around who shouldn't be, who regard, say, one's perfect pitch, or one's ability to hear the slightest distonation, as an affliction or, at best, an atavism totally out of touch with musical life as it is now lived, with present-day biological requirements as it were; the trouble is that many of them have every right to be around and are justly 'leading' — in a state of affairs where unmusical music has a part to play, whether you like it or not, because much music has become too weak to be able to survive without the help of unmusicality or extra-musicality; more of that in Section IV below.

Meanwhile, it cannot be gainsaid that even aside from Cage, the firmament of our century's second half is full of stars which, at any previous stage in the story of our art, would just not have been visible. Personally, I should go so far as to include Karlheinz Stockhausen among them, an intrinsically artistic personality if ever there was one, but not sufficiently gifted musically to make the kind of complete musician a composer had to be in the past; from the moment *Kontra-Punkte* for 10 instruments, an early work (1952-3), appeared upon the scene

('Counter-points', the hyphen being deliberate), it was clear to me that he wrote more than he heard, and his ear has never caught up, which is why, for a time, he sypmathised so much with the Cageian type of chaos. Nevertheless, he has secured himself a niche in the history of composition. He fancies himself at its centre, of course, in the true tradition of German megalomania — or perhaps not so true, for the intriguing thing about Germany's self-appointed genuises, such as Beethoven, Wagner, and Schoenberg, is that the musical world's successive parliaments came to confirm their appointment, however vociferous the opposition at every new division and in the intervening debates which — at any rate so far as Wagner and Schoenberg are concerned — still have not ceased. But against Stockhausen and the smaller semi-musical fry, figures like Berio and Hans Werner Henze stand out with their untimely, downright lonely musicality.

The moon is one thing, a painter's picture of the moon quite another, and György Ligéti is a third. His is the only meaningless — or at least truthless — music that deserves unreserved acceptance, the only chaos that is not empty, the only place outside heaven and earth that is not hell. I do mean his music — not his type of music. For it has become a type, whose imitation can, in our open musical society, both multilingual and languageless, become a self-saving addiction — but these more or less clumsy copies don't save anybody else. I see dozens of them on my daily rounds, I see them go round in formless circles, pathetic attempts at refinements of sonority which will remain as unheard as they were when they were written. What Ligéti really exposes is his ear, and it is quite an ear to expose — compared to which Stockhausen's doesn't

210

exist, and Boulez's, of course, harmonically speaking,
doesn't either. I well remember my outright rejection of
Ligéti when he first burst on the creative scene, though I
did not say much about it in public — just in case I didn't
understand. However Mátyás Seiber, then my closest
musical friend, was powerfully impressed by his ex-
compatriot's novel approach to composition, violently as
it contradicted his own, and we had a heated argument. I
said there was no form, no structure in the sense of
something happening to thematic material; in fact, there
was no thematic material. He said, in effect, so what. I
said the work was superfluous, a replacement of music.
He said so what, what is music, nowadays, and he was
right — and still is, after all these years, the situation
having remained much the same in this dynamic age,
when one era succeeds, indistinguishably, another,
as a 'new' concerto grosso by Vivaldi succeeded its
predecessor.

Ligéti creates an improved moon: he arranges it in a
way which facilitates our meaningful projections. Having
come to the conclusion that God didn't create the moon,
he creates it instead. Having come to the conclusion that
structure is a deadly pursuit in any of the chaoses
produced by the Schoenberg trauma, he concentrates on
texture instead, confines himself to it. And his textural ear
is wellnigh unprecedented, his capacity for textural
differentiation unsurpassable. He may not be saying
anything to speak of, but he expresses or insinuates our
chaotic condition itself with the utmost clarity: if he does
not bring order into chaos, he gives us a chance to order
our ideas about it. Like Stravinsky's in a very different
way, his approach to composition is absolutely unique,
and anybody who has tried to follow either's has done so

211

at his peril: neither has had a successful successor. But where Stravinsky worked by way of what I have called suppressionism, Ligéti simply works by way of exclusionism — the exclusion of the laws of musical thought as we know them, and hence the exclusion of consecutive thought itself.

Nevertheless, by dint of his textural ear, he succeeds where some of the leaders of contemporary developments fail abysmally: his harmony, although it does not, of course, evolve or show any definable movement, is never accidental. His foregrounds are often so close to whatever backgrounds he captures within himself that virtually no tension results — but the two-dimensionality is there, on and off, though again it tends to confine itself to texture, to the so-called diagonal aspect of music. In fact, his music can metaphorically be described as a diagonal without anything around it. He delights in the sounds he confidently makes, and in nothing else: his is the art of original craftsmanship — by no means superfluous at a time when the borderline between art and chaos is not easy to find, and craft, more often than not, is a euphemism for skill at games. Ligéti does not play games; he masters chaos by smilingly accepting it, and ignoring that which it endangers — meaning. 'I am so wonderfully decadent' he said at question-time after one of his lectures. To have, at this point, such a musician's ear in creative action is certainly wonderful; we'll worry about the decadence later, next century. The future of music is not only threatened by chaoses, but also by sheer unmusicality; there is no more musical composer than Ligéti around, none who is less concerned with any extra-musical aspect of his music — anything that doesn't sound.

## IV. Crutches

Paradoxically, then — the adverb has already occurred thrice in this chapter, but that is our age's fault — Ligéti's music, though virtually structure-less in the accepted sense of the concept, is more independent of any extraneous assistance, verbal, visual, or indeed spatial, than that of any other leading figure of the so-called avant-garde. His Second String Quartet (1968) is, in this respect, quite a unique achievement — in a medium which, as has been pointed out (pp. 179 f.), is gravely endangered by our contemporary upheavals in general and, it might be added, by the lack of concrete, instrument-conscious musicality among our composers in particular. The string quartet's texture is at once the most difficult to handle and the most rewarding when handled well, and though Ligéti's Second Quartet has no formal background to speak of, the mere fact that it is, throughout, supremely and successfully alive to texture has turned it into a milestone in the history of the genre's struggle for survival, an achievement compared to which many a more frequently played (and easier) quartet, brimful with one-dimensional, formal preoccupations, is negligible. Ligéti's Second Quartet stands, if not as pure music, then as the next best purely musical thing — indistinguishable from the real thing at any given moment, though not perhaps beyond that moment.

Ligéti, in short, does not use crutches: since he does not care two hoots about structure, since he lets texture take its place, he has no need to agonise over how to prevent his structures from falling over — a fear which, of course, is violently in evidence all over the place.

The romantic composer's need of words or programmes, as explained by the history books, is a partial illusion, at any rate so far as the great composers were concerned. They did not need extraneous *assistance*; what they needed was extraneous *inspiration*. They did not need anything to complete their music or support it; they needed something to inspire them towards its completion, or else to establish a mere formal framework for music which, without it, would not have proved easily acceptable to their musical society — though Mendelssohn's *Songs without Words* succeeded in just that, in showing that the words were really, ultimately, irrelevant from the musical point of view, even in small lyrical forms: his civilised manner makes us overlook the revolutionary shape of his matter (which is in evidence all over the place, including the wrongly hackneyed fiddle Concerto with its first movement's cadenza serving as lead-back overlapping with the recapitulation, or the theme of the last movement turning into an accompaniment in its own recapitulation). Schoenberg, himself the creator of a *Song without Words*[39] which assumed a symbolic position at the stage where twelve-tone technique was born and the help of the word abandoned, summed up the creative situation when he recounted that 'he was deeply ashamed' on the day he discovered

in several Schubert songs, well known to me, that I had absolutely no idea what was going on in the poems on which they were based. But when I had read the poems it became clear to me that I had gained absolutely nothing for the understanding of the songs thereby, since the poems did not make it necessary for me to change my

[39] The sixth, adagio movement of the Serenade, Op. 24, for seven instruments (1921-23) — a crucial work in the development of twelve-tone technique.

conception of the musical interpretation in the slightest degree. On the contrary, it appeared that, without knowing the poem, I had grasped the content, the real content, perhaps even more profoundly than if I had clung to the surface of the mere thoughts expressed in words. For me, even more decisive than this experience was the fact that, inspired by the sound of the first words of the text, I had composed many of my songs straight through to the end without troubling myself in the slightest about the continuation of the poetic events, without even grasping them in the ecstasy of composing, and that only days later I thought of looking back to see just what was the real poetic content of my song[40].

The 'song composer' Schubert, though marginally pre-romantic, is indeed an outstanding example of what the words did and did not mean to the total musician; he, too, came to create songs without words — within his large-scale symphonic compositions, extending varitions of the strophic principle into instrumental music. In the first movement of his A minor String Quartet, for example, the basic tune, which is composed against the clearly audible background of a song, occurs 9 times over, 8 times in the tonic (minor and major). And at the beginning of the body of the first movement of Schumann's A major String Quartet, a two-note song, an emphatic vocal call (is it too fanciful to hear 'Cla-ra!' in the background?), is contrasted with an intrinsically instrumental consequent[41]; the foreground-background

---

[40] 'The Relationship to the Text', *op. cit.,* p. 144.

[41] Antecedent and consequent: terms which have reached us from America (where they probably arrived from Germany: *Vordersatz* and *Nachsatz*), denoting the two parts of a musical statement that stand to each other in the relation of question and answer.

215

tension is heightened by the vocal phrase being a leap where you would expect it to proceed stepwise, and the conjunct motion[42] being characteristically instrumental where you would expect it to be lyrical, vocal.

It is, of course, easy to think of great romantics and post-romantics who seemed to depend on the word to the extent of appearing a little helpless in their instrumental music — even within the German tradition with its powerful instrumental orientation. Weber, Wagner and, in our own century (if you will allow me his greatness), Hans Pfitzner spring to mind; the fact, incidentally, that we have reached the last quarter of this century without an English production of his *magnum opus,* the opera *Palestrina* (1912-15), is a cultural scandal.

Upon closer inspection, however, we find that the word or verbal drama was as much of an inspiration in their cases, and as little of a crutch, as in the case of a Schubert, Mendelssohn or Schumann. Not only does their operatic music make complete sense as music alone, enriching the word rather than being enriched by it, but the inspiration of verbal drama gave rise to complex, *purely instrumental* edifices where, without such inspiration, these geniuses behaved far more primitively when writing instrumental music. Examples are the instrumental masterpiece that is the *Freischütz* Overture, the *Tristan* and *Mastersingers* Preludes, and the Prelude to, and interludes from Pfitzner's *Palestrina* too—which, despite our neglect of this opera, have become concert pieces in this country.

For 1975's chaotics, the role of the word and of other extra-musical means of communication or stimulation,

---

[42] Conjunct motion: steps. Disjunct motion: leaps.

aural or visual or both, was altogether different. (Tactile means haven't come in yet at the time of writing; on the contrary, they went out with the instruments — in electronic music.) Like old, cantakerous men — which is what they were with their long, heavy past which they couldn't bear but frequently kept either recounting *ad absurdum.et nauseam,* or else denying by acting young —like geriatrically attested intruders into society, they used their crutches not only for the purpose of walking or, more often, just standing up, but also aggressively, violently: with their help, they tried to knock some sense into music, come what may. Gone and future are the days when music showed (and will show) itself capable of knocking sense into the most idiotic words—of which there are many in Mozart's *Entführung aus dem Serail* and even in the sacrosanct *Magic Flute* (blessed are those who don't really understand the original German), as well as, self-created, in Wagner, the bit about German art in the third act of *The Mastersingers* taking, perhaps, the cake. In fact, great music about rotten words used to be, if not the rule, at least one respectable rule among many, whereas our century, heeding music's loss of potency, has decided, unofficially, to let rotten music about great words go with impunity: where music had the power to turn nothing into something, it now manages to turn something into nothing.

When the words are not in the music, they are around it. It is almost unimaginable that there was a time, not so very long ago, when a composer did not feel joyfully obliged to explain who and what he was and wasn't, when his own programme note, and/or his pages of instructions in front of the score, did not form part of the work, which was sufficiently two-dimensional to explain itself

217

—i.e. for the background to explain the foreground. Schoenberg, with all his theoretical preoccupations, with his need, acute and chronic at the same time, to justify what he was — or rather, had been — doing, left most of his music without verbal introductions, one of the few exceptions being the note for the first performance of *The Book of the Hanging Gardens* (1908), the so-called Stefan George Songs, where listeners were told about that plunge into the boiling sea; but there was nothing specific in this note about the music itself, which had to be taken or left and, admittedly, was left — at any rate for the time being. By 1975, it was only the conservative composer, usually insignificant (all background) but, once or twice, of towering significance (Britten, to a lesser degree Tippett and, among the too little known, Robert Simpson), who left his music unsurrounded by explanations of what it meant.

Otherwise, even on the highest level and in palpably opposing positions, our guiding lights have continued to illuminate their darkness verbally — or have tried to, anyway: when all is said and little done, the respective laws of musical and verbal thought remain in deadly opposition, and while it is possible both to describe and (inadequately) to analyse music in words, it is impossible so to explain its content — unless it's bad music, attempting to express a substance which ought to have been conveyed verbally in the first place, in which case it's the music itself that finds itself at a loss to explain much.

These palpably opposing positions are, for instance, Boulez's and Stockhausen's, both of whom continue to introduce what, sometimes unjustly, they fear to be inaccessible music; in any case, their words aren't all that accessible either. In the case of Stockhausen, in particular, the verbal introductions and explanations can be of a vagueness and inconsistence which, fortunately, the music but rarely shares; anybody who has tried to translate them into another language will immediately see what I mean, translation being a uniquely powerful agent in the fight against pollution of the intellectual atmosphere (gas and hot air)—especially translation from the German. At the same time, it must be admitted that when you listen to Stockhausen talking about what he has done or wants to do, you are not left in the slightest doubt about the force of his artistic personality — which, alas, has not been granted commensurate talent, either musically or verbally: he can't get it all out, either way. In this respect — and never mind the idiom — he has always reminded me of Vaughan Williams, whose artistic personality, likewise, was stronger than his talent, with the result that only sympathisers, those attuned to his creative character, get the whole message — the unarticulated part, too.

There are private as well as public verbal crutches: arrested in his development by the effect of the Schoenberg trauma, by the split-up and partial extinction of language and the accompanying loss or lack of security in this wide-open musical society, the weaker composer (i.e. everybody barring the strongest) has turned into the eternal student, projecting his musical superego on to whatever father figure is available — or, at the very least, on to an elder-brother figure. The *sequela* is compositional consultation — unknown, again, at any previous critical juncture in our history. Composers' Weekends, Composers' Workshops, Composers' Seminars, International Festivals of Contemporary Music where it is 'good to meet', Donaueschingen Festivals where it is equally infantile or adolescent to meet, interminable exchanges of technical information and, below all, an infinite variety of endless teaching and 'learning' about what is happening and what ought to happen and what oughtn't—all these and many more private verbal crutches keep the lifelong youngster on his legs, though, by their nature, crutches can't keep his music afloat. Throughout my teaching years, more composers have come to see me and, more or less ambivalently, asked my help than should have done, and few have felt able to leave me as early as they should have done, in an attempt to anticipate my making them get rid of me[43]. My 'shoulds' are, of course, idealistic, in that they dream up a grown-up state of compositional affairs which, *pro tempore*, is clearly utopian — a few encouraging exceptions apart. Jonathan Harvey, for instance, first weaned himself and then left me as he grew up creatively; it is no surprise that he has grown into one of our most individual composers. On the theoretical side, Alan Walker, now a highly independent, trans-academic professor of music at McMaster University in Canada, did likewise, as he came to notice the dangers of dependence.

Verbal dependence, our age's unceasing need for parental protection, had of course been there from the moment go — from the very instant of the Schoenberg trauma. On the highest plane, where in calmer times any such dependence would have been inconceivable in a composer once he had passed his student years, the description 'Second Viennese School' is indeed

[43] Cf, Chapter III, p.129.

appropriate so far as its chronic schooling aspect is concerned: if such a thing can be said of those deeply gifted composers, Berg and Webern, we must concede, if we take their potentialities into account, that they never fully grew up; their psychological and verbal dependence on Schoenberg was lifelong. In Berg's case, this perpetual transference situation resulted in an unrealistic and ultimately inhibiting loyalty to dodecaphony. In Webern's case, where there was quite a little negative transference too (his barely suppressed anti-semitism is being kept a careful secret, probably because it had to be kept from Schoenberg in the first place[44]), we have Schoenberg's privately expressed sigh that 'I only have to tell Webern something about what I am doing and he applies it and exaggerates it out of recognition; I oughtn't to tell him anything any more.'[45]

But such silence wouldn't have been the solution. The need for verbal crutches, parental and extra-parental, is an inevitable function of the crisis, and symptomatic treatment won't resolve it. For the moment, it seems that the crisis can only be smoothly resolved on the genius level. Nikos Skalkottas left Schoenberg with eventual ease, and without a trace of the dependence remaining: that much is clear from what we know of his mature music. We know the opposite from the music of Berg and Webern.

Visual crutches come in expected and, to begin with, unexpected sizes and shapes. What was expected was the

---

[44] My Swiss pupil Hansjörg Pauli has made a special study of Webern's real life; when I last talked to him he intended to produce a television documentary about it.

[45] Oral communication to me by Erwin Stein.

help of the stage, or of visible dramatic action anyway: ever since Boulez announced the death of opera, which apparently took place after Alban Berg had unfinished his opera *Lulu*, composers (except for those who, like Britten, didn't notice) have been careful to keep their visibilities out of the area to which the four-letter word *Oper* could apply—or, if they just couldn't move too far away, they've called it 'music theatre', and will continue to do so, in the hope that theatre music may be allowed to be less than music.

But visual drama is not confined to impersonations. Mere personations, if I may so call them, are another type of widely used crutches, aided and abetted in their turn by our 'new' space-consciousness which, in reality— a reality with which every simple music lover is familiar —is as old as are the opposing choruses in the St Matthew Passion. It is, of course, the performers that are the personators: they enact their own role, moving around or standing up—anything to take your mind off the absence of two-dimensional music. Not always, though; let me hasten to bę fair. As with words, what is a crutch to one composer becomes a functional — here visual — background for another: in this country, Thea Musgrave, in particular, has achieved distinctly musical person-ations.

Spatially organised music itself, whether it has a visual aspect or not (and with the help of stereophony, quadrophony etc. it can dispense with the visual dimen-sion altogether), should not arouse our *a priori* suspicions just because most of it limps along with the help of these spatial crutches; again, some of it makes space as intrinsic a part of the music as instrumentation is or should be: Luciano Berio emerges once more as an

222

outstandingly natural manipulator of spatial possibilities. But if space can be as important as instrumentation, it is also as unimportant. An episode during Schoenberg's class teaching springs to mind. 'What is "good music",' asked a student, 'could you explain, define?' Schoenberg was ready with an anti-academic answer: 'If you transcribe something for the zither, and it still sounds like good music, that's good music.' If you hear a spatial piece on your mono set and it still makes sense, that's meaningful music.

'Mixed media' is a ridiculous innovatory term, however impressive one or two specimens (not more!) of the genre: as if Wagner hadn't mixed his media! But though he called the mixture *Gesamtkunstwerk* (the total work of art), he accepted, in effect, the primacy of music — fortunately so: the *Gesamtkunstwerk* has meanwhile been forgotten, but his music will always be remembered. John Brown is unlikely to succeed where Wagner failed, although he has added plenty of media to Wagner's, mixing them even within the acoustic dimension, by adding electronics, radiophonic tricks, and a vast assortment of odd noises to what, without them, would be a blatantly thin score. The very phrase 'mixed media' has had a magical effect, that of an omnipotent crutch; in 1975, this English term travelled round various languages on the continent of Europe. No wonder: it comprises the widest assembly of contrasting crutches upon the contemporary scene. Cagery apart, a mixed-media work is the only possibility of saying absolutely nothing — if, that is, you are sufficiently unmusical. If you aren't, occasional meaning will emerge from behind your pretensions to meaning.

Before we leave visual aids altogether, and penulti-

223

mately in our array of crutches, let us glance at what, to the more musical among us, is the most surprising of them all — sheer notation. What, musically, cannot escape the suspicion of being a downright swindle — guilty unless proved innocent by the ear — ranges from picture music, which is the musical interpretation of something that looks good as an abstract pattern, regardless of its musical implications (if any), to innovatory symbolology, which looks jolly complicated while you peruse the score's introductory pages explaining it all, but which, more often than not, is more primitive *in toto* than the highly developed system of notation, or those parts of that system, which it replaces. Notation should continue to develop, of course — but only as a result of specific musical thoughts which cannot be adequately represented by conventional notation; the obverse relation, to wit, the hopeful conjuring up of musical thoughts by novel notation, signifies our extreme need for crutches. For the rest, the beautiful picture which a manuscript by Bach or Wagner presents cannot, of course, be denied; the point is that it does not improve the music in any way, or one's experience of the music: Beethoven's manuscripts, often illegible except to the initiated, hardly turn the composer into a second-rater.

And so to the last, purely aural pair of crutches; at least, it usually is a pair, for this particular type of crutch but rarely appears singly. It is not, perhaps, an altogether surprising type; what is surprising, and at the same time depressingly significant, is that it has remained wholly unnoticed. Composer and listener alike seem to need these crutches frantically, which is why the listener, be he critic or mere recipient, passes them over in silence. Yet they are the most easily detectable of the lot. No expert knowledge, no particularly refined ear is needed to spot them, even if they may not always be precisely identifiable. As a matter of fact, their whole purpose would come to nought if there were any particular difficulty in perceiving them; they depend on being heard, and consciously heard, for what they are. 1975 was full of them, but so was every preceding year of the past half-century — yet nobody (except for myself in a lecture centrally addressed to composers) has ever talked about them. Why am I going on like that, without immediately saying what I'm talking about? Because I want the reader to take part in an experiment whose result, alas, I shall never know; but *he* will, and that is good enough, functional enough for our present purpose. If he still doesn't know what these ultimate crutches are, that is to say, I have proved my case in advance: he himself needs them so much that he regards them as a natural element of composition—contemporary composition, at any rate.

What I am talking about is quotations — simply musical quotations, which have pervaded our century's compositorial scene ever since the Schoenberg trauma. In fact, arrestingly enough, that very trauma itself was introduced by a quotation, and a glaringly meaningful quotation to boot. In the scherzo of Schoenberg's Second Quartet, as things are beginning to hot up before the finale's plunge into the boiling sea, Schoenberg quotes and treats the opening of the Austrian folksong, 'Ach, du lieber Augustin, alles ist hin' (Oh, my dear Augustin, all's gone), which is said to date from the time of the plague in Vienna. There is, one gathers, a biographical reason for the inclusion of the song, i.e. the involvement of Schoenberg's first wife with a painter, Richard Gerstl, but we know from Freud that psychic events are

225

'over-determined'[46], and the other, musically obvious determinant is perhaps of more lasting interest: it cannot possibly be imagined that the insertion of a song about all being gone just before all (key) goes, before the home (key) is broken up, does not point to a causal connection. It might, on the contrary, even be suggested that the domestic tragedy precipitated the musical trauma, in which case it would be poor Mrs Schoenberg the First who would be partly to blame for Schoenberg's having come too soon — his atonal self, anyway.

The supreme analytic interest of this use of a widely popular folksong, universally known in German-speaking countries, is that it occurs at the brink: the universal language is about to be lost, together with the backgrounds it has provided. 'Ach, du lieber Augustin', on the other hand, is a common background if ever there was one.

Schoenberg, then, was the prophet not only of our age's revolution, but also of its reactive conservatisms, of which quotations are both the most widespread and the most literal example: what better conservation is there than quotation? It would be impossible to give a representative list of our era's quotations: they are well-nigh all-pervasive — so that it would be easier, in fact, to compose a list of, say, those of 1975's works

---

46 It is a highly descriptive term, but cannot be accepted as reasonable, in any way tenable: things are either determined or aren't; they can't be over-determined. If you remove a cause and the event still happens the same way, it isn't a cause — though, in other circumstances, it could be. Thomas Szasz's objection (oral communication), moreover, is that it is absurd to imply that any psychic event can ever have a single motive and no more than that. He thinks my objection is more logical and scientific, I think his objection is psychologically more illuminating.

which don't quote. And even those which don't, tend to throw yearning glances at the possibility of quotations, aware of the efficacy of these strictly musical crutches — the only intra-musical crutches available in 1975's rich warehouse. The 'popular' beginning and end of Berio's afore-mentioned *Chants Parallels* (1974-75), for instance, are as-if quotations: helped by the human voice and pentatonicism, they are experienced as a background which, itself, is composed against the close background of a folksong. However, people do not, of course, only quote from the remote past, but also, self-assuringly, dependently, brother-seekingly, from the present — and, of course, from themselves. When Elisabeth Schwarzkopf appeared on 'Desert Island Discs' the other year, she chiefly played her own records; many a contemporary composer, stranded on his own island, has evinced the need for similar narcissistic withdrawal: if one talks to oneself, the risk of misunderstanding or downright incomprehension is reduced. Karlheinz Stockhausen not only distorts national anthems, but also gently reintroduces material from his own work — though it must be conceded that he makes it form a legitimate background, so long as you are acquainted with it (which, needless to add, he assumes as a matter of course).

I have left quotations last in my catalogue of crutches, not merely in order to finish this part of our investigation on a modestly hopeful, i.e. musical, note, but also because they prototypically demonstrate the precise relation between the need for crutches and the anxiety over lost, endangered, or ill-defined backgrounds. What, in other words, the crutches are supposed to do is to replace, strengthen or clarify backgrounds. This, at any rate, is the creative hope; it has to be jolly creative in order to prove realistic—which is another way of saying that our time's tragedy is, pre-eminently, the tragedy of the not-so-great composer.

One radical solution is left. You can throw away all crutches and sit or even lie down for good. The artist's abandonment of art, and the art lover's too, is the age's unique extreme reaction to its unique crisis. We can, in fact, trace the con-fusion (from *confundere*, to pour together) of art and life all over the place, replacing art about life, art that sees through life—and, incidentally, democratically abolishing the need for artistic talent, let alone genius. The inevitable result is neither art nor life: more or less primitive games, or any of the other chaoses, replace either, until the individual in question, whether creator or recipient, is safely embedded in the delusion that he is pursuing and experiencing both. In any case, once there is no communication, the river between the land of creation and the land of apperception evaporates: nothing remains to be crossed. Instead, there is the do-it-yourself kit—and the work of art postulated by the previously-cited psychoanalyst acquaintance of mine or by Thomas Szasz (see my opening remarks in Section I): we must grant these psychological observers the right to base their definitions of art on contemporary experience, on the dictates of the spirit of the times—or of one of those spirits, anyway: they are many and they are in disarray.

Or must we? We have no right to be victims of the times. Victory in the face of victimisation is among the ultimate human achievements. Our psychological friends have given in to the abolition of art, of the need for unique communication; they identify that which provocatively hides (the patient's free associations, judge Schreber's delusions) with that which discloses, and no longer see the fundamental difference between somebody who is trying to say something old to someone, any-old-how, in order to save himself, and somebody who is succeeding in saying something new to all who can take it, and says it as translucently as possible, in order to serve and save them—in order, simply, to serve a truth that concerns them. A Beethoven, a neurotic patient and a psychotic don't share any traits which enlighten us about the essence of art—numerous as are the boring traits which they do share.

## V. Closed Worlds within an Open Society

What the disintegration and fragmentation of our musical society with its linguistic turmoil has produced is, paradoxically again, the overwhelming need for the kind of primitive protection and psychological legitim-isation which, alas, only a closed society is able to offer. The result is the worst of both worlds—linguistic estrangement and alienation on the one hand and the inability to be, think, or work alone on the other. The one thing which the typical contemporary composer cannot bear is the loneliness of individual thought; the absence of a collective language frightens him out of his wits and into one or the other form of linking up with someone, something, anything, so long as he can justify his creative existence that way—really or imaginarily. By the typical contemporary composer I mean, of course, the 'instand-ing' one, as it were; outstandingness cannot, by defini-tion, be typical.

Schopenhauer said that you couldn't possibly

judge a nation (the Germans!) by its geniuses; nor indeed are they ever characteristic of their times. Most of the interest of the work of a Dittersdorf or Boccherini is historical: it lies in these composers' representation and expression of their times, and the more background-ridden their foregrounds are, the more they tell us about that particular stage in the history of our musical world. The time-boundness of a Haydn or Mozart, on the other hand, is the least interesting aspect of his work; in fact, up to the age of 19 in the case of Mozart, and 40 in the case of Haydn, there is a great deal of time-boundness and a proportionate amount of boredom: genius had not yet erupted. But thereafter, it is these composers' timelessness that grips us. No act of the so-called historical imagination (is there such a thing, or is it imaginary imagination?) is needed for you and me, as distinct from Pierre Boulez, to be deeply excited by, say, a Mozart string quintet from his mature years: to us it is as contemporary as is a Schoenberg string quartet, if we understand it.

It is what removes these composers from their times (and, mark you, doesn't move them into any other) that involves us—their extremely individual foregrounds contradicting the backgrounds that are their times, and the days before their times.

Nevertheless, the instanding composers of Haydn's and Mozart's era (the Dittersdorfs and, I assure you, worse) had this to be said in their favour—that they worked like beavers in order to provide Haydn and Mozart with the backgrounds they needed for the sharply defined foregrounds whose understanding has proved independent of temporal circumstances. It was a thankless task, but they didn't notice—and, in any case, it was a much easier, more self-solving task than that with which a Mozart or Haydn saddled himself, dissatisfied with the automatic solution of his earlier years. A judge Schreber creates and exposes imaginary problems which he fails to solve; a creative, inspired judge of the artistic situation discovers, and keeps to himself, real problems which he proceeds to solve: we only hear about them once he's solved them and presents us with the solutions.

But nowadays, the solutions are difficult for the most inspired, because our Dittersdorfs and Boccherinis, who are legion, are not in a position to supply backgrounds. Instead, they err about in their backgroundless foregrounds, seeking help, support, parents and siblings wherever they can find them—seeking, above all, the illusion of comprehensibility, or else the illusoriness of the very act of musical comprehension, the legitimisation of futility and of any game that makes us forget the aimlessness of it all, at least temporarily.

The upshot is, yet again paradoxically, that the loss of a collective language has produced a wellnigh total lack of individualism, except on the very highest level, where newly old backgrounds are being carved out slowly and painfully. Elsewhere, our recognition of a composer's personality usually depends on our ability to identify his mannerisms—of which there tend to be quite a few around in all conscience. But such frantic attempts at individuation apart, he will invariably turn out to be a member of one or more collectivities which, themselves, rarely evolve far enough to produce a proper language and, with it, a reservoir of backgrounds; rather, they extend a protective umbrella over anybody who subscribes to their particular aim in art, which is almost always a so-called 'technical' aim (whatever that may

231

be), and which satisfies the middle-aged young composer's externalised conscience simply by giving him something to do, something to play around with in his backgroundless foregrounds—something, also, not to do: prohibition is one of the most blissful drugs, even when it prevents one from using a drug, because it enables one to assert with certitude what others are doing wrong. Thus, while we live our art without a framework, in a free for all, it is not everybody for himself, because he rightly fears he may go under, psychologically and professionally, if he isolates himself; needless to add, he may go under anyway.

Surprisingly, however, the situation is most overtly encouraging at the Cageian end, not only because we encounter elemental (and elementary) attempts at communication where the composer aims at the opposite, yet can't help himself, his expressive self, but also because even those who succeed better than most in saying nothing, whatever it is they want to do instead, sooner or later betray an instinctive if rudimentary conscience about there being something amiss, however dutifully they follow the laws of their collectivities and, for the rest, try to let their consciences rest in peace.

A young composer—20 or 50, it doesn't matter—comes to see me to 'show me his work'—a sufficiently ambiguous phrase, always, to guarantee anticipatory ambivalence: I am not to know whether I am to act as a consultant, adviser, teacher, guinea pig—or simply as an establishment pig: if the establishment but knew that I am considered one of their pigs! In any case, naive as I try to remain, I invariably look forward to the experience. I open the score and first attempt to read and memorise the instructions, which are usually a lesson in new notation. The task turns out to be superable, because I have seen most of them before, as trademarks of one or the other collectivity of my acquaintance.

So far, things don't look too Cageian, but as I reach the first pages of the actual music, occasional half-hearted attempts at the definition of a motif or the characterisation of a phrase apart, there seems to be no firm creative intention, far less any desire to achieve continuity on the one hand and contrast on the other; instead, there is the inevitable sporadic shock treatment, the latest type of old-fashionedness, to which there is much collective commitment, without regard for the fact that all naughty shocks are over, spent, have been assimilated. Now and again, however, there is this elemental flash of attempted communication, as distinct from mere exclamation akin to the bark of a dog, and I am encouraged to treat the score as if it were real music, and to react to it as if I were supposed to understand it. 'This', I say with trepidation, pointing to a passage that comes out of nowhere and returns thereto, 'doesn't make sense.'

The composer's reply is immediate and triumphant: 'It isn't supposed to.' 'So what is it supposed to do?' 'Exactly what it does to you. You are bewildered. You've been pulled up.' Residual charity prevents me from suggesting that I am merely bored—and, in any case, I would only be told that that was precisely what I was supposed to be. I do, however, venture a question: 'If you know that I am asking for sense and can anticipate my reaction, and if you don't want to make sense, what do you come to see me for? What do you want to pay me for? If I am mere audience, isn't it me who ought to pay you? Except that I haven't asked for the entertainment.'

233

There is no reply to this one—which is what I find encouraging: there are father figures and father figures, and the composer has come to see me, not in the hope of finding a suitable father, but because he still has a bit of a real artistic conscience about my unsuitability—about sense. The desire to make sense is human, exclusively human: it is unlikely that humanity will, for ever, renounce it.

It is for opposite reasons, then, that eighteenth-century mediocrities on the one hand and, on the other, 'advanced' twentieth-century composers anywhere below the level of superior talent are not readily distinguishable —the former because they all write more or less the same background and little else, the latter because they all write one or the other fashionable foreground and little else.

At the same time, across the cleft produced by the Schoenberg trauma and still not closed after the better part of a century, real composers don't even recognise each other, in either sense of the verb—even though their recognisability may be quite exceptional. Take Boulez and Britten, both far above any collectivity, both, on a conservative estimate, among the age's supreme talents. I think enough time has passed, enough aggression been spent, to tell a relevant story of self-evident significance. When I first joined the BBC, as Music Talks Producer, I had the idea of inviting one or two leading composers to take part in a symposium on the problems which form the subject matter of the present essay.

I first invited Mátyás Seiber, who said yes. Next I wrote to Benjamin Britten who, surprisingly, did not say no—perhaps because he didn't want to hurt me; he certainly was not enamoured of verbalisation — about

234

music, anyway, which was why he liked my wordless method of analysis.

Last, I wrote to Pierre Boulez in Paris, whom I did not then know. I told him of the two likely participants, and expressed the hope that he would see both the central interest of the subject and the absolute need to have sharply contrasting, leading creative personalities discuss it.

He replied by return of post—but I have to quote from memory, as I have since committed his letter to the waste-paper basket. However, I don't think he will contradict me when he comes to read these lines; all they will produce will be an unremembering smile:

Dear Mr Keller,
I agree that it would be very important to have a discussion on the subject of contemporary composition. But I only discuss this subject with musicians; since I cannot find any among the names you suggest, I have to decline your invitation.

Mátyás Seiber just laughed when I told him: his view of our open musical society and the isolated musical positions within it was complete. Britten I never told at all: I did not want to intensify his prejudices against the avant-garde.

Pierre Boulez has grown milder, more charming, less defensive, more straightforwardly human as a person— but I don't think his deaf spots have changed in the slightest, and these spots have an imposing diameter. He does not, in 1977, recognise the stature of Benjamin Britten any more than he did eighteen years ago (remember all those dead operas Britten wrote after Alban Berg's *Lulu!*), and I should hazard the guess that

235

he would not be able to recognise Britten's mature music when he heard it—except, perhaps, if he happened to come across one or two of those characteristics of Britten's which he would be able to misidentify as mannerisms. Britten himself remained too polite to express himself about Boulez's music — and I should think, too wisely indifferent from his own point of view, but again there is, conversely, no doubt that he could not grant it artistic recognition, and would not in fact have been able to recognise it as Boulez's. Such total mutual incomprehension would be a tedious story — incomprehension is never exciting except to those who don't understand — but for its glaring symptomatic significance: there could be no more violent illustration of the total closures that are possible, on the highest level of ability and achievement, within our wide-open musical world.

## VI. Second-round Marxism: the Crisis of Commitment

The most hermetic of these closures brings us back to the starting-point of our reflections on 1975 — Chapter II. Just as the Schoenberg trauma had, by way of extreme reaction, produced Dadaism in music (of all the arts!), and then, generations later, a second round of this anti-art movement, i.e. the Cage wave, so the musical society opened up by Schoenberg has given rise to two eras of musical Marxism; we are in the middle of the second. Only a single composer in either era succeeded in partaking of both worlds, the Schoenbergian and the Marxist: it was the highly talented Schoenberg pupil Hanns Eisler, who died in East Germany in 1962, and who thought his revered teacher politically naive; whereas Schoenberg thought it naive of Eisler, a born composer, to concern himself with politics. Otherwise, the closest the not so open Schoenbergian world got to the closed Marxist world was through the Italian communist, Luigi Nono, marrying Schoenberg's daughter Nuria—in itself, perhaps, an act of more than personal significance, in that every budding Marxist seems to need a lavish measure of ambivalence, which he calls dialectics: Marx, Lenin, and Engels themselves had given the cue to unconscious two-facedness, appealing as they did to the more primitive layers of the human mind without wanting to—at least in the case of Marx and Engels. Nono himself, as we learnt from a book published in 1975[47], has resolved his ambivalence by way of delusion: Schoenberg's *Moses and Aron* and his *Survivor from Warsaw* are turned into downright Marxist achievements!

Italy harbours another outstanding communist composer, and 'harbour' is the word: Italy is the haven to which he has escaped from his much behated Germany —in the best tradition of Germany's leading spirits (many of whom have, down the ages, sought refuge from the blessings of the fatherland, including even Wagner, whom we wrongly regard as a raving nationalist, whereas he was, in fact, a socialist). But then, every developed mind is a refugee from one or the other type of collective oppression, whatever its flag, its alleged claim to cultural or civilisational fame.

Advisedly, I have not mentioned Hans Werner Henze before: within the context of this essay, he is a test-case for the arguments submitted, not least because of his vast, intrinsically musical gifts. He is the German or

---

[47] Jürg Stenzl (ed.), *op. cit.*

European Britten, if you like, though for my part, I should insert one drastic qualification into this comparison: he's got all or most of Britten's wide-ranging talents—without Britten's genius. This circumstance made him that much more assailable by contemporary, even ephemeral developments, musical and extra-musical. But while he survived his environment's musical influences and interventions, simply through assimilation, because he is big enough (where Britten largely ignored them because he is bigger enough), the extra-musical attraction of second-round Marxism proved too much for the man who had grown up disgusted by Nazism: he did not subordinate his political ideas to the evolution of his musicality, but his musicality and everything else to his political ideas—which weren't his anyway; individual conscience was surrendered in the usual way, moral ends transformed into—dare I so call them?—immoral means towards the all-sanctifying collective ideal.

Of this I had some first-hand experience. As chairman of the international working party which plans the European Broadcasting Union's International Concert Seasons, I was responsible for the choice of Julius Patzak, an old man by then and one of our age's greatest performing musicians (a total musician in spite of being a tenor!), for the part of the speaker in Schoenberg's *Gurrelieder*, which we (the EBU) mounted in 1968. His interpretation (which, as a vocal musician, turned out to be his last, and has fortunately been retained on disc, as part of the complete recording of the event) was quite staggering, beyond verbal description; musically, in terms of notes, one could, I think, describe, though not reproduce it. Suffice it to say that he (who had never done

238

the role before, and was looking forward to it like a youngster) allowed himself slight, but almost compositorial changes in the part, which overwhelmingly enhanced its meaningfulness: at crucial harmonic junctures, he introduced harmonically important *notes* into the speaking part, which thus received an immeasurably sharper profile—nor were they always melodic notes but, on the contrary, concentrated on harmonic definition regardless of melody. One remembered that in his youth, before he decided to become a singer (self-taught: he never had a single singing lesson with anyone), Patzak had been a composition pupil of Schoenberg's coeval Franz Schmidt—now a 'new' name on our musical horizon.

After Patzak's performance, I suggested to the EBU working party (I refuse to call it 'my' working party and to assume leadership outside the authority of my knowledge) that we might commission a work from an outstanding composer which would include a part for speaking voice specially written for Patzak—who, of course, was no longer able to sing.

The choice fell on Henze, with whom I proceeded to discuss the proposition in great detail, in the course of a three-hour lunch which yielded more musical agreement that one would have expected from a Marxist and an extra-Marxist musician. Henze, in short, accepted the commission, and the road seemed clear towards the creation of a work of enduring musical substance which, at the same time, would enable Julius Patzak to crown his achievement with something he had never tried until his old age. We had not, of course, chosen Henze because of his Marxism; that bored the pants off all of us. But we certainly did not want to commit the Marxist mistake of underestimating any talent associated with a dislikeable world-view—sorry, 'ideology'; and we, all of us, thought (and still think) that Henze is one of the age's most important composers, slightly neglected (despite all the money he is earning) because he is out of sympathy and touch with all our 'advanced' societies, and they with him.

The job was duly done, for Henze is what is known as a 'thorough professional' (I call it a master, Wagner not having called his relevant opera 'The Professionals'). Or rather it wasn't, for a Marxist thorough professional, although he gets the job done, does it his way, or rather Marx's or Mao's or some Cuban communist's way, whatever the cost in terms of not meeting the terms of the job. That is to say, what we got instead of what we had asked for was, believe it or not, *The Tedious Path to the House of Natasha Monster (Natascha Ungeheuer* in the original German), without a trace of a part for Patzak in it. We had little reason for musical complaint—the blatant ignoring of Patzak apart. There was, in fact, a great deal of weighty music in this score, and if there were long empty stretches, some of them one would have expected from Henze anyway, Marxism or no (and there was plenty of no before his Marxism started). We took the ideology of the work as something unavoidable — as the price of the ticket for the event, as it were. So there was no complaint: if you commission music nowadays, you're jolly glad if you get music—some of it, anyway.

The fact remains that while we hadn't been cheated (after all, Patzak was not in the contract), we had, as gentlemen, been disappointed, and so had Patzak, without being aware of it. The even more disturbing fact remains that all that mattered to Henze was Natasha

240

Monster, rather than our gentlemen's agreement; it even seemed that Natasha mattered more to him than his own music. For he sacrificed some of it as well as some of our requirements on the altar of his religion, just as he and other believers think nothing of getting as much money as at all possible out of capitalist society, just as the crusaders thought nothing of killing off people in the process of saving mankind. It is said that Beethoven still owes the Royal Philharmonic Society £50 or so, *re* the Ninth Symphony. These musicological preoccupations don't interest me, so I'm afraid I can't report any precise details, nor pass an opinion on whether litigation is advisable (he's got a lot of heirs by now), but what I know as a musician is that in the most dire circumstances, he was incapable of not following the conscience of his individual genius, and that we all owe him a little more than £50 for that—whereas when Henze decided to owe us Patzak for ever, he must have decided to silence his individual conscience, and probably his musical conscience into the bargain, in the service of an ideal which, whatever its merits, has countless deaths and psychological mutilations to answer for, as have virtually all collective ideals that have attained the necessary power.

But then, you may say, Henze is not a genius. I don't know what his own position vis-à-vis the problem of genius is—whether he thinks he is one, or whether he thinks there is none anyway. He is so prodigiously gifted that it's extremely unlikely that he is capable of denying the most incisive gift, for the greater your own insight, the more you respect that different category of insight we call genius, the more you appreciate Schoenberg's differential diagnosis: 'A talent learns from others, genius from himself.' But if he does recognise genius, he is, thereby, committing a heresy, and good luck to him: it hasn't happened since Shostakovich.

However, so far as our neo-Marxists are concerned, the Soviet variety of the creed is out anyhow: just another form of capitalism, and who are we to argue with that. In any event, to the neo-Marxists, genius is absolutely inadmissible. I never really knew, but two dreamlike experiences on the eve of 1975 brought the fact home to me—dreamlike because it was difficult to accept, on those occasions, that one was moving in the real world of art.

One happened at London's Institute of Contemporary Arts, where I was invited to take part, as the only Briton, in a symposium held within the framework of a German Fortnight—West German, that is, but it was communist all the same: the other lecturers, my discussion partners, were all German composers whose music I didn't know, but who, despite lively differences between them, were all representatives of the very newest left, as anti-Henze, in fact, as they were anti-Stockhausen (with whom, like our own leading musical Maoist, Cornelius Cardew, one of them had collaborated). In my innocence, now long lost, I operated, as a matter of intellectual course, with the concept of genius. I might just as well have used the concept of witchcraft. Much as my colleagues disagreed among themselves, they were fervently united in their oh-so-scientific conviction that they had a quasi-medieval character in their midst, and but for the support of the public and, subsequently, the press, I might have come to the momentary conclusion that I had been born into the wrong age; mind you, in that case, I should still have thought that it was the age that was wrong, not I.

The other experience was my perusal of our own

242

Cornelius Cardew's so-called book (a collection of disparate, near-illiterate essays by sundry faithfuls) entitled *Stockhausen Serves Imperialism*. It seems that nobody except for myself has read it, which is rather a pity, not only because the 'áuthor' is, after all, one of the more interesting creative figures upon the contemporary scene, if only potentially so, but also because its very primitiveness enables one to view the collectivist danger to art and life under that microscope which his lack of sophistication places at our disposal.

When Cardew comes to criticise Cage, one of his two ex-good fathers he has duly turned into bad fathers, his projections (with which his writings, like every collectivist's—Hitler's!—abound) produce the mildly amusing and deeply depressing result that what he finds wrong with Cage, we are forced to find wrong with him, centrally so:

The aspect of Cage that engages our fury is his denial of the conscious role of the individual, of responsibility; in denying this, he is guilty of a vicious deception.[48]

This is it: the aspect of Cardew and his band that should engage our well-considered fury is his own denial of the conscious role of the individual, of individual responsibility unsullied by dogma. By abandoning his duty to think as an individual, and enacting the role of a parrot lovingly kept by the late Chairman Mao, Cornelius Cardew is guilty of at least temporary death—his own as well as the death of those whom his thoughtless explosions encourage to surrender (or hire out) the unique value they possess: that of their own individuality and, hence, of their own irreplaceable contribution to the solution of man's problems.

---

[48] *Op. cit.* Latimer New Dimensions, London, 1974, p.46.

It is as simple as that. Everything is, so long as you remain uncorrupted, un-preoccupied with what happens to be the line of least resistance from the standpoint of your own psychological make-up. Self-preoccupation, which is preoccupation with that which one isn't, but *was* in childhood, is original sin, above all when it manifests itself in collectively calming 'selflessness', dehumanising depersonalisation—just as independent thought is original virtue. Your self is the only thing you have, and once you lose it, you cease to respect other selves and their singularity, and even proceed to ignore the highest level of individualism, that of genius and its new insights. Within the same chapter, in the essay which gives Cardew's book its title, he gets down to this very question of genius, telling us that

concurrent with the development of capitalistic private enterprise we see the corresponding development in bourgeois culture of the individual artistic genius. The genius is the characteristic product of bourgeois culture. And just as private enterprise declines in the face of monopolies, so the whole individualistic bourgeois world outlook declines and becomes degenerate, and the concept of genius with it.[49]

All this apropos of Stockhausen, of course. Those of us who never considered Stockhausen a genius in the first place had no need to rid themselves of the concept of genius in order to get rid of Stockhausen—or put him in his place, slightly below the one he assigned for himself: that he appointed himself a genius doesn't invalidate the concept, merely his talent for self-appointment. It is, in short, possible to arrive at an uninflated estimate of

---

[49] *Op. cit.*, pp. 52f.

Stockhausen without gleefully participating in Cardew's 'struggle against the old and decrepit' (belated shades of Nazi language): the vast majority of our music lovers and musicians, however 'imperialist' and/or 'bourgeois' in Cardew's parlance, have no difficulty at all in doing so; if they brought themselves to read this book, they would immediately realise that he was saddling them with his problems, and his problems alone—of how to rid himself of his late father, which is a time-honoured preoccupation of the self-preoccupied.

I have complemented Schoenberg's differentiation between talent and genius, indulging in a purely empirical comparison which I find equally workable—or found equally workable until I faced the problem of Henze: what most attracts our attention in a talent's output is what his works have in common, whereas what is most interesting about a genius's works is the difference between them, the meaningful contrasts on top of their unmistakable unity.

Henze is the exception that doesn't upset the rule—for reasons which retain their interest even if we aren't much taken by the rule. The difference between his pre-Marxist and his Marxist works, that is to say, is fascinating—more so than are the obvious similarities between them. Before his political priorities developed, and in spite of having faced the Schoenberg trauma frontally, absorbing as much of it as he could for the purpose of maximal creative discomfort, he instinctively retained a sufficient variety of distinctly implied backgrounds to be able to compose without crutches, and both with and without words. The weak spots in his pre-Marxist scores, of which—as later—there are plenty, are nothing to do with any crisis of communication within him; they are just due to the fact that as a creative personality, he is not very discriminating—the opposite of Brahms, you might say: where Brahms's self-criticisms were insistently in action, at times to a fault, Henze's enjoyed many a restful slumber. He would, in fact, have produced a similarly uneven output if he had been safely embedded in the eighteenth century. At the same time, as a crutchless walker, even runner, he was quite exceptional among the post-traumatic composers of our age, second only to its few geniuses. Once the un-needed crutches had been acquired, however, his output became glaringly different—intermittently dependent on what he needn't have depended on, thinned out in musical substance to an extent he previously would not, instinctively, have tolerated.

One might have hoped that he shared one other strength with genius, i.e. immunity from collectivism in general and Marxism in particular: Shostakovich, the one genius who showed no such immunity, had no psychological alternative, since he knew no other world; and, as we have seen, he suffered, as a genius, from the consequences ever after. Henze had enough autonomous size to create without crutches, but, in the event, not enough to recognise a crutch in disguise, and the burning question is, why not? The answer would also tell us why so many smaller musical spirits have fallen for the redecorated religion, some of them losing their music altogether in the process, shutting themselves up in this extra-musical, closed society within our musically open one: Cornelius Cardew himself, for instance, hardly concerns himself with music at all in his book—nor, one might add, in any recent compositions one has encountered; there are only crutches and, for the time being, hardly anything is left to lean on them. General paralysis, we need not remind ourselves, is beyond the need for crutches.

When asked the persistent question, 'What is musicality?' I tend to answer that music is to a musical person what water is to a fish—more natural, even, than verbal language, more instinctive, more spontaneously acquired: where there are no inhibitions, the musical child sings, and accurately remembers, 16-bar melodies before he can speak—fitting, in performance, a single word or syllable to the tune in order to make it conceptually respectable to his verbal environment. If he didn't have to grow up in a conceptual world, he would probably dispense with verbal adornment altogether; in any case, by not worrying about the sense of the word he uses, he shows the way towards the primacy of music—which some of us have lost, de-musicalised by a growing-up process which, in harassed times, includes quite a bit of growing down.

So long as there was a general musical language, there was no conceivable psychological need for a musical person, creator or not, to worry about what music was about—unless his personality required him to wonder what anything, everything was about. By 'general language' I simply mean common backgrounds; I have no sympathy with the anti-atonalists' view, still widely (if less and less assertively) held, that diatonicism is more 'natural' than anything that came after. It felt more natural because it was more broadly and deeply understood; but it wasn't better understood because it was more natural. After all, those seemingly eternal and exclusive diatonic scales which produced our past's closed musical society were themselves but two church

247

modes[50] that owed their continued vitality to the survival of the creatively fittest—and what is music without continuing creation?

With the Schoenberg trauma and the ensuing crisis of communication, however, the musical person became aware of his musicality as something to be treasured and preserved, as something threatened by forces which he rightly or wrongly regarded as unmusical, because they presented obstacles in the way of instinctive, childlike musical understanding. It is surely significant that neither the concept of musicality nor that of musical understanding played any role in the eighteenth or nineteenth century: things get names when they threaten not to be there.

Prior to the Schoenberg trauma, whether the age or musical region was dominated by the church or not, there was only one lasting, indeed perpetual aim to which great music (as distinct from utility music used for work and play) attached itself if its creator felt so inclined: I shouldn't call it religion, because the denotation of the term is too narrow, its connotation too specific, but I would call it metaphysics. Throughout the history of music as we know it from actual experience, there has been, to put it as mildly as possible, the distinct suspicion that music comes from God and, having explained or exposed metaphysical reality, goes back to Him, or him, or it, or whatever meaningless word you want to attach to the unverbalisable—goes back as a prayer, if you like.

It is at this point that the typically contemporary, eminently secular reader who has borne with me so far

---

[50] The church modes were the basis of early music until about 1600, and the so-called Ionian and Aeolian modes became our major and (descending melodic) minor scales respectively.

248

and I, the extra-contemporary writer, temporarily part company. It does not really matter: if he will ignore my excursion into metaphysics and turn to page 251, he will be able to resume where he left off: inevitably, I consider my metaphysical declaration essential, but not essential to my argument which, I submit, remains valid whether my metaphysics are an illusion or not—though it must be admitted that if they aren't, the argument does receive additional support, 'over-determination' in Freud's sense.

I think I have developed fairly dependable, objectively verifiable criteria for the evaluation of music—for deciding, that is, what is good music and what isn't, and indeed what is bad music and what isn't: in 1975, there still was a broad no-worth's-land between not good and bad. The special case of Ligéti apart, I have not yet, touch steel, made a demonstrable mistake, nor indeed have I been accused of one, except by one or the other composer of a work I have judged negatively; the majority even of the so criticised have come to agree with me.

But when it comes to the differentiation between great and merely good music, my analytic criteria prove useless, in that I can only show that what's there in good music is there to a far greater extent in great music. However, we know that great music isn't just greater than good music; it's different, to the extent of there being not so good music that's great, as distinct from demonstrably good music that's undemonstrably small. In terms of my theory, there is music that is good in the best sense in that it does not merely meet implied expectations logically, but drastically contradicts them, just as logically; yet, apart from showing that great music contradicts them far more complexly, I am powerless, incapable of expressing the difference in kind—the difference between supreme talent and genius, supreme or not. The difference between, say, Haydn before the age of forty and after, between mere mastery and genius, is of such a fundamental nature that if we gave in to the abolition of the concept of genius, we'd just have to invent a term to indicate what is basically unlike what, who quite unlike whom, despite their shared attributes of high quality. But a term doesn't explain; it merely suggests or confirms agreement.

In order to explain, to myself, the essence of unmistakable greatness or genius in music, I can get no further than remind myself of its revelatory quality, of its direct disclosure, convincing at once, of a plane of reality of which, otherwise, I have no knowledge. In fact, if anything, I have anti-knowledge otherwise: if I can imagine myself to be what I am without being a musician, without being musical, I should be a well-considered agnostic, if not indeed an atheist in the purely scientific sense. As it is, I have to acknowledge, by inference, the reality value at the heart of the religions I detest on humanitarian grounds—which is more or less all of them. I cannot make twice two come out five, naturally as I should feel inclined to do so.

The history of great composition, of great composers, seems to confirm the fact that the essentially metaphysical quality of music cannot be denied. The few among the great whose conceptual attitude towards religion and metaphysics was negative made sure to leave a side-door open to transcendentalism, should it wish to enter despite the occupier's obstreperousness: Brahms's ambivalent *German Requiem*, anti-religious and relig-

250

ious at the same time, is perhaps the most impressive example. In our own age, secular until the day before yesterday when the new, preferably Eastern mysticism came in, the two counter-poles of music postulated by Theodor Wiesengrund Adorno in his *Philosophy of New Music*, Schoenberg and Stravinsky, were heavily committed metaphysically, indeed religiously; and now Karlheinz Stockhausen, justly or not the most prominent figure among the 'classical' (i.e. middle-aged) avant-garde, has joined the mystical ranks. Perhaps, by way of a bridge-passage that will lead the more sceptical reader back to the main course of the argument, it may, more non-committally, be asserted that all the greatest music is philosophically orientated, whether it is overtly religious, like the B minor Mass, the *Missa Solemnis*, the Stravinsky Mass, Britten's *War Requiem*, and Schoenberg's *Moses and Aron*, or indeed more comprehensively philosophical, like a late Beethoven quartet—perhaps musical philosophy's most climactic achievement to date.

If, then, during the era of the closed musical society, within which there was a universal language, great *and* merely good music involved itself in anything outside itself, it was the indescribable—and therefore not really outside itself, since the indescribable could only be described in music.

In dramatic and programme music, insignificant specimens apart (even though they were, of course, in the majority), it was the indescribable behind the describable that was sought—again that which can only be expressed in music. But dramatic action, the word, the story were never the masters, always the servants of good music. The only master, if any, was God, the universe, philosophy, what have you: ultimate truth (Bach, Mozart, Bruckner) or the search for it (Beethoven, Schoenberg). My distinction is inspired by Friedrich Schiller's philosophical differentiation between the 'naive' and the 'sentimental' artist: the former (in my words) is all there, naturally, while the latter, searching, striving, is trying to get there, letting us witness the struggle. Schiller rightly described himself as sentimental, and wrongly (sentimentally!) called Goethe (the creator of the most insistently striving soul in all literature) naive.

Below the genius level, in any case, ultimate commitment was a rarity: music was music and did not oblige one to fit it into the scheme of things. But with the crisis of communication, inevitably, the question, and the crisis, of commitment started: music wasn't music any more, not in the old sense, so what was it, and why was it?

It was, in fact, this crisis of musical commitment which produced the first round of musical Marxism about half a century ago, and the selfsame, continued crisis produces the same result now. And, as we have remarked, the same opposite result: Dada in the twenties, anti-communicative, chance operations still going strong today, if slightly weakening.

Between these two unmusical extremes—extra-musical commitment on the one hand, and meaningless music on the other, our century's prolonged twin crises of communication and commitment have been raging, with only the greatest of the great rising above them. Now Henze is not one of them: he is too worried to be able to see that as a musicality, he needn't be all that worried. Between the small and the great there is that fascinating tiny group of unassessables, all tragic figures: because

252

they aren't great, they don't grow as big as they could. Is there a more moving example of pure tragedy?

It is self-evident that in proportion as the West's general musical language—the reservoir of generally available, graspable backgrounds—disintegrated, all but the strongest creative personalities' sense of insecurity had to increase: 'How do I make myself understood?' led, inescapably, to 'What is it I am trying to have understood, anyway?' Paradisical ignorance of what music was about, eminently musical indifference towards this question, had ceased, had to cease. The two extreme answers have been 'Social change and revolution!' (from the sophisticated Hanns Eisler down the ages to the ultra-naive Cornelius Cardew, and not in Schiller's sense either) and, on the other hand, a hopefully liberating 'Nothing!' (from Dada to Cage and far beyond).

Naturally, where music has become mortally unsafe, musical security is being sought outside music, or else musical insecurity—the dissolution of backgrounds—is being made a virtue of, apotheosised. In the history of the Western world, ours is the first century to pay homage to the God of Non-sense, compared to whom the Golden Calf was a veritable testimony to humanity, for at least it embodied human aspirations, not sheer contempt of them. The Dance Round the Bloody Nonsense fires the other—Marxist—side all the more effectively, and unmusically, to make verbally demonstrable sense, i.e. conceptual sense, with the music either slavishly and pleonastically serving the words, or actually being there in place of words, which are then duly used to demonstrate the sense. In this way, it quite often happens among the untalented, at times downright unmusical composers of the newest left that they logically demonstrate a sense which, without the demonstration, doesn't exist in the music: verbal crutches driven well beyond the extreme limit delineated by the metaphor. Cornelius Cardew's book, for instance, contains, simply, programme notes by various composers and co-believers— on music nobody knows, or indeed need know after he's read the notes, since the notes themselves evidently contain all that the music is supposed to mean.

Now it might be thought that among all the frantic exertions to find fitting crutches, not too short and not too heavy, those of the newest left have this to be said in their favour, that they preserve the dignity of the art at least inasmuch as music is made subservient to a worldview—as, after all, Bach's and Beethoven's and Stravinsky's and Britten's and Schoenberg's was. Indeed, in his most ambitious works, the responsible Marxist wants to encompass the whole world, as Mahler said (to Sibelius) a symphony should; what is more, he 'wants to focus attention on the world's problems', and to 'supply a Marxist solution'. [51]

But there are two decisive differences, the second of which I have tried to adumbrate, between the intrinsically musical approach to philosophy and psychology and the secondarily musical approach, which owes absolute allegiance to scientific materialism. In the first place, that is to say, the metaphysical and/or psychological (operatic) composer's utterances are of *individual* discoveries, whereas the Marxist, and quite especially the neo-Marxist, makes a *collectivist* statement for the purpose of propaganda. The B minor Mass does not

---

[51] Patrick J. Smith, 'Viewpoint: A Question of Sincerity', in *Musical Newsletter*, New York, Spring 1974 (IV/2).

make propaganda for God, and its collectivist text is used for the purpose of accommodating exclusively individual discoveries about the human psyche and its transcendentalism, which are placed in the situation defined by the text: every phrase shows that, bearing the sublime trademark of a Bach discovery.

Thus, in the Marxist's hands, music abrogates its role as a discoverer of truth and becomes, instead, the slave of *professed truth*, of trans-personal dogma: in this sad sense, one obtrusive difference between Marxist music and religious music is that Marxist music is more religious.

But then, there is that other decisive difference between musical music and Marxist music—that at its best, Marxist music, the intended part of its communication, its declared *raison d'être*, still is the expression of something that can better be said by other—verbal—means; whereas musical music, art for art's sake only on the surface, expresses the otherwise inexpressible, verbally or pictorially. It follows ruthlessly that all Marxist music that does not go beyond its intentions (as Nono's or Henze's or, of course, Shostakovich's does) is music by the stupid for the collectively stupefied: if its creators and its listeners moved on a more intelligent plane, they would not rest content with second-hand communication, with mere translations, necessarily inadequate, of conceptual contents into music.

The ultimate degeneration of music as a means of discovery into music as a means towards destruction is unambiguously implied in a dictum of Mao's which is lovingly quoted by Cornelius Cardew:

An army without culture is a dull-witted army, and a dull-witted army cannot defeat the enemy.

Do we realise what this means? The ultimate degradation of truth-finding, of what all un-ideological culture is about. The ultimate conversion of love into hate too, since there is no discovery without love, and no discovery of an enemy without hate. And so far as our own art is concerned, it means the degradation of music into psychological *Gebrauchsmusik*, utility music, Music while you Kill, instead of music without any 'while': they had this in the Nazi concentration camps alright, where Alma Rosé, the daughter of the leader of the Vienna Philharmonic, and at one time the second fiddler in his world-famous quartet, was forced to be one of the performers.

One wonders what, in the end, the enemy is being defeated for: when all victories have been achieved, the need for culture will have peacefully expired. Meanwhile, the perfect neo-Marxist composer, as described at both that symposium at the Institute of Contemporary Arts and in *Stockhausen Serves Imperialism*, is the perfect bore, of interest only to those who aren't really interested in music. There is no substitute for music as an independent mode of thought, just as there is no substitute for conceptualism as an independent mode of thought—not even music. Neo-Marxist musical society has closed its doors to music itself, for music itself is music as such.

## VII. Unmusic

I am leaving out the hyphen in order to indicate the prevalence — not, admittedly, of the word I have, in fact, just invented, but of that which it denotes: just imagine we spelt un-happiness with a hyphen, not to speak of un-musicality. Yet in 1975, the stage was reached when,

256

compared to unmusic, unhappiness and unmusicality were rare phenomena in our civilisation.

Music While You Kill instead of music without any while—that would be one kind of unmusic, safely out of the way for the moment for most of us. But the discomforting fact remains that there is more and more music while you do plenty of other things, and less and less music without any while: the composer's crutches are balanced, on the other side of the communication barrier, by the listener's own crutches until, in frequent extreme cases on either side, it is the music that becomes a crutch without which, say, the other nonsense in a multi-media production couldn't move, and without which a school-girl couldn't do her homework. Thus, the crutch turns into a drug.

In my boyhood in Vienna I knew a complete and totally knowledgeable musician. They don't make them like that any more, and the reason is, as I shall explain, unmusic. If they did, Benjamin Britten would have been one of them.

The Viennese musician was the composer Franz Schmidt. For many years, he had also been a cellist in the Vienna Philharmonic, and he still was a piano virtuoso when I knew him, though he was an old man. He played quartets with Oskar Adler, Schoenberg's first (coeval) teacher and quartet leader; I have never again heard quartet-playing of comparable freedom and imagination. When Schmidt was a young man, Mahler had noticed his cello-playing too; though Friedrich Buxbaum, the Rosé Quartet's cellist, was the Vienna Philharmonic's principal cellist, Mahler insisted on Schmidt playing the solos. The result was not exactly a lifelong love-relationship between Buxbaum and Schmidt; nevertheless, such was the stature of Schmidt's musicality and musicianship that the Rosé Quartet invited him to play the second cello in the Schubert String Quintet with them, as well as the piano in the 'Trout' Quintet.

Schmidt's achievements, though they depended on his unceasingly burning imagination, would not have been easily possible without his downright universal knowledge — and by 'knowledge' I mean, as the recollective reader is aware, knowledge of, not knowledge about. In fact, so far as music was concerned, he knew it all, but didn't bother to know anything about it: as the aged composer, teacher and musicologist Hans Gál regretfully pointed out to me in 1975, the one flaw in Schmidt's make-up was that he was not an 'intellectual'. Maybe he had no need to be.

In any case, when you discussed music with Schmidt, any music, he knew it, every bit of it. He didn't talk in generalities anyhow; he talked in terms of the notes and what they meant and why they were there and how they should, or rather shouldn't, go in performance. You might mention a Bach cantata, a Haydn quartet, a crucial point in a Mozart opera, or a late Beethoven quartet (or an Op. 18 one, for that matter), a Schubert symphony, a Schumann song, a Mendelssohn overture or quartet or quintet, a Brahms, Dvořák, Bruckner or Mahler symphony — invariably he'd get up, waddle across to the piano, and play the passage or entire section one was discussing in an instant piano arrangement, note-perfect.

The reader may now agree that they don't come like that nowadays, not even on the highest level. And what I am saying is that Schmidt could not possibly have acquired his knowledge exclusively or mainly from the

study of scores; on the contrary, in my experience —
weekly, stretching over years — he never used or
consulted a score in quartet rehearsal or in any other
context, except when he conducted and, non-conductor
that he was, wanted to make doubly sure. The way the
bulk of his complete,.detailed knowledge was acquired
was through the ear — by automatically, invariably
listening with total, exclusive concentration, whether as
orchestral or chamber player or indeed as a 'mere'
listener: not so mere, with the activity involved in *his*
kind of passivity. But then, that was before unmusic had
come in as a way of life, before the capacity for
concentration — yours and mine too — had degenerated.

I have stressed that the history of music is a
meaningless discipline without the history of listening;
we needn't have worried about any crisis of communication if things were otherwise. To concern oneself with the
quality of creation without being concerned about the
quality of its reception is to accept a new, delusional
dimension of 'art for art's sake': to hell with the listener,
including the ideal listener — who, in musical reality,
should be as much the aim of artistic communication as
is the perfect (or imperfectly great) work of art itself.
Music that is not written for the listener's sake need not
worry about demands for clarity, or indeed for anything
else: it is, in aesthetic principle, indistinguishable from
the psychoanalytic patient's free associations, or the
delusions of judge Schreber — who while his fantasies
were undoubtedly supposed to make a point, has not yet
found much of an appreciative audience for it.

If, then, we are agreed that we have to treat the history
of music itself two-dimensionally, as both the story of art
produced and the story of art understood or misunder-

stood or just not understood, we find that in our century, for the first time in the entire history of our art, there are two powerful, complementary forces at work which aim at reduction rather than production — at the reduction of music to unmusic.

One force has been generated by the Schoenberg trauma itself, and by the crisis of communication it engendered. The trauma was, in fact, the last straw; so far as listening habits were concerned, the development towards an unprecedentedly critical situation was clearly perceptible throughout the latter part of the nineteenth century and the early years of the twentieth. What was happening all along, that is to say, was the setting up of the progressive isolation ward, of which our own Radio 3's indefinite series, *Music in Our Time*, is continuing evidence — as if that were needed.

The isolation ward started with the Schoenberg trauma; in fact, his own Society for Private Musical Performances was the first such ward to be opened. What the majority of listeners turned to, and still does, was and is the music of the past. Boulez and others have called it 'museal art', but this is a thoughtless over-simplification, the only thought being, if thought you can call it, the desire to plead specially. In a museum, we view things at a psychological as well as a temporal distance. That may happen to Boulez and to many an avant-gardist too when they are confronted with classical music, but for the lover of traditional music, this is his life, musically speaking, and for the mere user, consumer, of traditional music, who turns it into unmusic, this is his favourite drug: familiarity breeds forgetfulness and so, eventually, unfamiliarity.

His favourite drug, though not his only one. Even

though the consequences of the Schoenberg trauma have pushed the consumer away from contemporary music, he doesn't mind it so much if he needn't understand it: he will take it as background music in a film or on television or even at a higher-brow cocktail party, so long as he is invited to concentrate his attention on something else. The crisis of communication has caused him, the listening counterpart of John Cage, to renounce communication and understanding altogether, and when he returns to traditional music, all he wants to hear is its familiar idiom, and never mind its substance, or whether it has any: he will take Telemann or Vivaldi as happily during his cocktail party as he will take Bach, hardly noticing any difference between them — whereas if he went by type of substance, he would notice far more similarities between Bach and Schoenberg than between Bach and Telemann: Alban Berg uncovered the former similarities early on. In terms of my theory, the drug-taker has deafened himself to the tensions between the foregrounds and the backgrounds of traditional music; he either confines his automatic attention to the backgrounds, the resolutions, the meeting of expectations, or else he has heard or unheard the work in question so often that he more or less vaguely knows what's coming next and treats the foreground as background, merely enjoying the meeting of the expectations which his memory produces, and not aware, or no longer aware, that they contradict implied expectations which are not rubbed in, and not so easily audible behind the din of his unthought-provoking party.

He has heard the work in question so often: here lies the other force aiming at the reduction of the art of music — the mechanical production and reproduction of music, especially by gramophone record and tape, but also by radio, if it is misused at the production end or the reception end — or, most easily, both. The secondary danger is ready availability; the primary danger is repeatability. Both entail the indefinite postponability of concentration, an inevitable decline in the quality of listening, even where the music is not deliberately misused as background music — where the listener is, in fact, trying to concentrate: 'I'll hear it another time, I can play it back again, I'm not missing anything if I miss anything.' The concert-goer's or player's incorruptibly focal consciousness, 'This is it, if I miss it, I've had it', has gone for ever. Franz Schmidt did not try to concentrate; he instinctively concentrated, and for the duration of such concentration nothing else existed.

Nowadays you encounter people, distinctly musical people, who hear Beethoven's Fifth Symphony ten times a year and know it far less well than did those listeners, a couple of generations or longer ago, who heard it once a year. When one reads, in Louis Spohr's *Autobiography,* how much he heard in that symphony after a single hearing, in spite of being out of sympathy with the work and not really understanding its style and construction, one gets a measure of the deterioration of the quality of listening, which my previous example of Britten's receptivity to Alban Berg's *Lyric Suite* does nothing to mitigate: Britten was fully in sympathy with the work, creatively all agog.

I am not recommending a drug law against unmusic, but there is a difference between the abolition of prohibition and the running of alcohol out of every water tap. The metaphor, moreover, is instructively incomplete: alcohol is alcohol, cannabis is cannabis, heroin,

262

heroin, but unmusic was music once — some of it.

The muzak part of unmusic is no less devastating in its effect, even though it is less degrading: rotten or meaningless music cannot easily be misused or abused. *But one can be.* In 1974, I went on a very compressed lecture tour to Canada — about one lecture a day in different places, and two lectures in different places on the same day. It was brilliantly organised, and in a world without unmusic I should have had a wonderful time. As it was, I was on the run — at any rate in my hotel, which should have afforded rare moments of simultaneous relaxation and concentration on tasks ahead. I remember one particular extended moment of unrelieved torture. I was sitting in the hotel's café, because I wanted to think to the accompaniment of a coffee. But there was that other accompaniment — a particularly revolting piece of repetitive kitsch, it so happened. I drank up and stormed out — into the lounge which, from afar, looked particularly peaceful and attractive, with people reading, doing their own work, or quietly talking. When I got there, they weren't talking all that quietly: they had to make themselves heard over the selfsame tune's uncontrasting middle section which was just entering its first repetition. By now I was in a state of acutely realistic persecution mania. I rushed to the lift to reach the safety of my own room before the threatening recapitulation of the principal section. In the lift itself, the middle section's second repetition was in full swing. Never mind, I thought, just another ten floors. But in my distraught state, I had forgotten that my having locked the door of my room might not have kept the tune out: as I entered, there it was, the unmodified and unabridged recapitulation itself, background with a vengeance; not

263

the meeting of expectations, but of one's worst fears.

Yet you meet people in the same kind of situation who, far from noticing anything amiss, are not even aware of the presence of unmusic; and the same kind of situation is difficult to escape — in shops, at the hairdresser's, in airport lounges and aeroplanes themselves (music therapy before take-off and touch-down!), restaurants, pubs, sun terraces and beaches even . . . The only element of contrast is between background music and music pushed into the background: when I had my passport photo taken the other week, the photographer's instructions were accompanied by the F minor Quartet from Haydn's Op. 20, provided by Radio 3. Since I also sit at the other end of the medium which thus entertained me (I hope the mass media are still capable of a singular), I could not help wondering what one ought to do in order to prevent radio from encouraging unmusic; the whole-hearted abandonment of generic broadcasting — serious music on one channel, speech on another, pop on a third — would certainly be a step.

But so far as I can see (which, in this respect, is jolly far), the world's radio organisations couldn't care less about the quality of listening, the irreplaceable power of spontaneous concentration. Remote are the times when J. C. W. Reith told his listeners that it was a good idea to switch off the light when turning on the radio — and that turning off the radio itself was just as important as turning it on: today, such an attitude on the part of the one-time head of the world's most important radio organisation seems gravely old-fashioned. But then, it is only those who cannot transcend fashion who think in terms of what is or isn't old-fashioned.

In 1975, every radio station in the world was happy —

thought it had done its job — if it had convinced the potential listener that it was more important to turn (or leave) the radio on than to turn it off. Considering the broadcasting organisations' exertions to make people listen, and their delight at maximal audience figures in any given area — including, of course, culture-conscious minority areas — one might think that they felt it to be a self-evident truth that one's aim in life should be listening to the radio, the only conceivable alternative being the viewing of television — if, that is, the organisation in question was running a television service. I don't think that the genuinely self-evident truth has yet dawned upon them that the ultimate aim of broadcasting — as of teaching — should be to make itself unnecessary, to encourage the listener to decide upon mental activity rather than passivity — to arrive, after due consideration, at this momentous conclusion: I have something better to do; I might even have to think.

Instead, and in view of the rival attraction of television, the world's radio people now tend to concentrate on their single assured captive audience — captive, that is, so long as it can be prevented from wanting to be alone with its thoughts, if there are any left: the car audience. I do not deny that plenty of useful information is being dispensed to listeners in their cars — especially, of course, traffic information. But unmusic, designed as ever successful music therapy (drug therapy, too, is ever successful), is considered a well-marketable commodity for drivers and their passengers. Music a commodity! Need one say more? Is philosophy a commodity? Prayer? Science? Love? Revelation?

The result of unmusic has not merely been a progressive insensitivity to music, an incapacity to take it in as

265

music, as communication. What it has stimulated at the same time is the latent fear of solitude, of facing life by thinking things out, of thinking things out beyond the need of the moment. The Sunday papers were, themselves, a powerful means of paralysing people across the weekend; now they are accompanied by unmusic — as is everything else, the washing of that car which contains the acoustic tranquilliser, every domestic occupation which is not too loud to render unmusic inaudible, and some occupations which are. So general is the malaise that it is not even realised that sustained thoughtfulness is no longer characteristic of the higher levels of our civilisation which, by now, is unwilling to accept that there are values beyond tranquillity, artificially induced. Chairman Mao wanted culture to fight the enemy without; we seem to want music to silence the enemy within, to silence silence. But silence is a more powerful stimulant towards thought than all the so-called intellectual stimulation in the world — if, that is, one is capable of thought. Under the influence of unmusic, our civilisation is, in fact, becoming ever more stupid without, of course, noticing it, too stupid to listen to music in the first place, too stupid for the extended development of silent thought in the second: what, today, is called intelligence is the adjustment to, and solution of, a topical, momentary problem — the faster, the better, no matter what the cost in terms of lasting insight. A 'quick intelligence' is one of our most beloved tautologies, in that we self-love the idiotic slyness with which we imply that it *is* a tautology.

John Cage has indeed a point with his *4'33' (tacet) for any instruments* (1952), and with his demand for aural sensitivity; unfortunately, he is himself a victim of the insensitivity against which he has struggled — insensitive to music, which he opposes as if it were unmusic, insensitive to sustained thought, which he happily replaces by fragments of aphoristic thoughts, their open ends hiding their own lack of intelligence.

In fact, so long as sense is excluded, there is no lack of enthusiasm about sensitivity to sound among the unmusic-lovers, especially if the sensitivity is not yours, but a machine's: the disproportionate development and conventionalisation of hi-fi, stereophony and, of late, quadraphony are witness to that.

In the highest, culture-dispensing circles, I have heard stereophony compared to colour TV. What nonsense! Quick intelligence, this, quickly recognisable. The implication is that what colour is to the eye, space is to the ear. It has not even struck those fools that what space is to the ear, space is to the eye, and what colour is to the eye, colour is to the ear: not for nothing has the word 'tone-colour' developed as a technical term. If you see a Rembrandt in black and white, the experience is not equivalent to hearing a Beethoven symphony in mono; it is equivalent to hearing a Beethoven symphony played on the piano — as plenty of people did before the gramophone came in. The difference between hearing something in stereo and hearing it in mono is the difference between seeing a football match in the stands and seeing it on television. Of course, colour, the shades of tone, help to define visual space, but equally, tone-colour helps to define acoustic space.

Now, just as it is not difficult for the practised eye to conjure up space where there is no space, to predict accurately, when watching television, that the ball is going to hit the post or go just wide, it is easy for the

267

musical ear to hear the space that isn't there; in all but definedly spatial music, moreover, the spatial dimension is incidental rather than essential — as it is at a football match. Which is not, of course, an argument against stereophony or quadraphony, still less against hi-fi with its definition of tone-colour, but it is an argument against getting things out of proportion to the extent of turning incidentals into essentials, and essentials — sense — into something incidental. The unmusic-lovers are legion who will pay the minutest attention to magnificent sound reproduction, regardless of what is being reproduced, and will welcome the greatest music, or any old music, as a background to their devoting the minutest attention to something else. High fidelity, spatial and colouristic, in due honour, but it has to be inside you in the first place, and if it is, its partial absence from the sound that hits you is quite easily compensated. Needless to add, I prefer the imaginary stereophony and high fidelity in my ears to the distortions of both space and colour, however slight, which most stereo reproductions impose on me. And the highest fidelity should be that to the meaning of the music and the manner of that meaning's clarification (quality of sound included, of course) — but in this relationship between art and its addressee, the high-fidelity fans are, more often than not, the gravest infidels.

The escape from musical thought and conceptual thought into unmusic takes many forms, then — and, although unobtrusive, is frantic. In most respects, there were at least two sides to music in 1975; but so far as unmusic was concerned, one can only report unhampered progress. It is by far the worst aspect of the de-musicalisation of music which we are witnessing —

the only aspect that does not hide possibilities of re-musicalisation, of a recapturing of the dignity of the art we recognise as soon as it says something to us when it speaks, and says it with the voice of irreplaceable authority. If music is going to hibernate, unmusic will have to take an inexcusable part of the blame, if only because nobody will notice: unmusic will simply have replaced music, with stimulation taking the place of communication — for one can be stimulated into sleep too.

# CHAPTER V

# Football, 1975

## I. Vienna, 1975

Virtually without my help, this book came full circle in the closing days of 1975 — or was it half circle, the other end of the diameter?

On December 16, that is to say, I was in a taxi taking me from Vienna's Schwechat airport to Austrian Radio's Broadcasting House, where a sub-committee of my EBU Working Party was going to plan the 1977/78 season of our International String Quartet Series: my mind was on serious matters. The driver was commiserating with me over the five-hour delay of the plane, and clearly expected me to prefer his extended commiserations to my serious matters. In order not to seem stand-offish, which I am not but occasionally seem to be, I conveyed to him, in not altogether broken German, that I was grateful for his concern — and hoped that I could now return to the quartets. 'You have an excellent German accent, sir, for an Englishman. It even sounds a bit Viennese.' 'I was born in Vienna, where I spent the first nineteen years of my life.' 'Ah! That's more like it. When did you leave?' 'In 1938.' 'Oh dear. Yes. What that lunatic has done to the world!'

There was little doubt that, having been identified as a Jew, I was going to be regaled with a speech on the holocaust, culminating in a demonstration of the driver's pure anti-Nazi soul; little doubt, too, that he — about my age — had been a good Nazi teenager: who hadn't been? However, the problem with which he was going to confront me, apart from being his rather than mine, was a few decades out of date, and the tedium of the drive to town promised to be unbearable. Any thought of quartets had to be abandoned in any case, and the inescapable conversation had to be switched to something of common interest. 'What's Austrian football like nowadays?' I asked. 'Good God. It's a sorry story. Do you remember our "Wonderteam" of the thirties, the one which beat Scotland 5-0 and drew with England 0-0? Sindelar, the artist? Schall, the goal-scorer, the "front-runner", as they call him nowadays? Zi . . ., Zi . . ., what was his name?' 'Do *I* remember?' I grew stern: 'Do *you* remember! Here goes: Hiden, Rainer, Blum; Mock, Smistik, Gall; Zischek, Gschweidl, Sindelar, Schall, Vogel — Gschweidl playing at centre-forward for Vienna F.C. and at inside-right in the Austrian national side. Nowadays, we tend to have no centre-forwards at all, whereas at the time, we had one too many. But then, Sindelar was a deep-lying centre-forward, midfield distributor and striker rolled into one — the rich man's Charlie George, an individual genius, and selfless at the same time.' 'I don't know who that Charlie George is; otherwise I agree with you. But — I hope you won't mind me saying so — it's been English football, and particularly England's victory in the 1966 World Cup, that's caused this terrible deterioration. You and your "team spirit"! It's had a disastrous influence. No more room for *persons*, for talent, for the finer arts of the game — for a Sindelar. Instead, you get tough, hard, rough styles. Forgive me, sir, but where is that famous English "fairness" for which we have no word, when it comes to

271

your football? It's dirty, your game, that's what it is, and everybody else has learnt to play dirty, "physically", as they say — including ourselves, of all football nations. And how boring it is without personalities! I don't go to matches any more.'

The time had come to interrupt this particular speech, too, even though I was conscious that he was writing the last chapter of my book, the rest of which had just been finished, on a holiday. We had reached Vienna proper, and were passing through the XIth district, Simmering. 'Does the Simmering football ground still exist? In my childhood, Simmering F.C. used to fight my own club for a place at the bottom of the First Division: my entire boyhood was wasted on a struggle against relegation. Once we even *were* relegated, but the next season, we didn't drop a single point in the Second Division.' I felt a glow of pride in my face and was glad that he was sitting in front of me: he might have thought it a few decades out of date. 'Yes, of course, the ground is there alright.' He pointed in its direction — and asked after a pause: 'Which was your club, then?' His tone had gone a shade fatherly, which I resented. 'Hakoah,' I said — and added, by way of rehabilitation: 'When I was four and you two, they won the championship, with the fantastic Fabian in goal, Scheuer at full-back, Béla Guttman as domineering centre-half, Eisenhoffer as striking centre-forward, and Nemes (also known as Neufeld) at outside right — the man who scored five goals in ten minutes in the 5-4 win over Slavia, Prague — Hakoah having been 0-4 down 10 minutes from the final whistle.' 'Béla Guttman? Is that the Béla Guttmann who managed Benfica, Lisbon, when they won the European Cup in the sixties?' 'Yes. It's also the man who said in 1966: "If

272

England win the World Cup, it'll be a tragedy for football".'

'Tell me, sir, you remember all these players from the age of four? You remember those Hakoah matches?' 'No. One or two of the players I saw at later stages. The stories I had from my uncle.' These playing personalities must have been strong enough to survive mere avuncular reportage. Hakoah, incidentally, was a Jewish club. The Hebrew word means 'strength', 'power' — an ironical reminder in this conversation about the modern power game: power meant something different then. Anyhow, having disclosed my childhood allegiance, I was, after all, treated to a detailed description of my driver's pure anti-Nazi soul.

Two days later, on December 18, the EBU job finished, I was on my way back to Schwechat airport. My driver, in his early thirties, was as loquacious as his predecessor had been. We were passing through Simmering. 'Does the Simmering ground still exist?' Anything rather than whatever he was talking about. 'Yes, of course, it's over there.' 'Are you interested in football?' 'Yes and no. I was a First Division player, you know, for Schwechat F.C. But I gave it up. Not enough money in it.' 'Also, the current power game, de-personalised, isn't all that fascinating, is it?' 'Oh, I don't know, I'm all for power. I'm a power player. The English have taught us that. I played in goal and later, after I permanently injured my hand in a tussle,' he held up his right hand, 'I played on the right wing. Very strong.' 'Goalkeeper and right winger? You possess a rich diversity of talents.' 'Oh, I don't know. I was a strong player.' 'A power player in goal? How did you do that?' He got animated, almost turned round in his seat: 'Do you know the Schwechat ground?' 'No.' Schwechat F.C. were nowhere near the

First Division in my time, if they existed. 'Well, it's on the smallish side. In one league game, three years ago, helped a bit by the wind, I punted the ball over the other cross-bar.' 'Fantastic,' I said, with ill-disguised lack of admiration. It didn't seem to have struck him that all he had achieved was a goal-kick for the other side — and you can take this profound observation in more metaphorical ways than one.

## II. The New Mediocrity

Our civilisation, stupidly open-eyed, gaping, is walking straight into a mortal danger — *the dictatorship of mediocrity*, which more or less hidden collectivism inevitably produces. Whether you look to the responsible liberalism of the mass media, which give the public what responsible mediocrities think the public wants, or to the new, Maoist left which, as we have seen, has once again abolished the concept of genius, we are faced with a pseudo-democratic conspiracy against individualism. Yet — we must not cease to remind ourselves — there is little collective talent, and no collective genius: in this sense, the new left knows what it has abolished.

They are all the same, all collectively mediocre — the establishment and the anti-establishment establishment, the official culture and that unofficial sub-culture which is our culture's secret delight, because any mediocrity left to its own brand bores itself to death. It all started when art became (don't-leave-me-to-myself) entertainment, and it got worse when, self-consciously and sterilely, entertainment started to call itself art.

By now, even football has advanced to the status of an art, except that it doesn't tolerate individualism any more easily than does any other sphere of our life. So how do we get art and collectivism together? By calling any old collective illusion 'folklore', and playing along with this fantasy game to the best of our assumed naivety. After a factual study of the 'Busby babes' (eight of whom died in the Munich air disaster in 1958), John Roberts [1] adopts the expected stance: 'Manchester United have something far more potent than success. They have folklore.' From this piece of conventional vapidity it is only a step — four pages, to be exact — to a wish-fulfilling prophecy instead of any reasoned forecast: 'Soon new idols may emerge to thrill us all.' Manchester United have meanwhile made good, dramatically so — but idols there are none. Why should there be? For more than a decade — a football generation — they have consistently refused to emerge in this country, while not so old idols like Jimmy Greaves, George Best, and Rodney Marsh submerged themselves, with despairing zest, in voluntary, early retirement — albeit sometimes in the shape of a magnificently pensioned American football existence and, in 1976, a nostalgic return to the English scene at a lower (Second Division) level.

The reason is the New Mediocrity which, in football, was able to establish itself earlier, and with less opposition, than in the rest of our society, because football is just a game, whereas the society game has to be played more metaphorically, and is proportionately more complex, more liable to be complicated by the sinister forces of anti-mediocrity — of talent and even genius. History is not unmade in a moment, even though it takes frighteningly little time to regress (but also, as we shall see at the very end of this book, surprisingly little time to progress,

1 *The Team that Wouldn't Die, The Story of the Busby Babes,* Arthur Barker, London, 1975.

275

if the proper stimulation towards individualism is there). In England, the job was, in fact, done within a few months early in 1962, when Ipswich Town slipped in between Tottenham Hotspur (who were preoccupied with the European Cup, which they didn't win, and the F.A. Cup, which they did) and Burnley (preoccupied with the F.A. Cup, whose final they reached), to win the First Division Championship. Under the leadership of Alf Ramsey, who was capable of making second-raters play, collectively, above themselves, mediocrity had triumphed. In due course, he was appointed England's team manager, and a repeat performance ensued four years later: mediocrity won the World Cup. Here were, perhaps, the first World Champions without a single great player in their striking line, a single individualist, Jimmy Greaves having been got safely out of the way; there is no English striker today, at the time of writing, who can remotely match his scoring average per international game (.77, as against Allan Clarke's .58, Martin Chivers' .54, Mike Channon's .41, or Kevin Keegan's — a midfield striker's, as it were — .18). The only people who had a public inkling of this tragedy were the afore-quoted Benfica manager, Béla Guttmann, Brian Glanville, Danny Blanchflower, and myself.

Meanwhile, the former champions have, of course, become folklore, with the result that Nicholas Mason, in an otherwise fascinating history of the entire family of football games,[2] has come to the lapidary conclusion that in 1966, 'coolness and analysis were the only way to triumph over teams with greater flair and equal skill'. Equal skill? Did we have a striker anywhere near the

---

[2] *Football! The Story of all the World's Football Games*, M. Temple Smith, London, 1975.

class of, say, Eusebio of Portugal — a team we knocked out of the World Cup? England operated, in fact, through the successful destruction of skill, and we have never looked ahead since — except, possibly, in a match of which I shall remind ourselves as I take my leave.

What James Walvin, in his own meticulous social history[3], calls 'the British preoccupation with their own game' saw no reason to weaken, since a 'genius' (Matt Busby's description) like George Best was never asked, never searched for, his real reasons for his discontent; the psychiatrist he was pushed into seeing was hardly interested in them.

I have my information about George Best contemptuously seeing a psychiatrist from Michael Parkinson's biography[4] of one of the two greatest British players our age has produced. Its most riveting sections are, naturally, Best's own contributions, which are injected into the text:

I wish I'd been born in Brazil. I really do! Things might have been different then. The way they play the game with the emphasis on ball control, skill and talent, is what it's all about. You watch the Brazilians in form and you can set it to music, can't you? I mean if you were sitting at home and it's fifty-fifty whether to watch the telly or go to a game, you're going to go a million miles to see players like Pele and Gerson. But say it's fifty-fifty and the top two clubs in the first division are playing in your backyard, you'd want your bloody head testing if you got out of your chair . . . .

Of course you can make a good argument that it is no good learning the skills nowadays because you're only

3 *The People's Game, A Social History of British Football,* Allen Lane, London, 1975.

4 *Best, An Intimate Biography,* Hutchinson, London, 1975. p. 28f.

going to get yourself kicked for your trouble. And it's true. I was one of those players who was marked down for what's called 'special attention'. This means that the nearest man kicks him.

The moral is culture-wide: look at the top two anybodies, anywhere.

Our other greatest player said in the same year[5]:

The modern football player isn't allowed to develop an individual character. I was allowed to, when I first started playing. I could say, 'Look, I'm playing my way — you can either like it or lump it.' I was given the opportunity to express myself, and it's an opportunity that young players just don't get now. They're moulded from an early age into a uniform way of thinking, and any individual character they might have had is worn away; they're channelled into thinking as a team, not as individuals.

I think this shows itself in goal-scoring: you get players now who are prepared to run back and tackle and do what I would call a defender's job for him — and be satisfied with that. No way would I ever have done that.

The retirement, semi-retirement, or temporary retirement, within a few years, of Greaves, Best, Marsh, even Pele and Gerd Müller — all supremely skilled, great strikers — is a symptom, obvious to the naked eye, that ought to interest the reader uninterested in football. 'Team spirit' can be a euphemism for an ultimatum to individual talent: 'Adjust or get out!'. But our civilisation, complete with anti-culture, will not survive as more than its own shadow, which is mediocrity, if it does not come to sense the need to adjust itself to that which made it: talent and genius.

---

5 Jimmy Greaves in the *Radio Times*, October 25, 1975.

## III. Not Playing the Game

It takes three people to kick individual talent out of the game — the kicker, the talent, and the referee, with the football laws and their current application behind him. A few years ago I gave a lecture on football law reform to an assembly of referees. I enjoyed it so much that I was incapable of noticing whether it was a resounding failure. It probably was; at any rate, I had the vast majority derisively against me. The few who agreed with me were — no, not the young ones, but the oldest. That made me think: conservative youth. If you've just made it and feel insecure, you join the establishment. If you are on top of your job, you may be able to see the need for change. But if you've grown old meanwhile, you've mastered the craft of opportunism: what's there is good, if only because you know your way about it.

Thus, with constant support right across the generation gap, the world keeps going round rather than up in a spiral. Minor changes apart, the football laws have, for generations, remained rigid, God-given, while the game itself has changed out of recognition. Inconsistencies are legion, and rather than do anything about them, we try to gloss over them by changing the interpretation of the laws; the result is another level of inconsistencies.

An example right outside any controversy about hard and dirty play. The rule covering the offence of handball is clearly covered by Law 12, Clause (i): 'A player who intentionally . . . handles the ball, i.e. carries, strikes or propels the ball with his hand or arm . . . shall be penalised by the award of a *direct free-kick.*' First-level (legal) inconsistency: there is no differentiation between a wilful interruption of the game and an incidental offence against its rules. Second-level (procedural) in-

279

consistency: nowadays, a player who catches the ball is invariably cautioned, whereas a player who commits an incidental handball offence isn't — although in law, both have committed precisely the same offence, i.e. intentionally handled the ball.

Now take my thought a stage or two further. If you cripple an opponent by a tackle which is not intended to hurt him, which can be shown, or understood, to have been an (unsuccessful) attempt to kick the ball, you go scot-free, whereas if you catch the ball without harming a soul you are cautioned, although the Law only provides for four types of caution, none of them concerned with catching the ball — unless it be assumed that you are guilty of 'ungentlemanly conduct' when indulging in this activity, in which case I don't know what's so gentlemanly about risking your opponent's limbs in an attempt to play the ball.

Indeed, if, without touching him, you raise your foot tummy-high in close combat, you are 'playing in a manner considered by the referee to be dangerous', and you are penalised by the award of an indirect free-kick, but if you break his leg in a so-called 'fifty-fifty ball', you are not only a gentleman, but are considered not to have played dangerously. In virtually all 'dangerous play' decisions I have seen, nobody was hurt, which means that if you hurt somebody without fouling him, you can rely upon being considered not to have played dangerously. The moral: hurt, harass, intimidate without fouling — without showing intent. 'All fouls must be intentional': one of Dennis Howell's 'comments' on Law 12 (he's merely repeating it). 'It is impossible to jump accidentally at an opponent.'[6] Very special pleading, this, from a leading referee and government minister: it is not im-

6 *Soccer Refereeing,* Pelham Books, London, 1968, p.126.

possible to trip an opponent accidentally, and you know it.

None of this I said to the referees: I wanted to escape alive, so I confined myself to reformational thoughts which I (and only I) regarded as obvious. But in autumn, 1975, a statement by a leading footballer removed my residual inhibitions. John Craggs, the Middlesbrough defender, analysed the game in which his club achieved West Ham's first away defeat of the 1975/76 season: 'We didn't allow them to play and, like most teams of their type, they were unable to compensate. One or two of their players dropped their heads when things started going against them.'

The ultimate achievement: you don't allow people to play football, in the hope that they will be unable to 'compensate'. This inability to do something (strictly legal) instead of playing removed the afore-mentioned Greaves, Best and Marsh from our clouded firmament. The times when a silent gentleman's agreement between opposing players ensured a free display of individual thought and skill are over — nowhere more decidedly so than in the country which introduced the concept of 'ungentlemanly conduct' (Law 12, Clause 4 (m)). The old joke, 'Never mind the ball, get on with the game', will soon be indistinguishable from a managerial instruction. But a law which makes possible the statement 'We didn't allow them to play' is itself lawless: the sole function of football law should be not to allow the players not to play — to prevent them from 'compensating', as Mr Craggs euphemistically has it.

The problem is that of the nature of skilful and imaginative interception — the kind of constructive defence which the Brazilians practised throughout the

1970 World Cup and again in their match against England in the summer of 1976, and which Bayern Munich showed us in their successful European Cup Final in 1976: more of both these games in Section IV below. Meanwhile, as soon as Law 12, Clause (1) — 'playing in a manner considered by the referee to be dangerous' — were to apply, *not only to dangerous play that might have resulted in injury, but also to dangerous play that actually has,* it would no longer be possible not to allow a side to play.

At the moment, the law book's one pitiable example of dangerous play is, in its own English, 'attempting to kick the ball while held by the goalkeeper'. But if you attempt to kick a ball shielded by an opponent in a way which, if you fail, reliably produces a double fracture, you aren't guilty of any infringement at all, unless you 'intentionally throw him or attempt to throw him by the use of the legs or by stooping in front of or behind him', in which case it's unlikely, anyway, that you attempt to kick the ball at the bottom of it all. In short, all demonstrably dangerous play should be 'considered by the referee to be dangerous': legal and procedural reform rolled into one. Just consider that we have reached the stage where one's got to write about this daring proposition — so daring that I dared not mention it to the refs.

## IV. 1975/1976 and 1976/1977

The degeneration of English football has brought about a decline in the quality of football-*watching* which made it possible for the commissionaire at my office — the father of one of the youngest Spurs players — to say that he wasn't going to turn on the television relay of the

1976 European Cup Final: 'These Continentals have no speed, no power. Yes, they're ball-players alright . . .' To play the ball has become a recognised handicap amongst those who love to see people rushing around without it and playing the man instead. 'May the worse side win!', a wish hiding behind support for the underdog, itself conceals the inability to appreciate the better side, where there is one left.

A Second Division club winning the Cup was regarded as a national triumph by the press, even though it was bound to result in our making fools of ourselves in Europe, in the European Cup Winners' Cup — as the European exploits of Sunderland had shown the other year. Mind you, it wasn't a bad Cup Final in 1976 — compared to the Cup Finals of the preceding ten years, those traditional, massed village festivals to which an importance is attributed at which all other football-loving countries smile with incomprehension: why don't we regard the winning of the championship as the major event? Unless all the participants are themselves of the highest calibre, a knock-out competition is accident-ridden, especially when giant-killing becomes easier in proportion as the giants grow smaller and smaller, the killers tougher and tougher.

Yes, unless the participants are of the highest calibre: the leading European knock-out competition is another matter, in that all its participants have won the very opposite of a knock-out competition — their country's league. The match which my commissionaire refused to watch was in fact a feast, the towering climax of the European football season for an uncorrupted spectator, even if he had seen a great deal of international football in the course of it. But the press, almost as one man, reacted as my commissionaire would have done, had he watched because he was going to be paid for it. Solidly behind the underdog, St. Etienne, who are known in their own country as 'the club with the English style', our professional spectators complained about Bayern Munich's lack of pace and passion, suggesting that the old crafty Bavarians were lucky to beat the young heroes.

St. Etienne could indeed have killed the giant, but *they* would have been lucky, because the giant is tall even amongst giants — as his semi-final performances against Real Madrid had shown. As for that much-longed-for passion (with which our commentators on radio and television adorn the game, whereas in hot-blooded, football-conscious Italy and Spain, commentaries are calm), I preferred my own passion rising as I watched Bayern's majestic captain Franz Beckenbauer stroll around the pitch, invariably in comprehensive command of the situation, directing his players even while he tackled an opponent without touching him, his foot magnetically drawing the ball into a position from which — defender changing into attacker — a pass ensued, be it over ten or thirty yards, which spotted the most auspicious possibilities of counter-attack, his thoughts two or three moves ahead of the opposing players' — sometimes even his own players', which was when his passes could go 'wrong'.

Now in my opinion, Don Revie has participated in the degeneration of English football, but as a spectator, he was still well ahead of my commissionaire and his press colleagues: at half-time, he disclosed that he had kept an account of Beckenbauer's passes, of which there had been over forty successful ones. I have often conducted similar statistical surveys, none of which showed such towering distribution, not even on the part of an exclusive midfield player — whereas Beckenbauer is, nominally, a sweeper. In reality, however, he is everything — *not* an all-round player, unspecialised, but one who has developed all the specialities, defence, construction, attack, and indeed scoring: his equalising goal against Rot-Weiss Essen, the week before the European Cup Final, would have ranked high amongst the exhibits of a Puskas, Pele, Greaves — or indeed Gerd Müller, the great Bayern striker, whose brilliant, disallowed goal in the opening minutes of the Final was glaringly on-side, yet remained unmentioned by all the professional spectators who drew attention to St. Etienne's twice hitting the crossbar.

There is, of course, no question that the French side was outstanding, but it is a matter of fact, not of opinion, that Bayern's football was altogether of a higher order — and facts are demonstrable. We read all about Bayern's victory being due to their strategy, their seasoned capacity to absorb their opponents' attacks. With their high crosses, so much beloved in this country, the Frenchmen did indeed seem the more dangerous attackers to the more primitive eye: high crosses sail towards the goal area and, to that extent, produce goalmouth 'incidents'. St. Etienne, admittedly, sometimes produced the most skilful variety of these crosses, but they didn't produce anything else — which is where my facts come in.

That is to say, aware from the outset of the finesse of Bayern's approach and indeed their approach work, I made detailed notes about the two sides' high crosses and through-passes respectively. It is hardly believable, but not one journalist noted the exceptional fact that throughout the game, St. Etienne did not attempt a single

285

through-pass: they out-Englished the English in this respect. Bayern, on the other hand, delighted us with six through-passes in each half — hardly evidence of defensive preoccupations! In the first half, only one of them was less than masterly, while three — all of them by Beckenbauer — created mortal danger, albeit without obvious goalmouth incident. The second half was a statistical replica of the first: five outstanding through-passes and one defective one. Meanwhile, St. Etienne indulged in no fewer than nine high crosses in the first half, three of them genuinely dangerous, and eight in the second half, with no more than two potentially convertible.

By this time, the sports commentators must have been the only people left who did not see what was going on. David Miller in the *Daily Express* saw Gerd Müller back into Oswaldo Piazza when the latter clearly fouled the awe-inspiring striker; and from Beckenbauer's ensuing free-kick, or rather free-pass, Miller saw Franz Roth 'hammer the ball low into the corner'. It was in fact a wonderfully gauged rising shot: the goal had such a traumatic influence on Mr Miller, who thought Bayern 'soulless', that he just couldn't see it, or couldn't remember it.

Beckenbauer, in the second half, showed his own, ever more favourable view of the course of the game with every movement: 'We had some bad moments, but we really dominated the second half, and by then I was sure we would win.' I do not understand why anybody who could not perceive this domination with its underlying invention ('soul'!) and ability should have wanted to watch the game at all, and what it was he watched. But then, a few days later, I equally failed to understand people's passion about what I thought was a match between a moderate First Division side and a typical Second Division side, high crosses abounding — until I discovered it was Scotland v. England, the worthy nadir of our own season.

That, then, would have been that so far as the 1975/76 season was concerned — had it not been for the most unexpected event of all, following hard on the heels of Scotland's Home International win over England: the England v. Brazil game in America's Bicentennial Cup, which was relayed live from Los Angeles. Brazil won 1-0, as Bayern Munich had beaten St. Etienne, and once again the entire press opined that the winner was lucky to win; once again, too, the entire press saw a different match from the one I saw. What I saw was the best, the most inventive, the most skilful, the most individualistic football team in the world — all the more unbeatable for surrendering none of its individualities to the team effort: I could have gone on watching them all night.

But the surprise was England: 'England played terrific stuff against the Brazilians', said Jimmy Greaves. 'But Brazil attacked and made us play.' The imaginative type of their attack made us change, lift, individualise the type of ours — if only, alas, for the duration of this match; we would have been ashamed to respond with anything less than inventive football, anything less than the character-istic skills of a Trevor Brooking or Kevin Keegan. Even as we had pulled the world down (Brazil themselves played uncharacteristically in the 1974 World Cup), Brazil now pulled us up, for a moment, made us play as we had not played for a football generation, showed us that there was one single group ideal — unreserved collective respect for contrasting individualities and their autonomy — that was not regressive, yet effective, downright catching. In the first place, of course, somebody, some body of people unlike each other, has to possess that ideal. Left without it, at the early stages of the 1977/78 season, notwithstanding the eminently English goalless draw with Brazil in the summer of 1977, we are as far back at the bottom as makes no difference.